THE FUTURE OF A TROUBLED WORLD

General Editor
HOSSEIN AMIRSADEGHI

The Future of a
Troubled World

Editor
RITCHIE CALDER

Contributors

Elisabeth Mann Borgese
Lester R Brown
Silviu Brucan
Nigel Calder
Ritchie Calder
Walter Perry
Gerard Piel
Shridath S Ramphal
Ninian Smart
Anthony Smith
Maurice F Strong
Jan Tinbergen

HEINEMANN: LONDON

William Heinemann Ltd
10 Upper Grosvenor Street, London W1X 9PA
LONDON   MELBOURNE   TORONTO
JOHANNESBURG   AUCKLAND

First published in Great Britain 1983
© International Communications Enterprises Limited 1983

SBN 434 10502 3

Photoset by Deltatype, Ellesmere Port
Printed in Great Britain by
Redwood Burn Limited
Trowbridge, Wiltshire

For my little Leila.

And for millions like her: small and tender; pure and
loving; temptingly naive; so full of simple hope.

Theirs is the quest for the future. Ours is the keeping of
the past and of tending to the present.

They are the beacons, the beckoning call. Our future fires
lighting the way to our heavenly desires.

To them we owe the future. For them we must survive the
present. Survive ourselves. We cannot fail them.

WE CANNOT FAIL THE FUTURE

Hossein Amirsadeghi

Contents

Contributors   vii

Preface   xi
by Hossein Amirsadeghi

Acknowledgements   xvi

1 THE OBLIGATIONS OF OPTIMISM   1
by Ritchie Calder

2 THE ACCELERATION OF HISTORY   10
by Gerard Piel

3 TO THE POLES OF TECHNOLOGY   31
by Nigel Calder

4 FOOD AND POPULATION: A TIME FOR REASSESSMENT   54
by Lester R Brown

5 THE FUTURE OF THE OCEANS   79
by Elisabeth Mann Borgese

6 COMMUNICATIONS IN THE YEAR 2000   90
by Anthony Smith

7 LEARNING AT A DISTANCE   112
by Walter Perry

8 NEW ECONOMIC POLICIES   121
by Jan Tinbergen

9 GROWTH AND THE QUALITY OF LIFE   144
by Maurice F Strong

10 THE FUTURE OF RELIGION   158
by Ninian Smart

11 IDEOLOGIES AND POLITICAL PARTIES   176
IN A CHANGING WORLD
by Silviu Brucan

12 THE POLITICAL MAP OF THE FUTURE   194
by Shridath S Ramphal

Index   211

Contributors

ELISABETH MANN BORGESE
Elisabeth Mann Borgese was born in Munich in 1918 and was educated in Germany, the United States, and Switzerland where she gained a Diploma in Music. In the United States she took up a Research Associate post at Chicago University in 1945. From 1964 she has been at Dalhousie University in Halifax, Canada, where she has been Professor of Political Science since 1980. She is Chairman of the Planning Council, International Ocean Institute; advisor to the Delegation of Austria to the Third United Nations Conference on the Law of the Sea; and Editor, since 1980, of the Ocean Yearbook. Her books include *The Ocean Regime*, 1964; *Tides of Change* (ed), 1975; *The Drama of the Oceans*, 1976; and *The Law of the Sea and the New International Economic Order* (with Arvid Pardo), 1977.

LESTER R BROWN
Lester R Brown is President and a Senior Researcher with Worldwatch Institute, a private non-profit Washington-based international research institute devoted to the analysis of emerging global issues. Formerly Administrator of the International Agricultural Development Service of the United States Department of Agriculture, he is the author of several books, including *World Without Borders*, *By Bread Alone*, *The Twenty-Ninth Day*, and *Building a Sustainable Society*.

SILVIU BRUCAN
Silviu Brucan, born in Bucharest in 1916, was a participant in the anti-fascist underground movement; in 1944 he became the acting editor of *Scinteia*, the most influential daily newspaper of Romania. From 1956 to 1959 he was Romania's Ambassador to Washington, and from 1959 to 1962 its Permanent Representative to the UN. He subsequently served for four years as head of Romanian television, and since 1966 has been Professor of Social Sciences at the University of Bucharest. Professor Brucan has published many books and has lectured widely in the US and other foreign universities. He is the author of two books in English: *The Dissolution of Power* (Alfred Knopf, New York, 1971) and *The*

Dialectic of World Politics (Free Press, Macmillan, New York, 1978).

NIGEL CALDER

Nigel Calder was born in London in 1931 and was educated at the Merchant Taylor's School and at Cambridge University, where he earned a master's degree in natural sciences. He served his apprenticeship as a science writer on the staff of *New Scientist* and from 1962 to 1966 was its editor in chief. Winner in 1972 of UNESCO's Kalinga Prize for the popularization of science, he seeks out the latest scientific knowledge from every continent and interprets it for his readers. He is author of the books *Einstein's Universe*, *Spaceships of the Mind*, *The Weather Machine* and *Nuclear Nightmares: An Investigation into Possible Wars*, to name but a few. His major science programmes for the BBC have wide audiences around the world.

PETER RITCHIE CALDER

Peter Ritchie Calder, who was created a CBE in 1945 and a life peer in 1966, began his career as a police-court reporter. He went on to become an outstanding communicator of science to the general public, and winner of the UNESCO Kalinga Prize for the popularization of science (1960). His concern for global poverty and the future of the Third World led him to undertake many missions and assignments for the United Nations and its agencies, 1946–60. He was Professor of International Relations in the University of Edinburgh 1961–67, Chairman of the Metrication Board 1969–72, and a Senior Fellow at the Center for the Study of Democratic Institutions, California, 1972–75. In 1977 he became Chairman of the Advisory Committee on Oil Pollution of the Sea. In 1980 he initiated the Edinburgh Conversations, that bring together leading experts from Britain and the USSR, to discuss the avoidance of nuclear war. Lord Ritchie-Calder died in 1982.

WALTER PERRY

The Rt Hon Lord Perry of Walton was born in Dundee in 1921. He studied medicine at St Andrews University and graduated MB, ChB in 1943, and MD in 1948. He served in the Colonial Medical Service from 1944 to 1946 and later joined the staff of the Medical Research Council. He was appointed Director of the Department of Biological Standards, National Institute for Medical Research in 1952. In 1958 he became Professor of Pharmacology at Edinburgh University and then Vice Principal from 1967–8. He was appointed

Vice-Chancellor of the Open University in 1968 which post he held until his retirement in.1981, when he was made a Fellow of the Open University. He holds nine honorary doctorates from universities in England, Scotland, Australia, Canada and the USA. He holds an OBE and Knight Bachelor.

GERARD PIEL

Gerard Piel, born in 1915, was Science Editor on *Life* magazine between the years of 1939–1944, and in 1947 he became President and Publisher of *Scientific American*. His awards include the UNESCO Kalinga Prize in 1962; the George Polk Award, 1964 and The Henry Johnson Fisher Award, 1979. He is a fellow of the American Academy of Arts and Sciences, the American Philosophical Society, the Institute of Medicine and a member of the Council on Foreign Relations. Notable books are *Science in the Cause of Man*, Alfred A Knopf, New York, 1961 and *The Acceleration of History*, Alfred A Knopf, 1972.

SHRIDATH S RAMPHAL

Shridath S Ramphal has been Commonwealth Secretary-General, the first from the Third World, since 1975. Born in Guyana (then British Guiana) in 1928, he was educated at Queen's College, Georgetown, King's College and Gray's Inn, London, and Harvard Law School. He became Assistant Attorney-General of the Federal Government of the West Indies in 1961. As Attorney-General of Guyana from 1965, he helped to draft his country's 1966 independence constitution; later to be appointed Minister of State for Foreign Affairs and then in 1972 Minister of Foreign Affairs, also holding the portfolio of Justice. At the Commonwealth Secretariat he has given emphasis to the Commonwealth's service to the world community and priority to issues of conflict resolution in both the political and economic areas. He has been prominent as a champion of the cause of development. He was a member of the Independent Commission on International Development Issues ('The Brandt Commission') and the Independent Commission on Disarmament and Security Issues ('The Palme Commission').

NINIAN SMART

Ninian Smart is Professor of Religious Studies at the University of California, Santa Barbara and teaches part of each year at the University of Lancaster, England, where he founded Britain's first major Department of Religious Studies. He has written extensively on the philosophy and history of religion and on religion and politics.

His most recent publications are *Worldviews: cross-cultural explorations of human beliefs*; *Sacred Texts of the World* (with Richard Hecht) and *Religion and Politics in the Contemporary World* (with Peter Merkl). He helped to plan and execute the television series *The Long Search*.

ANTHONY SMITH
The Director of the British Film Institute; formerly Fellow of St Anthony's College, Oxford and for ten years current affairs producer at BBC TV; he was responsible in the early 1970's for BBC-1's nightly television news background programme and continues to make films on questions relating to the media. Author of *Shadow in the Cave*—the broadcaster, the audience and the state; *Goodbye Gutenberg; the Newspaper Revolution of the 1980's;* and *The Geopolitics of Information*. A Board Member of Britain's new Fourth Channel.

MAURICE F STRONG
Maurice F Strong was born in 1929 in Manitoba, Canada. He is currently Chairman of the International Energy Development Corporation in Geneva, Switzerland, as well as being involved in a number of other organizations concerned with energy. Former posts include Executive Director of the United Nations Environment Programme in Nairobi, Kenya, from 1973–1975, and head of Canada's International Development Assistance Programme between the years of 1966–1970. At present he serves on many committees: Chairman to the North South Energy Roundtable in Washington DC; a member of the International Council of the Asia Society, New York; and Chairman to the Advisory Committee, United Nations University, Tokyo, Japan, to name but a few. He has received honorary doctorates from twenty-three universities in Canada, the United States and Europe.

JAN TINBERGEN
Jan Tinbergen, born in 1903 in The Hague, Netherlands, received a Doctorate in physics in 1929 from Leyden University. He was in charge of business cycle research at the Central Bureau of Statistics (Netherlands) between the years of 1929–1945, and was with the League of Nations Secretariat in Geneva between 1936–1938. He has been the Director of the Dutch Central Planning Bureau, and Professor of Development Planning. He holds honorary doctorates in social sciences from twenty universities, and was made a Nobel laureate in economics in 1969.

Preface

The future is fostered in the past and bred in the present. Every new hour, day or month we live presses against our mortal presence, pushing us ever deeper into the vortex of times past. We project our souls into the future in order that the past may live forever. For the future can never be surmised except through the prism of the conscious present and *Homo sapiens'* fossil-bound history. We know our pasts, for good or for bad. Can we glimpse the future?

Ever since launching this project I have attempted to reconcile my pessimist's determinism with my optimist's striving for the stars. Did I believe in a future? Could I claim a special concern for the human condition? Or was I, and a few billions like myself, too tied up with my own present and looming concerns, too sorely tested at every turn of the wheel, the cycle of despair, the grating passage of life's travails, to leap into the unknown.

Was it, indeed, rather presumptuous to attempt to undertake such a project? In bringing together some of the finest minds of science and learning I hoped to take a peep into the unknown; to conjecture a thought or two upon infinity. I hoped to bring some sanity to the Earth.

Considerable contemplation finally led me to undertake this challenging work, and I sought out a man of vision and compassion to steer the project through its many difficult stages.

A few to whom I spoke affected smiles at my supposedly naive intent. A book on the future of the world—just one book? A friend remarked that it would be more appropriate for a book to tackle some of the present problems 'we're bogged down in. . .'. How many times had I heard that exasperating expression? They told me to attempt something simpler, something with more relevance and immediacy, more practical and saleable. These were some of the early responses.

But all this strengthened my resolve to bring fresh thinking to the study of the future. Not by modelling or forecasting techniques, nor with computers and cybernetics theory, but through the experience of scholarship, learning and wisdom. Such experience might lead to a vision of science and politics; of economics and society; of religion and compassion. It might give an insight to life itself through the reflections of eminent thinkers of our time.

I was most fortunate to find a warm and distinguished scholar in the person of the late Lord Ritchie-Calder with his life-long optimism in the human condition strained by world events. Lord Ritchie-Calder over the next four years tackled, with me, the difficult task of gathering distinguished contributors for an exercise in heuristic thought, to produce an original perspective on future trends.

Meanwhile television brought more dead bodies, distended stomachs, man-made disasters and even more political chaos into our global living rooms. The agony of Iran had scarred my very soul as I saw hope turn to despair, beliefs sour into sorrow, massive energy transformed into streams of blood. I had seen the past, tasted the present and still the question nagged: 'What of the future?'

The motor of conflict seems irreversibly embedded in Man's psyche as one violent and bloody conflict succeeds another. His *animus dominandi* inexorably drives him to even greater self-inspired calamities. His lust for power blinds all others to his primal passions.

From bingo to war games *Homo ludens* plays out his Earthbound fantasies. And every so often, as if under some protean cue, conflict and conflagration break out somewhere, somehow. The cause is often trivial, sometimes pathetic, and the consequences are always tragic.

Is the future yoked to the past? Do the cycles of history have to repeat themselves? Will we ever find an escape from our circle of despair? Reinehold Niebuhr wrote of man as a pygmy who aspires to godliness to escape his foolish irrelevance. Thus condemned to a hypocritical existence we ride out the cycle of natural destiny from biological conception to physiological disintegration, meanwhile playing a fretful tune or two, wanting recognition, hoping to be remembered, and all the while trying to break out of our pitiable mould.

And what of survival? For two million years our ancestors in different sizes and shapes learned to kill better than their competitors, and so set themselves apart from the rest of the animal kingdom.

Modern man arrived only at the very end of that long apprentice-ship. And to prove his worth, his immortality, he set about building pyramids and giant temples, towers of worship and great golden gods. The pygmy who had aspired to godliness fitfully laid claim to his kingdoms. The territorial imperative translated into a celestial imperative.

The physical and spiritual combined to carve out empires, to build Babylon, Persepolis and Rome and to extend the faith. 'My faith is better than yours; yours may be superior to his.' So it went on enslaving the living to strive for deferred promises of fresher pastures, the greener grass for future generations. Man was never satisfied.

This is how it was through millennia as empires came and went, and new faiths destroyed older ones, making yesterday's truth a present heresy. The great religions followed one another, each taking its toll of human suffering in the name of its gods. By the sixth century BC monotheism ushered in an age where man-gods in the guise of kings and emperors lorded it over the people, as the proclaimed earthly representatives of God. They ruled in their numerous forms for over twenty-three centuries.

By the seventeenth century dying for kings was replaced by dying for one's country. The twentieth century saw whole continents mobilized in orgies of blood-letting in the name of ideological nationalism. For Man's greatest suffering at the hands of Man we can thank the ideologues and the religious zealots. These people are certain of their righteousness and are eager to impose their will on others. They seek to rule the body and the soul.

Thus we have reached the present, often floating on seas of blood while still seeking the shining promise, our Garden of Eden. The mass of humanity, poor and always wretched, is still promised eternity. As unfulfilled dreamers we shall pass to succeeding generations the eternal torch of hope shining in the oceans of despair.

The wonder of it is the task that men set themselves in their quests for better futures. The voracious physical and spiritual needs of societies present such formidable problems that overcoming them will need Man's total ingenuity as well as any reserves of collective goodwill that may exist.

The last century has seen the phenomenal rise of the super-society, the cosmopolitan ethos, liberation from spiritual tyranny and a spreading vision of the true cosmos. We've glimpsed the promised land and we want to see more. Earthly dreamers, our environment has been harnessed to our ends, and through sheer will—the will for power and the power to will—some nations have reached previously unimaginable heights of material satisfaction and physical well-being.

But the irony and the bathos lie in the knowledge of our insignificance; the more we know, the less we know; the bigger we become, the smaller in relation to the expanding universe.

We still fear the same dark shadows, remain exhilarated by the same passions and desires, and yet shrink from learning about our true nature from the psychophysiologists' penetration of the chemical and mental processes of emotion. Only the outer shells have been disassembled, only surfaces scratched. And the result? From present perspectives, age-old intuition seems to have served our ancestors no worse than all the behavioural sciences do for us today.

History knows best, but the pathos of novelty still reigns supreme. Narcissistic reflections of a thousand ages past blur in the pools of history. Insecure, spiritually dependent, physically insignificant, we build ever grander sand castles that crumble as the winds of time scour our mortal presence. The promise of change shapes our very thinking. Change for the better, for richer, for bigger. In spite of all that we have achieved we are never satisfied.

Original sin still pervades our very psyche. The Hobbesian cycle of fear and insecurity predates our history. The death-wish—Freud's thanatos—seems, through the experience of history, to consume his life instincts—his eros. Spinoza thought that men were not led by pure reason, but by their passions. Violence, he concluded, was a reflection of Man's nature. St Augustine conjectured that Man's love for so many vain and hurtful things led him to violence and the desire for power. Confucius would have added deceit and cunning as instincts that lead men to their own destruction.

We seek history's renewal in our future worlds, but always falter. As Comte said, 'it is the old that prevents us from recognizing the new'. Earthbound visionaries we claim to be, but we seem only to imagine the past and remember the future.

Are we therefore simply looking at the past by staring into the future? Do methods, styles and moods change but the principles remain the same? Are our actions the result of the invisible hand of evolution, or has Man launched a new cosmic revolution? Has the bazaar of life a commerce, a trade in death? Will the human race be decimated upon life's sacrificial altars, and bring near the hour of the flight of the Owl of Minerva?

Such was the stuff of my thoughts as I scrambled through life these last few years. Sometimes lost in a deluge of despair, I clung to the hope that my contributors would offer visions of more reasonable worlds.

Lord Ritchie-Calder did not share my pessimism, my determinism, nor my belief in original sin and the cycles of history. Yet when he died in 1982, as we neared our common goal, the irony of life and death, of renewal and restoration, seemed to me tragically real. Must there always be a present sacrifice to ensure a rebirth?

Hossein Amirsadeghi

Acknowledgements

This book owes a principal debt of gratitude to my late distinguished co-editor Lord Ritchie-Calder. He was the guiding spirit and the luminous light of my project.

Every one of our contributors is a person of high esteem in their international environ. Scholars, scientists, men of affairs and letters, they have co-operated patiently towards an exercise in lucid thought on a high plane concerning our future condition. Each deserves more credit than my humble thanks can convey.

Lady Ritchie-Calder and her son Nigel have helped complete Lord Ritchie-Calder's unfinished work. I hope that publication of this volume will in some small way ameliorate her sorrow at Lord Ritchie-Calder's loss.

And then there are those worthy people, names that often go unmentioned, but who must know that we owe them a debt too. Every part goes into making the whole.

Hossein Amirsadeghi
1st June 1982

The Obligations of Optimism

by Ritchie Calder

The younger generations might be excused for thinking that history began in the 1940s. In an important sense they would be right, if only their elders had shaken off their prehistoric ways of selfishness and hate. In the growing-up years of the war-babies and their siblings, four great revolutions took place, ushering in the Atomic Age, the Computer-Communications Age, the Space Age and the Biotechnology Age. Each was as epochal as the Bronze Age, the Iron Age, the Renaissance and the Industrial Revolution, but they happened all at once, bamboozling the politicians, the diplomats, the financiers, the economists and the social scientists.

The secret of matter was released from the nucleus of the atom as an apocalyptic bomb. The secret of life, written in DNA, became for genetic engineers a means of manipulating the essential nature of living species. The computer, initially a cumbersome abacus, was transformed by miniaturization, transistors, solid-state circuits and microchips, and it acquired a prodigious memory capacity, so that it is possible to envisage the knowledge of all the world's libraries being contained in a casket no bigger than a human skull. Electronic senses amplified, refined and extended the range of the human senses, reaching out even to Mars and Saturn, to scrutinise, record and telemeter their findings back to mission control.

Man stood on the Moon and saw the blue planet, Earth. In the moment of his most spectacular achievement, he discovered true humility for he saw the world diminished to its real proportions. Through the swirl of clouds, he made out mountain ranges reduced to wrinkles, on a globe of which seven-tenths was covered by oceans. Among forests, hot deserts and cold deserts, a meagre tenth of the land surface was under cultivation. Such were the limits of humanity's family estate.

That Moon's-eye view of the world came into sharper focus with the help of man-made satellites patrolling closer in, fitted with remote-sensing devices for examining the Earth's surface. From satellites little can be hidden—as the military have had to recognize and accept. Geologists use remote-sensing devices to help in their search for minerals, petroleum and underground water. The meteorologists see, in the cloud pictures, the movements of weather fronts, hurricanes and rain storms. Foresters and agronomists can determine what kinds of trees and plants are growing in an area, quickly spot signs of blight or fire, and estimate harvests. Oceanographers map ocean currents, marine life and pollutants. Geographers analyse patterns of land use. With such means we are now in a position to chart, classify and quantify the Earth's resources and, one might hope, to make better use of them in the interests of all Mankind.

Satellites in low orbit go around the world in ninety minutes. The continents are separated from another by no more than a few hours of jet travel, or a few minutes by intercontinental ballistic missiles. Using communications satellites we can sit in our armchairs and see instantaneously on our television screens events happening on the other side of the globe. The world has been reduced to a neighbourhood. Neighbours may be fractious, unfriendly, politically distasteful—or they may embarrass us by dying of starvation on the spacetime equivalent of our front-doorsteps. They are very numerous, and we are continually reminded that they are there. We can no more ignore the isobars of political and economic storms than the cold fronts of the weathermen, which come upon us equally unbidden.

The 'winds of change' to which Harold Macmillan referred when he was Prime Minister of a diminishing empire were, in fact, ethereal winds. Radio waves carried the epidemic of independence. The aspirations of freedom might be innate, but awareness of the success of other movements for colonial liberation was an encouragement. The initial approach to self-government in the Indian subcontinent was a long haul compared with the subsequent concessions to independence in Africa, as the timescale of change contracted. In 1945, one-third of the inhabited Earth was not self-administered, being mostly in the direct colonial possession of Britain, France, the Netherlands and Belgium, while other countries (including South Africa in Namibia) were administering territories under mandate from the pre-war League of Nations or vested in the Trusteeship Council by peace treaties. The dramatic changes since then are shown by the membership of the United Nations: the original fifty-one of 1945 have become 155, most of them new nations formed from the fragmented empires.

The awareness of change became pervasive. I have been with the dispossessed heirs of the Incas on the *alto plano* of South America, huddled beneath the gleaming bowls of a space tracking station and eavesdropping by transistor-radios on the gossip of astronauts. With sherpas in the Himalayas I heard accounts of a nuclear submarine going under the ice of the North Pole. I watched as Congolese in the rain-forest of Central Africa listened to radio news bulletins and then tapped out the messages on talking drums. In a pagan longhouse in Borneo I came upon youngsters enjoying western pop music by courtesy of the Voice of America. I was mushing with Eskimos in the Canadian Arctic when their sledges carried geiger counters to look for uranium—and portable radios to monitor its market price.

Radio communications fostered rising expectations of material, as well as political, betterment. The rich countries, with their competing ideologies, boasted in every language of their great achievements: of miracle grains, miracle cures, and abundant energy from nuclear reactors that would help the underprivileged of the world to 'leap across the centuries' to industrial prosperity. Neither the wealthy countries, with their abundant resources, nor the local national leaders, with their abundant promises, delivered the goods. Many people remained hungry and sick and miserably poor. Disenchantment led to resentment against the rich countries, and to unrest and instability in what came to be called the Third World. That very term, useful though it is, embodies the failure of understanding. There is only one world, the small blue planet that the astronaut sees.

*　　　*　　　*

Among all the attempts to conceive planet-wide institutions, the most enlightened innovation was the Economic and Social Council of the United Nations. Never before in international affairs had governments agreed to accept responsibility for peoples other than their own. They did the right sort of things with the temporary UN Relief and Rehabilitation Agency (UNRRA) but wound it up too soon, and with the more durable Children's Fund (UNICEF) and International Refugee Organization. Specialised agencies became part of the global apparatus, cursed with initials but blessed with good intentions: FAO, the Food and Agriculture Organization, UNESCO, the United Nations Educational, Scientific and Cultural Organization, WHO, the World Health Organization, and ILO, the International Labor Organization. They were semi-auton-omous, but the Economic and Social Council co-ordinated them.

More technical functions were embodied in agencies like the International Postal Union, the World Meteorological Organization, the International Telecommunications Union and the Inter-Governmental Maritime Consultative Organization. The UN system relied on more-or-less conventional banking methods, in the International Monetary Fund and the World Bank.

The Second World War coincided with revolutions in medical science, and the production of sulpha drugs, antibiotics and insecticides ranked in priority with munitions. These were outstandingly successful in preventing deaths from infections and pestilences which, in previous wars throughout history, had killed more fighting men than weapons had done. The war ended in 1945 with the pharmaceutical capacity to reduce the burden of disease in the developing countries, and UN agencies made the new drugs and pesticides available. With medical task forces recruited from all nationalities, the World Health Organization conducted campaigns against the killing and disabling diseases: malaria, yaws, cholera, typhoid, typhus, yellow fever, polio, and others. Smallpox was eradicated. The readiness of governments of wealthy countries to volunteer funds for such campaigns was humane, but it was also a recognition that infectious diseases know no frontiers and could easily spread from the poor countries to afflict the well-to-do. For whatever motives, we sawed off the peaks of the death-graphs.

The population explosion that we witness today is not a great orgy of procreation. Couples are not having more children than they used to have. Adults are living longer. More people are surviving the hazards of childbirth and infancy to marry and to multiply. More than half the population in the developing world is under fifteen years of age and presently they will be begetting. The rate of increase is the equivalent of twenty divisions of Martians arriving every day without their rations, to live off the land. In fifty years' time, if we continue to reduce mortality without lowering fertility, there will be four people in the world for every one now living. Amazingly we have, at least until recently, matched the increased population with increased food, but the race between production and reproduction seems never ending, and localised famines today foreshadow worse to come.

It would be nonsense to say that such effects were not foreseen. Brock Chisholm, as Director-General of the World Health Organization thirty years ago, knew perfectly well what would be the demographic consequences of medical intervention on a global scale. At that time, WHO was expressly forbidden to study human fertility, let alone promote birth-control methods. And John Boyd

Orr, as Director-General of the Food and Agriculture Organiz-ation, knew that he had to feed the multiplying millions. He wanted to help people to feed themselves by improving agricultural methods, by extending the food acreages, recovering deserts, providing irrigation and fertilisers, and supplying higher-yielding seeds. He wanted a World Food Board which, with enhanced resources from FAO, would appraise the world's food needs each year, tell farmers how much they could produce with a guaranteed income, and offer food to needy nations at stabilised prices. Reserves would be located throughout the world to deal with famine, or to be used as food investments in development projects. Distribution was what mattered. 'Global calories *per capita* are meaningless; what matters is what reaches each *stomach*,' Boyd Orr would say. He earned the Nobel Prize but his World Food Board was scuppered by vested interests.

Julian Huxley, as Director-General of UNESCO, was supporting the other agencies with campaigns on Food and Population, master-minded by Jacob Bronowski, later celebrated for *The Ascent of Man*. They spelled out the Misery-Go-Round of poverty. Sick people cannot work to produce, or earn, food and as a result they are undernourished. The sick and hungry cannot learn how to improve their condition, and so remain ignorant. And because they are sick and hungry and ignorant they remain poor and produce plenty of children as their only assurance for the future. With more mouths to feed, there is less food for everyone. So the roundabout of wretchedness keeps on turning, and today half a billion people are seriously undernourished.

* * *

When the Charter of the United Nations was signed in San Francisco in June 1945, four of the delegates, from among fifty-one nations, should have known that they were legislating for a world that no longer existed. They were President Truman, his Secretary of State Stettinius, Deputy Prime Minister Attlee and Foreign Secretary Eden. They were the only ones present who knew that a nuclear device was due to be exploded. They knew but did not understand its significance. Truman had been let into the secret when Roosevelt had died two months before, but he had been inadequately briefed. Stettinius had only as much information as Defence Secretary Stimson would let him know. For Attlee it was just 'a bigger bomb' and Eden knew it only from classified dispatches crossing his Foreign Office desk.

Within weeks, Truman and Attlee were parties to the decision to drop the A-bomb on Hiroshima. Attlee confessed, years later:

> We knew nothing whatever at that time about the genetic effects of the bomb. I knew nothing at all about fall-out and the rest that emerged after Hiroshima. As far as I know Winston Churchill knew nothing of those things either, nor did Sir John Anderson, who co-ordinated research on our side. Whether the scientists concerned knew or guessed, I do not know. If they did, they said nothing of it to those who had to make the decision.
> (Francis Williams: *A Prime Minister Remembers: The War and Post-War Memoirs of the Rt. Hon. Earl Attlee*, Heinemann, 1961.)

The Founding Fathers of the United Nations overlooked something else: the way the bomb was being produced by the technological crash programme called the Manhattan Project. Uranium fission was discovered in Germany in 1938. By July 1941, a British committee had established that a chain reaction, and hence a nuclear bomb, was feasible and had worked out how the fissile uranium-235 might be extracted from natural uranium. The Manhattan Project brought together hundreds of the ablest scientists, chemists, metallurgists and engineers, not only of the United States but of the free world. It secured a monopoly of Canada's supplies of uranium. It built a great plant at Oak Ridge, Tennessee, to use the huge hydro-electric resources of the Tennessee Valley Authority for the separation of uranium-235. By December 1942, the chain reaction was being controlled in a nuclear reactor at the University of Chicago and was producing another fissile element, plutonium. On the strength of laboratory samples from Chicago the Manhattan Project built a gigantic plant at Hanford in Washington State to produce plutonium. A bomb-development plant was established at Los Alamos, New Mexico.

On Monday 26 July 1945 at 5.30 a.m. the laboratory discovery of 1938 exploded with a violence a thousand times greater than any chemical explosive and 'brighter than a thousand suns'. The crater it made in the desert was a notchmark from which the future of Mankind would henceforth be dated. The Manhattan Project, by the mobilization of brains and skills in a concentrated effort unlimited by money or resources, had reduced the timescale of innovation from decades to years and from years to months. Later crash programmes would achieve rapid results in space technology and in the development of other weapons systems. Technical change could easily outpace political change.

In June 1945, working in the hot embers of the European War and with the Pacific still in flames, the devisers of the United Nations assumed that the Great Powers—the USA, the USSR, the UK, France and China—would combine to keep the peace through the mechanism of the Security Council. Abuse of the veto crippled the Security Council. The Military Staff Committee, provided for in the Charter, has never functioned, and for his peacekeeping interventions the Secretary-General has to behave like a short-handed sheriff in a Western movie, calling on reluctant member-states to provide a UN posse.

Failure to secure international control of nuclear energy was the crucial weakness of the new international order. The UN Atomic Energy Commission was set up in January 1946 when the only stockpile of nuclear weapons was American. The stumbling block, which has kept cropping up ever since, was the demand that international inspection should precede the dismantling of nuclear weapons and the banning of their manufacture. The Commission reported an impasse. The Soviet Union, Britain, France, China and other nations went on to develop not only the A-bomb but the far more powerful H-bomb, and novel methods of delivery for nuclear weapons of all kinds.

In place of collective security under the UN, we had the balance of terror. The only thing that the nuclear deterrent ever deterred was the other fellow's deterrent: the nuclear capability has been unusable for any lesser purpose. Since 1945, it has not deterred over 140 wars with an estimated thirty million military and civilian casualties. In that rehearsal for Doomsday, the Cuba Crisis of 1962, Soviet missiles were placed in Cuba and the Super Powers found themselves horn-locked on the edge of the abyss. They disengaged: the missiles were withdrawn. Khruschev said, 'People ask "Who won?" I say "Reason won." '

But not so as you would notice. The sardonic meaning of the Hot Line, installed between Moscow and Washington in 1963, is that when there is a mistake—a faulty silicon chip in the computer, an error in the programming or the wrong identification of a radar blip—the Man in the White House calls the Man in the Kremlin (or vice versa) and says 'Sorry about that multi-headed, multi-megaton missile which is going to vaporize you ten minutes from now. It is a technical error with no political significance.' Both sides are aware of the numerous occasions on which that has nearly happened, in the precarious system of early warning and instant response. Yet they have gone on adding to their stockpiles of weapons, in which the quantities are now so vast as to be irrelevant.

By default of political decisions in the late 1940s when the nuclear situation was still manageable, a generation later the nuclear arsenals contain 50,000 weapons, capable of turning much of our planet into a radioactive desert. Destruction is no longer at the discretion of Super Powers; despite the Non-Proliferation Treaty, at least a dozen countries have the capability to make nuclear weapons. Even the peaceful uses of atomic energy have become ominous: by the end of the year 2000, electricity generating stations will be producing enough plutonium to make, each year, thirty thousand bombs of the type that destroyed Nagasaki. Governments now realize that there is no technical way of preventing the spread of nuclear weapons. The solution must be political; internationalizing those parts of the nuclear cycle, especially the reprocessing of spent reactor fuel, which can produce fissile materials.

When military scientists devise new weaponry, pressures build up for its deployment. Politicians, pushed along by the momentum of military technology, then have to adapt their policies to rationalize this deployment. The Numbers Men calculate the 'acceptable casualties', reckoned in megadeaths, in allegedly 'limited' and 'winnable' nuclear wars, which are nothing of the kind. Thus have the high hopes of the 1940's been trampled upon by the military realities of the 1980's. The tragedy is a double one, because of what might have been accomplished if the money, skills and resources devoted to the arms race had been spent differently. By 1980, world military expenditure amounted to £500 billion a year. That was fifty thousand times as much as WHO expended annually in its successful ten-year campaign to eradicate smallpox from the world. In the global arms trade, about three-quarters of all transfers of major weapons are to the Third World—guns instead of bread.

The hopes for a better world were not, and are not, naive. On the contrary, those who regard world development as a deferrable option delude themselves, as do those for whom disarmament negotiations are a leisurely diplomatic game. Peace and prosperity are still the only realistic alternatives to unbounded war and woe.

* * *

The future begins now, with fingers fidgeting over the buttons of mutual destruction, and millions of our kind multiplying in misery. We are the victims of our own prodigious achievements, and the portentous comet is not Halley's but Adams's. In the first of the following essays, Gerard Piel recalls Henry Adams, the American historian. At the beginning of the century, Adams plotted human progress and likened it to a comet making a U-turn near the Sun, before heading back into darkness. H G Wells, in his later years when I saw a lot of him, shared his pessimism. He who had for so long believed in the social benefits of science and impending triumph of rationality, in the end despaired: 'Events now follow one another in an entirely untrustworthy manner'.

Temperamentally, I cannot accept the metaphor of the comet. Optimism is obligatory, because without hope we are finished. In any case, despite all of the disappointments of the past forty years, the reasons for living in hope have not altered. Wars are made by men and can be averted by men. The age-old afflictions of hunger, disease and ignorance can be tackled by available means. That is why I prefer to think of human affairs not as a comet, but as a rocket, subject to our remote control, so that we can change its trajectory and extend the curve, giving *Homo sapiens* more time to think. Imagine sitting in mission control: what midcourse corrections can we propose? What impulses can wisdom signal to it?

The intention should be to steer away from disaster and to keep hope alive, not to determine a destination in some idealized Utopia. In compiling this book I have sought the best thinking we can get on the options, in the belief that it can be convincing enough to counteract the prevailing pessimism, and realistic enough to influence policy makers. Consensus was not a requirement, but in the outcome most contributors share the restrained optimism appropriate for these purposes. They assert that progress can continue, given changes in direction that are matters of necessity, not idealism. If they are heeded, humanity's rocket may still be just at the start of a long adventure in spacetime.

2

The Acceleration of History

by Gerard Piel

Futurology places the everywhere evident increase in the rate and the scale of technological change at the centre of its attempt to secure a scientific footing for the ancient urge to prophesy. Technology is said to have its own imperative; its accelerating change (no longer 'progress') gives history increasing momentum, beyond deflection by any force or will. The future of the world, thus ever more strongly determined, comes ever more swiftly into sight. To predict it, one needs but to see it.

If futurologists find this a fair statement of their position they will find it better stated in two essays by Henry Adams; The Tendency of History and the Phase Rule Applied to History. Adams there propounded his proposition that the acceleration of technological change was forcing the acceleration of history. In these two essays, written at the beginning of the twentieth century, Adams also anticipated the futurologists in the millenarianism that so pervades their reflections about the future, with the inexorable and now near approach of the year 2000.

As in the last years of the first millennium, the people are summoned to the hilltops, from there to behold the dread riders of the black, the red and the pale horses mete out the last judgement to human wickedness and folly. In the secular apocalypse, mankind is to perish by population explosion, by exhaustion of resources, by pollution—unless it is spared such terminal misery by thermonuclear suicide. Cheery voices, it is true, can be heard against the basso continuo of despair. They tell us the technological fix is in.

Cultivated in the sciences as in letters, Henry Adams appreciated the powerful generalization in the equations of James Clerk Maxwell; he grasped the main ideas in the thermodynamics of Josiah Willard Gibbs; he was enthralled by the dilemma of the Ether in physics, and he was ready for the discovery of radioactivity. When Adams turned, late in his life, to seek the underlying sense or rule or law of history he was prepared, as few historians are, to relate his subject to science and technology. From his own collection of the data, he plotted the rising curves of coal consumption, of steam power, of the arrival of electrical power. Any schoolboy, he said, could plot such curves and see that 'arithmetical ratios were useless'; the curves followed 'the old familiar law of squares'. Adams accordingly ruled off the time baselines of his charts on a logarithmic scale, which accords equal space to the last decade and the last century (see Fig. 1). By this geometrical stratagem he was able to stretch out and display the detail of the stronger deflection of his curves that came progressively in the most recent times. It was a stratagem that served psychology as well, reflecting the compression of the past in the memory.

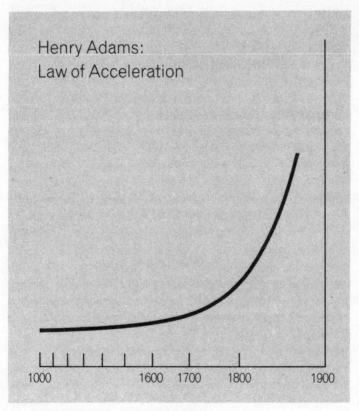

Figure 1

The acceleration of the seventeenth century, [Adams observed] was rapid, and that of the sixteenth century was startling. The acceleration even became measurable, for it took the form of utilizing heat as force, through the steam engine, and this addition of power was measurable in the coal output.

Acceleration was the law of history.

From his acquaintance with the work of Gibbs, he was prepared to grasp the metaphor in the change of 'phase' in thermodynamics that comes with change in quantity. History, Adams declared, was in passage through three phases (see Fig. 2). By reason of the acceleration of history each phase must necessarily be of a duration equal to the square root of the duration of the phase that preceded it:

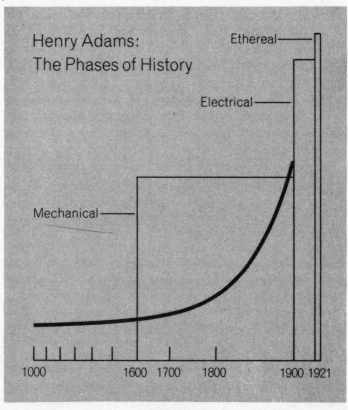

Figure 2

Supposing the Mechanical Phase to have lasted 300 years, from 1600 to 1900, the next or Electric Phase would have a life equal to $\sqrt{300}$, or about seventeen years and a half, when—that is, in 1917—it would pass into another or Ethereal Phase, which, for half a century, science has been promising, and which would last only $\sqrt{17.5}$ or about four years, and bring Thought to the limit of its possibilities in the year 1921. It may well be! Nothing whatever is beyond the range of possibility; but even if the life of the previous phase, 1600–1900, were extended another hundred years, the difference to the last term of the series would be negligible. In that case, the Ethereal Phase would last till about 2025.

By Adams' calculation the life of Mankind is on probation: we are living in the grace period between 1921 and 2025. Adams despaired of our capacity to withstand the overriding force of acceleration. In 1905, he declared,

Yet it is quite sure, according to my score of ratios and curves, that, at the accelerated rate of progression since 1600, it will not need another century or half century to turn Thought upside down. Law, in that case, would disappear . . . and give place to force. Morality would become police. Explosives would reach cosmic violence. Disintegration would overcome integration.

He likened the life of Thought to the passage of a comet:

If not a Thought, the comet is a sort of brother of Thought, an early condensation of the Ether itself, as the human mind may be another, traversing the infinite without origin or end, and attracted by a sudden object of curiosity that lies by chance near its path. If the calculated curve of deflection of Thought in 1600–1900 were put on the planet, it would show that man's evolution had passed perihelion, and that his movement was already retrograde. (See Fig. 3.)

The same nightmare vision recurred more recently to another man who might be reckoned among the precursors of *fin de siècle* futurology. That man, of all men, was H G Wells. In the last year of his life (he died in 1946), within twelve months after the first public demonstration of the new explosives of cosmic violence, he wrote:

Events now follow one another in an entirely untrustworthy sequence. . . . Spread out and examine the pattern of events and

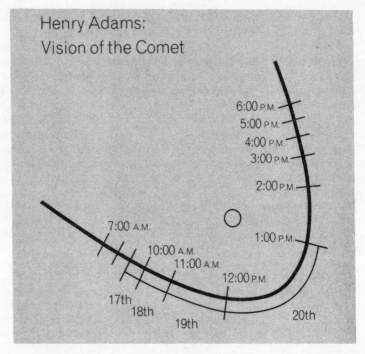

Figure 3

you will find yourself face to face with a new scheme of being, hitherto unimaginable by the human mind. This new cold glare mocks and dazzles the human intelligence. . . . The writer has come to believe that the congruence of mind, which man has attributed to the secular process, is not really there at all. . . . The two processes have run parallel for what we call Eternity and now abruptly they swing off at a tangent from one another—just as a comet at its perihelion hangs portentous in the heavens for a season and then rushes away for ages or forever.

Against such formidable authority at the founding of futurology, I have the presumption to press here another view of history and of the new technology of prophecy. Old Adam did not spring ready-made from the finger of Jehovah. He had a hand in his own biological evolution. His descendants have carried forward his supreme invention: with the coming of Man, purpose found its way for the first time into nature, at least in this corner of the universe.

Evolution therewith became history. History shows that purpose—human value—has always had its ultimate ground in the objective knowledge we call today by the name of science. History shows as well the accelerating expansion of human purpose as a force in nature. In the next millennium, our descendants will have their say about the course of the acceleration of history, which will depend upon the engagement of increasing numbers of them in the work that keeps it going. Percy Bridgman once asked what the consequence would be of 'letting loose in society an increasing quotient of intellectual integrity'.

The expansion of objective knowledge and of the control over nature inherent in that knowledge has transformed not only the relation of Man to nature but the relation of man to man. From age to age, discovery and invention have opened new scope and possibility to human life. Each new possibility has compelled

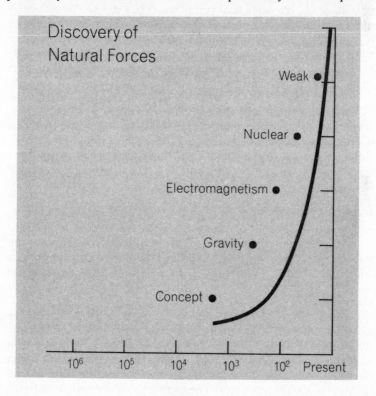

Figure 4

choice. In the succession of choices, values and the social order have evolved.

Now, the steeply accelerating advance of objective knowledge and of its uses allows no time for evolution. People and nations are compelled to the immediate re-examination and deliberate over-haul of the values and institutions they have carried into the present from the suddenly receding past.

Let us spread out and examine the pattern of events and see how it sustains this thesis (see Fig. 4). I have projected Henry Adams' curve backward to the classical period, 2,000 years ago, and forward 75 years to the present. A wealth of statistical data supports the ascent of the curve to twice the height at which Adams charted it at the turn of the century. Considering only the statistics for the United States, every index, from the consumption of energy *per caput* to the volume of scientific publication, has tripled in this period. Since few statistical series reach beyond 150 or 200 years into the past, the projection of the curve back behind 1600 must be regarded as largely symbolic. The projection is documented, however, by a number of crucial indexes, especially if one may reverse the Henry Adams rule of historical phase and count changes in quality as accumulations in quantity.

Consider what is shown here: the shrinking time interval from the discovery of one primary force of nature to the next. At the outset, there had to be the notion of a natural or inanimate force, as distinguished from the animistic and particular genius of the place, thing, or process; this elementary idea was first propounded in the science of the Greeks two millennia ago. Then, 300 years ago, came the Galilean-Newtonian great world system ordered by the force of gravity. Next, less than 200 years ago, came the Franklin-Faraday-Maxwell discovery of the electromagnetic force. Now, within this century, Einstein, Planck, Rutherford and Bohr uncovered the most energetic of the forces, that which binds the nucleus of the atom. Last, at this very moment, physics is comprehending the presence of the fourth primary force of the universe: the so-called weak force observed in the decay of elementary particles.

Consider, alternatively, the curve that is plotted by the successive isolations of the 92 elements into which matter is chemically differentiated (see Fig. 5). Perhaps as many as a half-dozen elements—carbon, copper, gold, silver, lead—had come into use in more or less pure form at the beginning of the agricultural revolution 10,000 years ago. The number rose abruptly to 20 with the beginning of modern chemistry 200 years ago. By the time

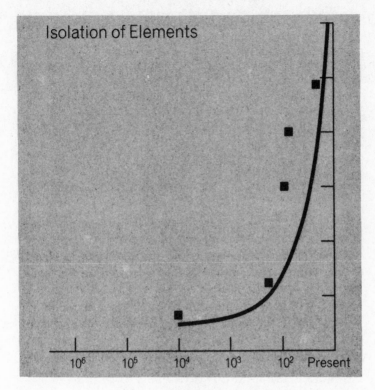

Figure 5

Mendeleev laid out the table of elements, a century ago, the number of elements isolated had more than doubled again to 60-odd. Today physics has carried the series out beyond the bounty of nature, adding a dozen so-called synthetic elements to the table—and the curve might be extended indefinitely by grafting on the lengthening table of 'fundamental' particles.

Consider still another curve—that plotted by the mastery of the major sources of inanimate energy (see Fig. 6). The starting point carries our projection back behind the beginning of history to at least 50,000 years ago when Man discovered the first uses of fire. With his own vital energy amplified by fire, Man must already, in that remote time, be reckoned as a geologic force. He used fire not only to warm his body and to cook his food but more significantly to burn forests and extend the grasslands over which he could hunt more safely and productively. The next point on the curve marks

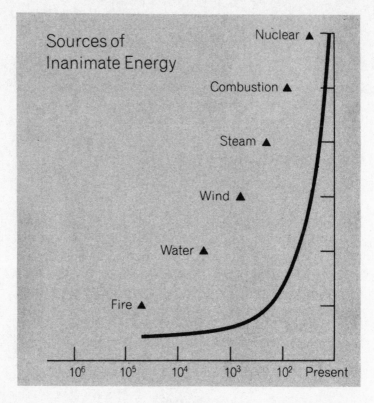

Figure 6

the harnessing of water power in the Bronze Age, 5,000 years ago. It was only 800 years ago that Man began to make comparable use of the wind (granted: the sail began to harness the wind as long ago as 3,500 BC); the invention of the windmill in twelfth-century Europe was something of a technological revolution, spreading in a century from Normandy to the Black Sea. The Industrial Revolution itself began, of course, with the harnessing of steam, 200 years ago. Direct or internal combustion—which generates as much mechanical and electrical energy as steam in contemporary technology—dates back only a century. And now the first nuclear reactors are delivering electricity to the power networks of the world.

The pattern of events shows history on a course of accelerating acceleration (see Fig. 7). The major developments in Man's

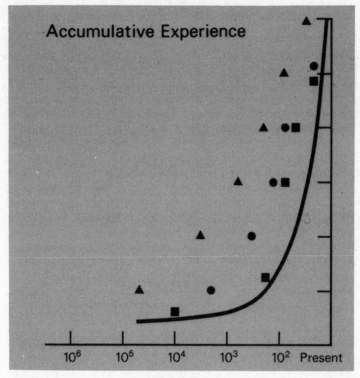

Figure 7

accumulative experience have occurred within the most recent times, and these developments occur at shorter time intervals into the very present. The pattern of events explains furthermore the exponential drive inherent in the inquiry after and the use of objective knowledge. The inquiry, as the chart shows, is accumulative. Objective knowledge, in the words of Benjamin Franklin, is useful knowledge; no useful knowledge has ever been lost. But, what is more, every discovery and every invention asks new questions and creates new niches inviting renewed inquiry and facilitating new invention. Thus it was mastery of fire that brought the first metallic elements in reach; it was the conductors, silver and copper, that opened the way to the electromagnetic force; command of that force led inquiry to the nuclear force. Like the chain reaction, fired by the two reaction-igniting neutrons that issue from each reaction, the inquiry proceeds exponentially.

This chart does not, of course, tell the full story of history. Plotting only accumulative human experience, it excludes the rest—the glory and tragedy, the shame and the honour, the bestial and the humane—and so, by some lights, it excludes all that gives meaning to history. Yet the exponential curve of objective knowledge, I believe, plots the mainstream of history insofar as history has not merely repeated itself. This assertion is confirmed when we place the brief period of recorded time in the perspective of Man's longer past. At the giddy vantage point on the vertical co-ordinate to which we have ascended in our lifetime, we are as far removed from the nineteenth century as our grandfathers were from prehistoric time.

The starting point of the plot of history may now be established two or more million years before the present, and proportionately closer to the time base line (see Fig. 8). At sites reliably dated to that

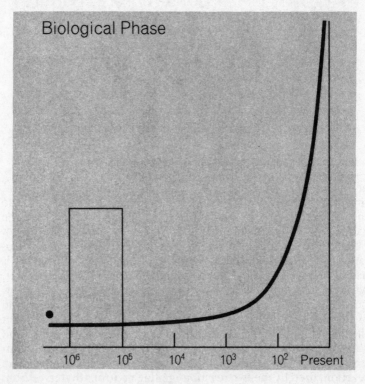

$$10^6 \qquad 10^5 \qquad 10^4 \qquad 10^3 \qquad 10^2 \qquad \text{Present}$$

Figure 8

distant time in the Rift country of Africa, anthropologists have been finding assemblages of stone tools. With these tools they have found fragments of the bones of the hands that made them. The hands are not human hands—not our hands. They are the hands of a primate who still used them at times for walking. In the old taxonomy of primates it was supposed that Man had made the first tools; toolmaking was the status symbol of membership in our genus. Now, it would appear, tools made Man. Certainly, toolmaking conferred a selective advantage on the maker of tools and of better tools. But the meaning of this phase of history goes deeper. The truth is: Man made himself.

The record as to bones of hands and skulls is scanty. There is an abundance, however, of the fossils of behaviour—the stone tools. In their increasing diversity, specialization, and refinement, they give evidence of the evolution of the hand and of the brain, of which the hand is an extension. The tools show, in time, that evolution has quickened because it has entered on a new mode. It has become cultural as well as biological, Lamarckian as well as Darwinian in that acquired characteristics—better tools and toolmaking—are transmitted from generation to generation by teaching and learning. Emergent Man has already discovered in his own head the notion of purpose, for which men have since sought validation in so many other corners of the universe. That extraordinary selective advantage, it must be conceded, gave Man an active role in his own biological evolution.

The increasing specialization of the stone tools implies, of course, a corresponding elaboration of technology employing less enduring materials. The mastery of new environments commanded thereby disclosed new possibilities and new ways of life—one must go so far as to say new goals and values—to the men who sired modern Man.

Homo sapiens himself came on the scene in the last 250,000 years, emerging in a population that probably never exceeded 500,000. On the way to *Homo sapiens*, it is estimated, some 30,000 million members of the emerging genus *Homo* were born and died.

As long as 50,000 years ago, the diversity of hunting and food-gathering technologies enabled primitive Man to make himself at home in every environment on earth (see Fig. 9). Some primitive cultures have persisted even into modern times on the Arctic shores of the northern continents, in the interior of the southern continents and on oceanic islands in the Pacific. These peoples have taught us to use the term 'primitive' with respect. There is no human language that is primitive; each has a grammar as well as a vocabulary. The aesthetics of these cultures is the more compelling because it so directly articulates the experience of life. Typically, their social order is the extended family, and the code of law and custom submerges the individual in the common identity and destiny of the group.

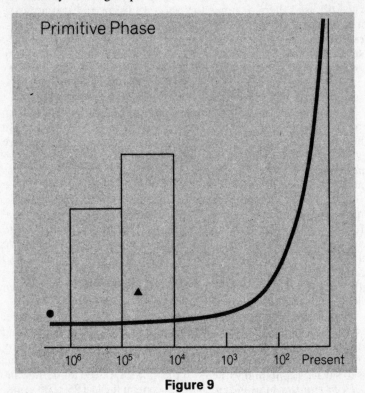

Figure 9

It has been shown that even in a continental environment as favourable as that of North America, primitive technology could not sustain more than one person per 10 square miles of territory. The aboriginal peoples, of course, never approached the limiting density. The world population may have reached 5 million, with life expectancy not exceeding 25 years, and 30,000 million of the *Homo sapiens* species were born and died in the course of these 200 millennia. The hazard and uncertainty of the hunting and food-gathering way of life is the common theme of primitive religion and art.

Imperceptibly, over tens of thousands of years, as certain of these

peoples came into possession of more intimate understanding of
their environments, they found a more secure way of life, as
herdsmen and cultivators of the soil (see Fig. 10). By 10,000 years
ago they had domesticated all of the plants and animals now grown
on the world's farms. There could be no doubt about the progressive nature of this development. It multiplied by 100 the potential
size of the population that could be sustained on the land. As history
was soon to show, the labour of four families in the field could now
support a fifth family in the city.

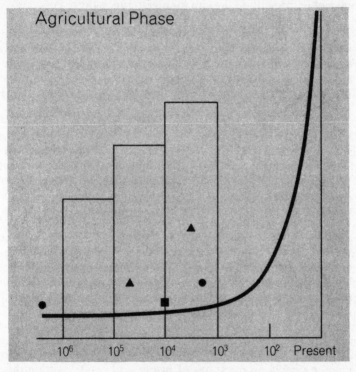

Figure 10

The transition to agricultural civilization was made in the same
2,000–3,000 year period in Asia Minor, in the valley of the Nile, in
the Indus Valley in India and in China; the transition was made
more recently in pre-Columbian America, apparently in entire
independence of events in the Old World. Wherever this revolution
occurred, it gave rise to essentially the same social and economic

institutions. The function of these institutions was to secure the inequitable distribution of the product of the soil. Law and custom speedily legitimized the necessary measures of coercion. But the primary compulsion, as we can now see, was supplied by the slant of the curve of discovery and invention. Over millennia or centuries, progress was substantial; in the lifetime of a man, however, it brought no appreciable increase in the product of his labour. Population tended always to increase faster than production, maintaining a constant equilibrium of scarcity. Bertrand de Jouvenel has described the situation with precision:

> As long as there is a fairly constant limit to production *per caput*, one man can gain wealth only by making use of another man's labour; only a few members of society can gain wealth, therefore, and at the expense of the rest. All ancient civilizations rested upon the inexplicit premise that the productivity of labour is constant.

The inexplicit premise of scarcity is stated plainly enough in the plan of the ancient cities. Invariably it shows the palace, the temple, and the garrison within the ruin of the walls and, outside, the traces in the soil of the hovels of the slaves. Thus four-fifths of the population was made to render up the surplus necessary to sustain one-fifth in the new enterprises of high civilization.

Put the other way around, agricultural technology and the social arrangements it sustained made it possible for some people to explore the protean potentialities of the biological endowment the human species had acquired in the long journey of evolution. For the small fraction of the population to whom such enterprise was open, it can be said that they made the most of the possibilities and opportunities. History is first and foremost the story of their extraordinary lives. They gave impetus to the advance of invention and discovery; they explored new realms of aesthetic experience, enriching the lives of all men with their vitality and sensibility; they pondered deeply on questions of justice and equity, setting their reflections down in codes of law and treatises on moral philosophy; they developed the arts of government and administration; they led their countrymen on bold adventures in politics, war, and conquest.

Of the 80 per cent of the population who were excluded from history—except when war loosed murder, famine, and pestilence on the land—history has little to say. It has even less to say about the underlying inequity of the social and economic institutions—whether slavery, serfdom, helotry or other form of pseudospeciation—that laid the burden of history on their backs. Laws were passed to regulate the treatment of slaves and serfs, but the gross immorality of these institutions was never called in question until modern times—not until, that is, the inexplicit premise of scarcity itself had been overturned and its annulment had made these arrangements morally as well as technologically obsolete.

By 1600, the world population had reached, it is estimated, about 500 million, and another 30,000 million had been born and died. Population growth continued at the near zero annual rate, with life expectancy still at 25 years and with the high death rate offset by resolute maintenance of a high fertility rate.

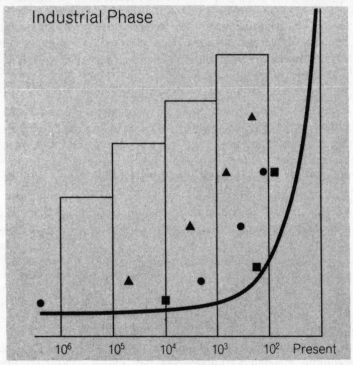

Figure 11

It is easy now to mark the turning point of history (see Fig. 11). But even in the seventeenth century people sensed the accelerative force of the contemporary deflection of thought. Without doubt, the most revolutionary idea in history up to that time was the concept of inertia advanced in 1638 by Galileo—then already past the age of seventy and writing in secret under house arrest for the lesser heresy of advocating the Copernican revolution. Galileo's great insight comprehended at once the swinging of a pendulum and the motion of the planets on their orbits. The idea of inertia not only changed men's view of nature; it placed a primary force of nature in their hands. Within a few generations they were setting much besides pendulums in motion.

The surplus gathered in by the institutions of scarcity found a new historic function. It became the wealth of nations to be invested in the increase of capacity to produce wealth. Though hindsight encourages us to place emphasis on the acceleration of the rate of discovery and invention in this period, we must not fail to credit the role of the institutions of political economy. In 1802, looking in satisfaction on the ascendance of Britain, then in the vanguard of the industrial revolution, Sir Humphry Davy astutely observed: 'The unequal division of property and of labour, the difference of rank and condition amongst Mankind, are the sources of power in civilized life, its moving causes and even its very soul.'

Industrial revolution soon brought on a biological revolution. The European peoples constituted 10 per cent of the 500 million world population of 1600; they were 30 per cent of a world population estimated by Thomas Malthus at 1,000 million when he wrote his famous treatise. Rising productivity *per caput*, and the popularization of material well-being it made possible, showed up first in decline of European death rates.

With birth rates following death rates downward, the European population explosion was passing its peak even as Malthus was writing. Population growth in the industrial rich countries has now returned close to the zero rate, with low death rates—and life expectancies in the order of 70 years—balanced by low birth rates. That commonsense and simple arithmetic are not the monopoly of European peoples is evident in the fact that the people of every industrial and industrializing country, including those of Asia, have followed them into the same demographic transition.

In the generation of the increasing affluence of industrial civilization, mechanical horsepower has almost completely displaced biological energy from the production of goods. Now solid-state electronics is taking over from human nervous systems the control of production and much of the new kind of work that is occasioned by the logistical complexities of industrial production, distribution and consumption. Typically the labour force in all industrial countries has migrated from agriculture and the extractive industries to manufacturing, and now from manufacturing to the services. In the United States of America, where this transformation has gone farthest, less than 4 per cent of the labour force remains on the farms and less than 30 per cent is engaged in production all told; in employment and input to gross national product, medicine and education are, each one, bigger than agriculture.

In the industrial countries, in sum, the economic problem is solved. For readers who might not have encountered that problem John Maynard Keynes found it necessary as long as 50 years ago to define it as:

> . . . that struggle for subsistence always hitherto the primary, most pressing problem not only of the human race but of the whole biological kingdom from the beginnings of life in its most primitive form.

The social and political institutions of industrial civilization remain, however, adjusted to the management of a technology of lesser competence. They have evolved but slowly against the friction of custom and vested interest. The accelerating advance of technology has now terrifyingly capacitated the inequity and cruelty built into those institutions from the beginning. While the ruling powers in all industrial countries, it is true, proclaim the sovereignty of the people and are compelled to rationalize policy and action by reference to democratic ideals, only a few of the smaller countries have sought and approached political and economic democracy in practice. Inequity destabilizes the social order in all the great countries. In political instability the Super Powers turn upon each other. No ideologue on either side accepts the admonition of Andrei Sakharov:

> The development of modern society in both the Soviet Union and the United States is now following the same course . . . giving rise in both countries to managerial groups that are similar in social character. We must therefore acknowledge that there is no qualitative difference in the structure of the two societies.

The overhanging threat of the mindless confrontation of the two societies lends substance to millenarian despair. It is as if the repeal of the historic premises of inequity were to be answered by an eruption of violence equal to the cumulative sum of that which held the great mass of Mankind in subjection throughout history down to this day. It may be, in the words of Abraham Lincoln, that 'all the wealth piled up by the bondsman's unrequited toil shall be sunk and every drop of blood drawn with the lash shall be paid with another drawn by the sword'.

By a kind of displacement activity familiar to students of animal behaviour, citizens who should know better turn away from the hard political and ethical questions to anti-rational disillusion and irrelevant protest. Popular opinion in the industrial world increasingly holds science to be amoral and even inimical to 'humane' values. Technology is said to obey its own internal imperatives in pursuit of aimless innovation without regard to utility or peril. Its giant intricate enterprises have no place in them for individual human conscience and responsibility. 'Things are in the saddle and ride mankind.'

For the three-fourths of Mankind who inhabit the poor nations of the world the economic problem remains, meanwhile, to be solved. Their still rapidly growing numbers have overrun not their resources—few of the new nations are as ill-favoured as Japan—but the agricultural technology and still earlier technologies they have brought with them into the twentieth century. Among these peoples, there is no recoil from the advance and use of objective knowledge. They look to it for answers to the great simplifying question that still rules their daily existence: 'When do we eat?'

The first modicum of industrial technology imported into their existence has already started them into the first phase of the demographic transition. Their death rates are falling and life expectancy has lifted above the age-old 25 years into the 40s and in some countries even into the 60s. How soon they will enter the second phase and bring their birth rates downward is a function of the rate of their economic development. For them, as for the rich countries, industrial revolution must precede biological revolution. Those in the rich countries who fear that the Earth's resources will not suffice to make the poor as rich as we are should be reassured to learn that some poor countries have established fertility control and secured decline in their birth rates at standards of comfort and security far below those at which fertility control began to be practised in the rich countries. If birth rates in all poor countries could be brought down to the zero-population-growth net reproduction rate of 1.0 by the Year 2000, the world population might settle at around 8,000 million by mid-century. The longer that date is put off the larger must be the world's ultimate population.

Economic growth of the poor countries turns upon the transfer to them of the catalyst of industrial technology that will bring their abundant manpower and unused resources into productive re-action. A generous large effort to this end was promised by the rich nations at the end of the Second World War. It goes without saying that industrial technology, incorporating the accumulative ex-perience of the human species from the first stone tools onward, is the common heritage of all Mankind. The poor nations are now suing for such action and are learning to use their resources and their weight otherwise in international politics to induce or compel the transfer. Industrial peoples, whose moral and economic equi-librium has been upset by the too-abrupt ending of their economic problem, could stretch out their entry into the next phase of human existence (see Fig. 12) by helping the poor countries end theirs.

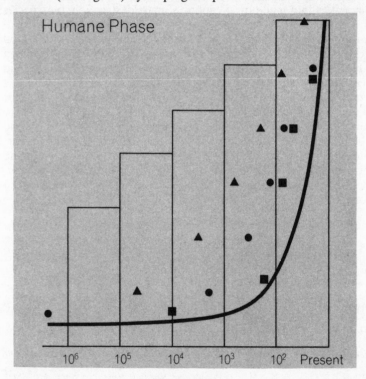

Figure 12

The acceleration of history has brought the human species to the fork in the road. One way from here goes to a dead end; on the logarithmic time base-line, history has not long to run. The other, less plainly marked, may yet show our species the way to realization of its humanity.

If history is indeed to end in suicidal conflagration, it will be from habit. Civilized communities have always employed force and violence, tempered at times by fraud, to hold their members together against the inequities that divided them. Inequity has had its historic role as well, freeing a few members of the community for larger enterprises when there was not enough to go around. The enormous forces and the violence now at the disposal of national states makes this way of organizing society and going on with history suddenly fatal.

At the same time, by exercise of the same supremely human capacities that made the weapons of mass destruction, our species has brought another future into sight. Understanding and control of nature have shown how to secure enough and to spare of material goods to permit the admission of every man into full membership in Mankind. Inequity is thereby denied its historic sanction. Force and fraud lose, correspondingly, their legitimacy as tools of domestic management and international politics. The accumulation of objective knowledge has now made it possible to cherish every human life. It is no longer possible, therefore, to justify the spending of any human life for the security, profit, ennoblement, pleasure, revenge or higher purpose of others. The humane dispensation of abundance reversing the iron law of scarcity, declares: One man can gain increase in well-being only by working for the well-being of all other men.

REFERENCES

Henry Adams, *The Tendency of History and the Phrase Rule Applied to History in The Degradation of the Democratic Dogma,* Brooks Adams, editor, 1919.

H. G. Wells, *Mind at the End of Its Tether,* 1945.

L. S. B. Leakey, Olduvai Gorge, *Scientific American,* January 1954.

Sherwood L. Washburn, Tools and Human Evolution, *Scientific American,* September 1960.

Edward S. Deevey, The Human Population, *Scientific American,* September 1960.

J. M. Keynes, *Economic Prospects for our Grandchildren,* 1930.

Andrei Sakharov, 'Letter to My Foreign Colleagues,' *New York Review of Books,* January 1982.

3

To the Poles of Technology

by Nigel Calder

'I got a flat on the flyover but of course Mary didn't believe me and when I arrived she had the stereo going full blast and was talking to her mother who's on a package in Corfu.' If ghosts haunting old inns were to eavesdrop at the bar they would be baffled by the conversations. 'It's classified, of course, but these squids will pick up a missile sub at ten miles and then you can nuke it—bad news for the felt-slipper navy.' And so on: the jargon decorates realms of human activity unknown to our forefathers. At the same pubs in forty years' time, you might hear them chatter about gollocking in the shribe, which is jabberwockese for how people will spend their waking hours in the twenty-first century.

Predicting the future of technology in any definite sense is impossible. To anticipate the less obvious discoveries and inventions of the decades ahead would come close to making them yourself—a tall order. And even if you had second sight about the intrinsic possibilities of technology, it would tell you nothing about the political, economic, social, environmental and other factors that will determine how the available techniques are put to use. Reason and common sense are imperfect guides: large cars and H-bombs, for instance, are undesirable in the abstract, but people want to have them. Nor is there any coherent theory of human nature and market forces that will explain why electric razors are big business and electric toothbrushes are not; why sailing is so popular that the crowded Dutch have stopped reclaiming the old Zuiderzee to leave water for it; or why the Indians excel in nuclear research and development and do all too little for the agrarian poor.

Human technological behaviour is labile as well as cryptic. Even if you could make sense of all the present patterns of the uses of technology, in all the different cultures of the world, extrapolation would not tell you the patterns of the twenty-first century. In some cases the limits of human resources will force a change in behaviour:

it is an economic and physical impossibility to give everyone all of the benefits—heart transplants, for example—that might in principle benefit them. If there is no metaphorical change of heart in other areas of technology, weaponry in particular, our civilization is probably doomed. If we survive, there will be brand-new enthusiasms—perhaps for communing with playful and artistic computers, perhaps for supergardening that aims to evolve new species of plants and animals, perhaps for guarding the planet against strikes by giant meteorites. These forms of gollocking will displace older activities because there are only a limited number of hours in the day.

In short, to speak predictively of technology more than a few years ahead, the forecaster would need to combine the inventive genius of a Leonardo with the business acumen of a Ford and the moral insight of an Old Testament prophet. For this reason you should be sceptical about forecasts that purport to tell you what *will* happen even (I might say, especially) when made by delphic committees of eminent experts. You are on safer epistemological ground if you let experts speak imaginatively about possibilities and then say what *you* think *should* happen. Everyone is entitled to his or her opinion about uses of technology to be favoured or disfavoured. But there are pitfalls of other kinds in this normative approach. The chances are that one's opinions are either banal or mere wishful thinking; if they are not, then one may be seeking to impose upon other peoples and other generations a Utopian update of one's own local and temporary way of life. Almost certainly normative forecasting pays too little respect to other cultures and does scant justice to the social and technological possibilities of the twenty-first century.

If I were as discouraged about technological forecasting as the preamble might suggest, this chapter should consist of a number of blank pages and an invitation to the reader to write his own future, on the assumption that technological possibilities are virtually boundless. Alternatively, one could imagine an elaborate logical tree of reinforcing and countervailing options which purported to let the reader discover what gollocking might be, through a succession of choices leading to a typical diary for a typical citizen in the early twenty-first century. But all that would be idleness akin to filling in crossword puzzles, and certainly inadequate for coping with fateful choices in the real world.

Fortunately a third approach presents those choices vividly and provocatively, without being either predictive or prescriptive in any naive sense. It is a matter of going to extremes, of asking, 'What if we went down *that* road as far as it could lead?' No need to say we ought to do so; only suppose that some people might want to go there. In this exercise the limits tend to be set by the laws of physics and biology rather than by current inventiveness or by the traditional economic constraints of materials, energy and space. One is carried far into the future and can accommodate imaginative inputs from any source. The details of the technological systems are relatively unimportant—it scarcely matters whether an electronic circuit runs on thermionic tubes, silicon chips or Josephson junctions. Most usefully of all, the poles of possibilities correspond with poles of virtues and vices and the effect, as in a parable, is to dredge up moral questions about human ambitions. Apply the method to a range of different opportunities and dangers and one begins to see an envelope of possibilities. As I hope to show, this 'polar' approach to the future of technology and society leads also to inferences that are instructive here and now.

The method has longstanding antecedents in social philosophy (Plato), satire (Swift) and science fiction (Stapledon). As a deliberate methodology for exploring the future it was adopted by the Marxist physicist J D Bernal in *The World, The Flesh and the Devil* (1929) and developed by the non-Marxist physicist Freeman J Dyson in a celebrated lecture of the same title (1972). In his remarkable autobiographical work *Disturbing the Universe* (1979), Dyson exhibits the method as the source of the boldest ideas about the technological future that are available anywhere, especially in space colonization, genetic engineering and robotics. While I extend the method into some other areas besides these, and offer some fresh inferences, my indebtedness to Bernal and Dyson is total.

The core of this chapter consists of a series of brief visits to some technological poles or extremes, namely:

1. Doomsday Machine
2. Santa Claus Machine
3. Green Machine
4. Climate Regulator
5. Space City
6. Anti-Comet Battery
7. Disembodied Brain
8. Cheap Thrills Machine
9. Self-Reproducing Robot Rocket Ship
10. Total Information System
11. Big Brother Machine

In beating the bounds of technology I cannot avoid trespassing into matters dealt with more thoroughly and knowledgeably in other chapters. There are further candidates besides these eleven machines but they suffice, I believe, to construct a rough 'polar diagram' around most of the fateful choices. They satisfy other criteria. The machines are all realistic, in two senses: one can point to existing systems that foreshadow them, and one could sketch block diagrams to show how a comprehensive version might be designed. And they offer plenty of contrasts and opposing tendencies without generating any flat contradictions. The eleven machines could in principle coexist, although that might make a lunatic world. I trust that we are past the stage when invention was the mother of necessity and anything that could be done, was done.

*　　　*　　　*

The *Doomsday Machine* began as a theoretical conception of nuclear strategists, for exploring the limits of deterrence theory. It is a system that destroys at will all human life, the user as well as his enemies and every neutral, in a culmination of spite. The technology is trivial, because there is no need to deliver it to any target, nor need the killing occur instantly. You can, for example, imagine a number of large and very dirty H-bombs doped with a material (cobalt, for instance) that is intended to cloak the world in intense and persistent radioactive fall-out. The machine makes possible a threat of the form: 'Do as I say (or desist from thwarting or attacking me) or we shall all die together.' If you even half believe the threat, you have to capitulate; it avails nothing to say, 'I have my own machine and I'll kill us all too, so there!'

Existing weapons systems approximate in a rough way to a Doomsday Machine, at least for northern civilization. The advent of highly accurate intercontinental missiles with multiple warheads, capable in principle of destroying the opponent's missiles in their silos, means that responses to threats have to be quick, thorough and quasi-automatic. National leaders are themselves prime targets in nuclear war and the notion of the Doomsday Machine reminds us that only a moral sense or sentimentality about the species preserves, in these doomed men, any concern for the survival of their fellow citizens and of neutrals.

Who would want such a Machine? The world has never lacked for clinically insane national leaders, and it should not be supposed that only the Super Powers are candidates. The proliferation of nuclear weapons means that any nation, except the very poorest and least well-schooled, could manufacture a Doomsday Machine. We shall never be certain that none exists, and the Jonestown Massacre showed that 'spiritual leadership' can inspire followers to co-operate in their own destruction. But insanity or religious zeal is not a prerequisite: the declared strategic policy that comes closest to the Doomsday concept happens to be that of the North Atlantic Treaty Organization, which promises to *initiate* the use of nuclear weapons in the event of a defeat in conventional fighting.

Discussions of the future usually take for granted that we shall avoid nuclear war, but to do so in the 1980s is a form of genteel irresponsibility. Of all my 'extremes', the Doomsday Machine is the nearest to realization and more technological skill is going into Doomsday-like projects than any other area of human activity. Extinction, at least of northern civilization, is now probable enough for one to suppose, actuarially, that an individual is more likely to die from the effects of an H-bomb than of heart failure, or in a road accident.

Even if we escape that outcome, there is another stern inference from the postulate of a Doomsday Machine. The threat to ignite it comes less unconvincingly from a madman, a zealot or a defeated Hitler than from any democratic government. In a game of deadly threats played by resolute men, the more amoral or ruthless side is bound to prevail and nuclear weapons and other genocidal devices are ultimately unsuitable for the defence of liberty. And if nuclear threats, unmitigated by moral factors or political dissent, are allowed to determine the political shape of the world we must prepare to live, if at all, under a ruthless global empire. Whether it is attained by war, by political conquest, by Super Powers uniting 'to keep the peace', or by well-intended efforts to give military supremacy to the United Nations, that is the most likely outcome. The empire will be obliged to employ totalitarian methods to ensure that no rebels can hope to make or steal nuclear weapons for themselves.

So, from hypothetical technology one is led back to present policies. If we allow the arms race to carry us ever closer to the Doomsday Machine we shall survive only at the expense of freedom. If we hastily switch to negotiated comprehensive dis-armament, we might expect to scrape through with both lives and liberties intact. The improbability of such a profound change of heart on all sides, least of all among those who might expect to rule the world, suggests that our creative, freedom-loving civilization is doomed, one way or the other. Nevertheless I go on to consider less violent possibilities for the future of technology, because I retain an ounce of hope, beyond reason, that my expectation is wrong.

The promise of industrial automation is summed up in the *Santa Claus Machine*. This name and concept, which I have from Theodore Taylor, an exceptionally imaginative and thoughtful engineer at Princeton University, help to bring into focus the hopes and fears about automation now prevalent in the richer countries of the world, with the promise of abundant material wealth and leisure on the one hand and the threat to jobs and social roles on the other. The Santa Claus Machine, then, is a large device that eats commonplace rocks and turns out any product that the operators can specify as a manufacturing programme: coffee cups, word processors, Rolls Royces or spaceships. Putting it simply, you draw a picture of what you want and the Machine makes it.

The engineering details are a matter of choice. The rocks to be consumed may be in a desert, in an uninhabited mountain range, on the seabed or on the Moon. Its energy supply may be solar, nuclear or anything else, but that is something that the Machine takes care of, for itself. A central feature of the system, at least in Taylor's own thinking, is the atomisation of the rocks followed by physical separation into all of the chemical elements; then, by chemical recombination, the Machine assembles any alloys, plastics, ceramics, dyes, drugs etc., that might be wanted, and computer-controlled tools and processes of extraordinary, but not incredible, flexibility complete the work. If there are aesthetic or environmental objections to eating up the Himalayas or the Sahara desert, the Machine can be programmed to landscape its own waste tips.

The best model for a Santa Claus Machine is not any existing factory but a bacterium, which takes in materials and energy from its environment and exudes distinctive waste products which may be extremely useful to other organisms. As the mathematician John von Neumann anticipated so uncannily in 1948, and biologists have amply confirmed, automation theory is the key to how living things work. So the Santa Claus Machine is a 'natural' way to do things, endorsed as thoroughly practicable by 4,000 million years of mindless life on Earth. Self-repair is plainly a desirable feature but I postpone the thorny question of whether the Machine should also be, like a living cell, capable of reproduction and multiplication. Suffice it for the moment to observe that in principle a Santa Claus Machine can make a Santa Claus Machine, so that capital investment vanishes and production costs virtually nothing, apart from the modest efforts associated with designing, transporting and distributing the products—roughly equivalent to handling similar weights of sand.

The Santa Claus Machine illuminates, in parable fashion, the present problems of unemployment and underemployment and all the talk of work sharing, shorter working weeks and old-age pensions at eighteen; and it highlights the mythic significance of industry in a materialistic society. Social systems, politics, the moral urge to work, the very existence and layout of many of our cities, are based on the primacy of extractive and manufacturing industries: wrench out the heart and remove it to the wastelands and what remains to be done, after automation has cut at least as wide a swathe through offices as through factories, may leave the general population with little sense of purpose. The religion of work is illustrated by those exhortations to 'work harder' that persist even in a period of runaway unemployment. When it is 'blown' one must expect disruption of ordinary life in the industrial countries. Violence and repression are likely, if only for the vulgar reason that the 'priests' who wield great power in the present work-oriented system—bankers, bosses of the multinationals, professional politicians, mandarin bureaucrats and trade union leaders—will not give it up without a struggle. As the Nora and Minc report to the President of France (1978) put it delicately, when social organization based on production is defunct both Liberal and Marxist approaches will become 'questionable'; more robustly these authors say that 'the traditional games of power' will be thrown into disorder.

Practical power will lie with the designers and operators of the Santa Claus Machine, or its piecemeal equivalents, and they may of course make the most of it. Kurt Vonnegut's disturbing novel *Player Piano* (1952) describes a fully automated age in which the population is divided into an elite of managers and engineers on one side of the river and, on the other, the 'Reeks and Wrecks'—the rest of the population dragooned in the Reconstruction and Reclamation Corps. But to give unlimited wealth and power to a few men and women who by chance have inherited, via the general culture, the engineering skills of their predecessors would be as bizarre for the post-industrial era as the reinvention of a feudal aristocracy.

There is no rational economic basis for allocating wealth among citizens blessed with Santa Claus Machines, nor for maintaining differentials between classes and crafts. But viable social systems not based on production are entirely feasible, and functions and prestige can be apportioned in ways that do not treat money-making, exam-passing and demagogy as the supreme human virtues. For instance William Morris's *News from Nowhere* (1891), although heavy on haymaking and sculpture, portrayed people using brains and hands as they pleased, and managing without money or central government, while an unspecified 'force' satisfied their economic needs. I would expect to see contrasting social experiments in sub-national regions, and perhaps a new polarization of the world into well-adapted, free systems in the manner of Morris, and regimented systems like Vonnegut's.

The *Green Machine* is the cousin of the Santa Claus Machine, its rival or its adjunct. At the zenith of biotechnology, it derives its energy from sunlight and draws its prime raw materials, carbon dioxide, nitrogen and water, from the air and from the hydrosphere. It may also employ microbes to extract supplementary nutrients such as phosphorus and trace metals from rocks or water. As in an ordinary living plant, the Machine uses pigments like chlorophyll to absorb the energy of daylight and then synthesizes sugars and other primary materials for energy and structural growth. Whether it will be more efficient to circulate natural algae for maximum rates of growth (as in current experiments) or to devise a mainly artificial equivalent of a giant green leaf, remains to be seen. The initial supplies of sugars can be used to produce energy in any desired form—substrates for microbes, alcohol for burning, electricity for light, and so on.

Food is the most important product of the Green Machine. It can be as conventional as people want: wheat, potatoes, tomatoes, steak. While one can imagine endless sausages growing by tissue culture of pork muscle, it is equally plausible to feed farm animals on microbial cultures and to grow vegetables indoors with outstanding efficiency, under artificial light produced from sunlight by bio-electric methods.

Because the use of solar energy and water is far more efficient than in any agriculture, the areas of land required for food and fibre production will be greatly reduced, despite growing populations. Moreover the Green Machine, like the Santa Claus Machine, can operate almost anywhere: in deserts, marshland, mountain slopes, the sea. The net effect will be to liberate the natural world from the sequestering of all the best land by farmers, with their axes, guns and chemical sprays. The most gracious new aim in life—the gollocking—may be to restore wild life to something like its condition before the invention of agriculture (Calder 1967). But human interference cannot be eliminated and we must expect to see biologists and their amateur helpers 'playing God' by transplanting species and engaging in genetic engineering with wild plants and animals, to guide evolution along new lines.

Besides food, other products of the Green Machine make a list of almost unlimited extent: apart from liquid fuel and metals extracted by microbes, there will be plastics, fibres, drugs and possibly nerve-tissue computers. Automatic tools appended to the factory can make up products in Santa Claus fashion but the most significant advantage of the Green Machine over the Santa Claus Machine may be its greater suitability for small-scale operations; it is quite easy to envisage village-scale and even cottage-scale Green Machines, making its social-revolutionary possibilities correspondingly wider. But to offer too sharp a distinction between the two would be foolish: any comprehensive production machine of the twenty-first century is likely to be a hybrid of 'hard' and 'soft' technology of steel and living cells. That leaves the abolition of farming as a special contribution of the Green element.

The *Climate Regulator* is a system, or assortment of systems, for managing or generally improving climatic conditions over substantial parts of the Earth. Existing concepts range from family-scale greenhouses in which people can live comfortably in a frigid climate, to global proposals for controlling the amount of carbon dioxide in the atmosphere, or for increasing the supply of sunlight by flying huge mirrors in space. Intermediate in scale are air-conditioned cities inside giant domes, and schemes for wringing moisture out of the desert air by promoting an updraught, perhaps by planting vast areas of trees, perhaps by painting the desert black, perhaps by setting up huge chimneys. Meteorological nuisances like hurricanes, tornadoes and fogs might be suppressed locally.

Although the term Climate Regulator may imply playing games with the air in particular, I would extend it to include large-scale manipulation of the water cycle, a theme that goes back to ancient Mesopotamia. One contemporary example is the project for towing Antarctic icebergs to Australia or Saudi Arabia; another is the controversial Soviet scheme for diverting the great rivers of Siberia. And the Ganges Water Machine, proposed by Revelle and Lakshminarayana, might rescue much of India and Bangladesh from the tyranny of fickle monsoons by using hydro-electric power from Nepal to run a system which stores water underground during floods and pumps it up again for irrigation in the dry season. (That could be set up, by the way, for the cost of two aircraft carriers.)

There is no reason to doubt that human beings could live comfortably and prosperously in any part of the world, from the Poles to the Tropics.

Policy issues about the Regulator transcend the technological possibilities and difficulties. One is a non-trivial question of taste: whether human beings should really want to escape from the differences, variations and extremes of the weather, which provide one of the prime sources of diversity in space and time. People contemplating artificial cities in space have suggested that weather-like processes should be governed by random-number generators, simply to mimic natural vagaries on the mother planet. This is a fragment of the broader question of whether Man on Earth is to settle down as a loyal participant in the global ecological system, or always to insist on putting his own comfort first. Note also the improbability, given the present political constitution of the world, of securing international agreement for schemes that affect the climate regionally or world-wide. On the contrary, the Regulator is more likely to be a cause of war or even an instrument of war.

And it is around human interference with climate that the natural problems of energy revolve. Within our envelope of technological poles, the present panic over energy seems obtuse. Direct and indirect use of solar energy and coal, backed up as expedient by nuclear fusion, should meet all foreseeable domestic and industrial needs, which are trivial compared with the energy required to launch a few small starships. It will be ironic if we fight a nuclear world war over strictly ephemeral oil supplies, when what we might be doing is mining the atmosphere of Jupiter for a clean fusion fuel (helium-3). No, the substantive issues about energy are climatic. Shall we, on the one hand, overheat the Earth in the next century by releasing too much carbon dioxide and non-solar energy? On the other hand, shall we have enough energy, coupled with climatological and geopolitical skills, to ward off the now-incipient ice age in a programme that would have to continue for thousands of generations? No one can answer either question with much confidence at present but, given help from outside the Earth, I think the Regulator could meet these major challenges.

The idea of the *Space City* was advertised by Bernal in 1929 and canvassed during the past few years by the Princeton group: a group of physicists, astronomers and engineers led by Gerard O'Neill of Princeton University. The basic physics was most vividly expressed by Dyson in 1959, when he reasoned that an advanced civilization could completely surround its parent star with a swarm of orbiting space platforms, so numerous as to black out the light seen from the outside. Seen from the inside the Dyson Sphere, as it has come to be called, exploits virtually all of the radiant energy of the star. Implemented by human beings in the Solar System it would allow for a million-million-fold increase in the population before it became necessary to move on to other stars.

The size and form of the individual platforms, or Space Cities, is arbitrary. Engineering studies by O'Neill and his colleagues, based strictly on twentieth-century technology, have emphasized the immense resources of space, not only in solar energy but in the materials of the Moon and the asteroids, which require less effort to heave them into space than do materials carried up from the Earth. Artificial gravity and other conditions of life in the Cities can be made to approximate as closely to conditions on the Earth as may be desired, for crops as well as for people. For space dwellers there is the promise of propulsion systems far better than present-day chemical rockets, including 'solar sailing' (propelling spaceships by the pressure of sunlight) and nuclear-fusion rockets.

There is no shortage of volunteers, young people who see living permanently in space as an exciting challenge and a natural continuation of the human expansion into new environments. Attempts to rationalise and mount a space-settlements project within the framework of twentieth-century economics seem to have faltered, but there is no obvious mechanical reason why it should not be accomplished early in the twenty-first century. By then there may be Santa Claus-like machines to make the work far easier and, what is more crucial, a better understanding of the ecosystems, including cargoes of humble micro-organisms that will be needed to ensure the biological survival of the Space Cities. Before the twenty-first century ends, there could be more people living in space than on the Earth, and a continuing explosive growth of Cities and human numbers out there would quickly thereafter make the Earth's population a small minority in the cosmic scheme. Already it is possible to outline methods of sending spaceships to other stars and colonizing the entire Milky Way Galaxy, in some millions of years. But there is really no hurry, just as long as our descendants get into space before any Doomsday Machine goes off.

As in most of my other cases, the technical problems are less than the social ones. In principle there are unlimited opportunities for quasi-Utopian experiments on the individual platforms. But what will the upshot be? Will most Cities be like *Mayflower* colonies or penal settlements? Will there be endless squabbles and nuclear wars in space, or will an unending, unopposed expansion moderate the urge to compete and dominate? The Earth can scarcely expect to rule, but will it be conquered itself by returning spacemen? They will be very different from the stay-at-homes—culturally and, in the end, genetically.

For present-day Earthlings, the most important inferences from these space speculations concern the material and biological riches of our home planet. Antarctica and the mid-Sahara, mountain peaks and the deep ocean, are all easy-going paradises compared with the Moon, Mars or the surface of an asteroid, with vast resources of low-grade minerals and solar energy remaining untapped. And when we learn to regard lowly microbes and invertebrates as indispensable crew-members for any long-lasting venture into space we may have greater regard for them in our terrestrial back yards. But exploiting the Earth to anywhere near its material limits is incompatible with maintaining respect for the Solar System's cradle of life. So the most decisive bifurcation in human history may occur when Earthlings opt for 'green' technology and natural ways of life, and space dwellers pursue mechanical, electronic and other artificial systems to the bitter end. But in one respect, at least, the two 'races' can make common cause.

A growing awareness that the inner Solar System is littered with substantial objects that cross the Earth's orbit and sometimes hit our planet prompts thoughts about an *Anti-Comet Battery*. The chances of a formidable space collision in, say, the next thousand years are better than two hundred to one against and we should wish that nuclear war were as improbable as that. But the very small piece of Comet Encke that hit the Earth in 1908 was equivalent to a fairly large H-bomb and had it fallen on a city rather than the remote Tunguska valley of Siberia it would have killed many people. An entire comet colliding with the Earth can release energy equivalent to about a million megatons of explosive; a 'spent' comet, captured in a small orbit around the Sun, turns into a dark Apollo (Earth-crossing) object with less energy of motion but a one-in-four chance of eventual collision.

The horrendous consequences of the largest impacts include a blast wave capable of killing large animals on the far side of the world, and vast quantities of dust thrown into the upper atmosphere, which can blot out the Sun entirely for months or even years. Persuasive evidence now suggests that the dinosaurs were wiped out in this way and all of the various geological periods, distinguished by characteristic forms of life, may have been punctuated by cosmic impacts. In keeping with our new perception of our place in the cosmos and amid life on Earth, the management of comets and Apollo objects to avert these rare but dreadful catastrophes has become a matter of small-scale study, notably in Project Icarus at the Massachusetts Institute of Technology. Large H-bombs carried by rocket can in principle deflect and perhaps disrupt an oncoming object and so 'save the Earth'.

My nominal Anti-Comet Battery consists of perhaps a hundred missiles with H-bomb warheads of various sizes from one thousand megatons downwards. They are stationed in high orbits around the Earth, ready to be launched on command to deal with any inanimate cosmic intruder that is liable to cause death and damage on the Earth. But this is only the 'sharp end' of a much larger ground-based and space-based astronomical militia. Because the objects are difficult to spot, and even quite small meteorites might be regarded as suitable targets, there is no limit to the amount of effort that could be devoted to this task. The obvious risk of the Battery being subverted by someone wanting to dominate the Earth from space can be weighed against the benefit of channelling into benign purposes the military urges of the human male, and his pyrotechnical fascination with large explosions.

For the precedents of this kind of activity one thinks of fire-fighting and lifeboats and especially medicine, which began with prayers and spells against natural misfortune and became a huge science-based industry. The wish to control earthquakes, volcanoes and ice surges may give rise to a similar programme, nearer home. But, in a much wider sense the Battery also represents that most misty class of future uses of technology which are true gollocking, as new absorbers of human interest and energy, virtually unperceived at present.

In a similar sense, the *Disembodied Brain* must stand for more than itself, which is literally a human brain transplanted into a life-supporting sensory and manipulative machine. It sums up and symbolizes all those tendencies in medicine, information technology and culture which emphasize mental rather than bodily life, postpone death at all costs, and adapt human beings to suit their circumstances rather than vice versa. Not far away are the ideas of reproduction by cloning, of correcting errors in human genes, and of suspending life by refrigeration.

Bernal was the first to admit that his speculations of 1929 about mechanized spacemen running on an artificial heart-lung–digestive system were distasteful. That made them no less apt and it is now difficult to see where to draw the line between artificial limbs for the handicapped and 'bionic' people equipped with infrared eyes, ultrasonic ears and bird-like wings. My earlier remark about spending all our time in transplant surgery was not meant lightly: it is easy to imagine a hypochondriacal and death-fearing culture in which all other interests are wholly subordinated to the survival of the individual brain. This selfish wish to live indefinitely contradicts the essential character of life on Earth and of human societies that continually rejuvenate themselves by birth and death.

The other lure in the direction of the Disembodied Brain is the power, sensory and physical, that might be achieved. It is but a short step from making an artificial arm that mimics a lost one to fitting a nerve-controlled mechanical shovel that can pick up dirt by the ton, or seven-league legs for striding or jumping about at high speed. Soldiers in particular might be candidates for this kind of surgery; and hybrids of humans and other animals of the kind envisaged by H G Wells in *The Island of Doctor Moreau*, are not out of the question. For life in space, there are apparent advantages in a Brain that can resist weightlessness and severe accelerations. For intellectual pursuits, direct nervous links between Brain and computer, or between clusters of Brains, could give a new meaning to the phrase 'too clever by half'.

One logical end-point for all this is to perfect bionic man and then exchange the human brain for an artificial one. Some engineers countenance the idea that our evolutionary destiny is to create 'superman' in the form of a highly intelligent robot, destined to replace us and take over the Galaxy. If Disembodied Brains and the proposed abdication of our species make your flesh creep, pay heed to that emotional response, while you still possess flesh that is capable of creeping. Cold reason is incapable of protecting us and our descendants from dehumanizing tendencies in medical technology and that in itself is a comment on everything in our culture which emphasizes operational and intellectual attainments at the expense of bodily and emotional satisfactions.

Emotional satisfactions may, on the other hand, be all too easy to come by if Mankind proceeds towards the *Cheap Thrills Machine*. In Aldous Huxley's *Brave New World* rations of the drug *soma* guaranteed public contentment. In the 1950s scientists in Montreal discovered the pleasure region of the hypothalamus deep in the brain; rats with this region wired for electrical stimulation would press a treadle every two seconds for twenty-four hours without stopping, and pass up food in order to maintain the stimulation. The dreadful manipulatory potential of that discovery did not escape the attention of thoughtful scientists. And in the 1980s, when neuro-pharmacologists have a far shrewder grasp of how natural and man-made chemicals act on the brain, speculation is rife about mood-controlling drugs that might 'liberate' the mind from the natural constraints of emotional and bodily chemistry.

The Cheap Thrills Machine, in its basic form, is a method of rewarding the most trivial action with elation. Park your car legally and feel as if you have just swum the English Channel or invented General Relativity; enjoy making a piece of toast as much as a ride in a supersonic plane. This satisfaction may come in chemical rather than electrical form and be either self-administered or meted out by those in authority to achieve high productivity and obedience to the law. The recipient gets 'high' without any of the side effects or impairments of performance that come with existing drugs, from caffeine to LSD.

In its broader application the Machine suppresses to the point of atrophy any disagreeable or disturbing emotions such as grief, fear or anger. Like the Disembodied Brain, it detaches the individual from the realities of life amid which our species evolved, but this time at the level of perceived values. Again, the possibility should make us reflect on the characteristic interplay of reason and emotion in normal human behaviour. In the short run, should we not tremble a little at the thought of pot-smoking soldiers in charge of nuclear weapons, and political leaders doped to their eyebrows with stimulants or tranquillizers?

The *Self-Reproducing Robot Rocket Ship* is a method of making easier the transplantation of human life from the Earth into the Solar System and on to the stars. Rather than sending men and women to do the uncomfortable, tedious and dangerous work of building Space Cities, you send what is, in effect, a rock-eating Santa Claus Machine that flies through space to a chosen destination, settles down to its labours and also multiplies its own kind, to accelerate the activity. While work at one place is still in progress —mining the Moon, for instance—some of the progeny set off to other sites, to Mars, perhaps, or the asteroid belt.

Operating far from the Earth, the Self-Reproducing Robot Rocket Ship has to be endowed by its designers with a great deal of autonomy, machine intelligence, decision-making power and capacity for self-repair. It is an enchanting idea—a family of mechanical slaves that furnishes the universe for human habitation. It is also fraught with extravagant dangers. Prudent engineers will want to regulate the operations of such a craft and its descendants by limiting their rate of reproduction and giving them firm instructions not to return and settle on the Earth. But any self-reproducing system, even a purely mechanical-electronic one, is subject to mutations and to the biological law of natural selection.

To make this more explicit, let me mention that modern compact, low-voltage computer memories are, like living cells, vulnerable to the cosmic rays that pervade space and rain on the Earth and other planets. The radiation particles, especially muons, create bursts of electric charges which do not damage the hardware but alter the stored information. Recent studies by IBM suggest that a large computer, using a thousand chips and operating at sea level, will suffer an error due to cosmic rays once every day or two. Error correcting codes, analogous to the gene repair systems of living cells, are standard circuits in large computers and can cope with most but, probably, not quite all of such errors. At high altitudes a significantly higher mutation rate must be expected, especially in outer space where the Ships operate.

Consider that a Ship from which the constraints on reproduction are accidentally deleted is, in a biological sense, 'fitter' than its brothers. (A close human analogy is in Robert Trivers' telling observation that if we ever try to regulate human reproduction by statute we shall become a race of cheats, because those who contrive to circumvent the law will outbreed those who abide by it.) The mutant Ship will multiply like a plague of space rats, and this 'variety' will quickly displace the normal Ships. After a few more mutations it may evolve into a new 'species' that escapes to the stars and runs riot through the Galaxy for millions of years to come. And when a mutation suppresses the prohibition against returning to the Earth, ravenous swarms of Ships will come and devour our planet entirely, in the course of a few years.

Thus self-reproducing machines are potentially extremely useful and extremely hazardous. Even special provisions like ordering 'infanticide' for any new Ship that shows mutant behaviour is itself subject to mutation. And the parable tells us that, in the twentieth century, we should already be very careful about entrusting computer systems with too much autonomy, intelligence or reproductive capacity. If we make a hyper-intelligent machine it will be capable of outwitting us in ways that we cannot even guess at.

For the person who wants merely to nourish his own undrugged brain in his own unmechanized body, the *Total Information System* unites all telecommunications, publishing, library services and mass-entertainment. It is a box that sits in your office or living room and gives you access to anything that can be communicated electronically, in alphanumeric, video or audio form. You can 'read', 'see' or 'hear' the news, fill up your pools coupon or tax return, buy shares or order milk, summon up a selected comedy show or coaching in Spanish, or instantly consult any paper, periodical or book extant in any language anywhere in the world. In conception the System is very simple, almost familiar, when compared with some of the other machines I have described.

But to the would-be user, an all-embracing System is formidable and bewildering. He needs someone to guide him through the raw information and make it significant and appealing to him; so there will be at least as much need for information 'middlemen' or 'midwives' as at present: journalists, authors, teachers, librarians, editors, graphic designers and so on. Yet, with a Total Information System it is not clear to me why many people should bother with written words, apart from scribbling electronic notes to friends who are out. At breakfast, an audio presentation like the present radio news is more compatible with toast and marmalade than newsprint is. In addition to the familiar counter-attractions of audio and video programmes, which will be freely available through the System, we must also expect a new treasury of computer games, gambles and semi-automatic arts to play with. Remember that only one side of the human brain is concerned with spoken and written words and most people through most of prehistory and history have spent their lives without even learning to read and write. Many of those who are still force-fed with those skills, to meet the diminishing needs of industry and commerce, read very little for pleasure or enlightenment. We shall easily revert to a dyslexic society unless written words serve the general public much better than at present.

Seen as a social system of publishing, education and control, the Total Information System can operate in ways that either decentralize or centralize power. Decentralizing opportunities include the handling of very local or minority-oriented material (television programmes with an audience of ten, for example) and the use of the system for elections and referenda. Centralizing tendencies include the quest for the largest possible markets for standardized information and entertainment, perhaps culminating in the imposition of English as the 'working' language for the entire world. What I find perturbing is not the cornucopia of information, which, properly organized, could have a liberating effect, but the national and global features of the System. These afford a last refuge for big business and bureaucracies threatened by the material cornucopia of the Santa Claus or Green Machines, and they will help to prepare the ground for national and global police states. Much of the hardware will be interchangeable with the Big Brother Machine, to which I shall come in a moment. The System also threatens to overwhelm those local cultures which, in my opinion, offer the best hope for evolving novel social policies appropriate to a world of Santa Claus. Beyond the Hollywood phenomenon, Nobel and Olympic medallists and 'recognized' artists already impose a hegemony of attainment, discouraging to those who are only the most talented people in, say, Yorkshire. So far from obliging everyone to speak English, we should perhaps be encouraging Yorkshiremen to evolve a distinctive language out of their dialect, as the Norwegians did. All in all, the likely benefits of a Total Information System are probably outweighed by the risks of its perversion for cultural and political repression.

The components of the *Big Brother Machine* already exist. All that is needed to bring about continual surveillance of every citizen, in the manner of George Orwell's *Nineteen Eighty-Four*, is a certain diligence, combined with a willingness to devote resources and manpower to it. The tricky little eavesdropping devices of the security police are the least of the possibilities. Surveillance cameras already operate in public and secret places and there is always a 'good reason' for them, whether to discourage shoplifters and muggers, to keep out robbers, terrorists or spies, to protect nuclear installations, to assure the safe running of a plant, to keep traffic flowing smoothly, and so on. Present military surveillance satellites are capable of imaging from orbit not only a car but a person standing beside it; before long the car number plate may be legible and honest citizens as well as law-breakers may learn to welcome cloudy days that blind the satellite cameras. Yachts taking part in certain ocean races have to carry radio transmitters that repeatedly notify the boats' positions to a satellite; similar equipment could be required for cars and bicycles. Researchers into animal behaviour attach small radio transmitters to individual beasts—why not to people, too? The Buck Rogers two-way wristwatch radio which some engineers foresee as the ultimate in citizen-band radio could become an electronic handcuff, automatically transmitting a person's identity and whereabouts to the police computer.

The computerized data banks alarm libertarians because of their ability impertinently to accumulate all manner of personal information, from the state of one's cardiogram to the level of one's overdraft. The police use data banks with increasing effect for fighting crime and terrorism. Laws and codes of conduct which discourage pooling of information from different data banks are pretty worthless, not just in a police state but anywhere, because they can be circumvented by maintaining data banks abroad, linked by satellite to the users. As credit cards replace cash, telex substitutes for letters and look-up systems take over from libraries, the pettiest transactions and interests of the individual will be, in principle, known to the authorities: telephone tapping is a bland precursor of the possible abuses of the Total Information System.

In practice, rather than tediously monitoring every shopping trip or seaside jaunt, the Big Brother Machine can be programmed to spot anomalous behaviour, whether of suspects foregathering near a sensitive installation or a driver stopping to urinate behind the bushes. Existing police states and several 'free' countries must be presumed to have developed the Machine to a greater degree than is generally known. Other grounds for anxiety about centralized electronic systems include computer crime, administrative blunders, and the extreme vulnerability of the systems to strikes, sabotage and the electromagnetic pulse of nuclear weapons. But the Orwellian nightmare of the Big Brother Machine is the 'black' extreme of information technology. It corresponds to the Doomsday Machine in material technology, with which I began this tour around the technological poles, and they stand side by side on the 'polar diagram', as the two most dismal manifestations of human ingenuity and also the closest to us in time.

* * *

I should be disappointed if, by this stage, many readers were not saying to themselves: 'Why is he holding forth about all these more-or-less far fetched extensions of high technology, when the most conspicuous features of the present world are the greed of the industrialized nations and the dreadful poverty of that majority of Mankind living in the rest of the world?' The disparity, and its plausible culmination in North-South wars using biological weapons that differentiate between races, is painfully clear to me; I also think it shaming for scientists and technologists that most of their work is devoted to pampering the rich nations and arming them to the teeth. But I have reasons for concentrating on what can loosely be called the technological problems of the rich.

One is that I see little hope of drastic reform of the present world economic system based on productive work, so as to favour the poor who work hardest of all. We may have to dismantle it and replace it with something better, and that is exactly what the Santa Claus Machine and its present precursors promise to help us to do. Secondly, the envelope of high-technological possibilities leaves no excuses whatsoever for allowing poverty, hunger and infectious disease to continue anywhere: the natural world is far richer in materials and energy than most people yet realize, and even the population explosion and the problems of pollution, lately offered by the rich as reasons why the poor should not expect to stop being poor, are readily absorbable by better technology. While it might be crazy for every Asian to have a Volkswagen, it is certainly not the impossibility that 'liberal' western economists would have us believe. Then there are direct practical applications of high technology for the benefit of the poor nations: for example the Climate Regulator, the Green Machine which offers ready adaptation to peasant economies and tropical ecosystems, and the Total Information Machine which should in principle make an engineer or agriculturalist in Accra as well-informed as any in Amsterdam. My chief reason for concentrating on 'the problems of the rich' is not selfishness or arrogance but the reverse. Contemplating the military, political and social disruptions with which the industrialized nations are now faced puts me in a mood of deep humility, when it comes to suggesting how the rest of the world might better itself.

'Appropriate technology' is the fashionable phrase among scientists and engineers with genuine concern for alleviating world poverty, and I want to close this chapter in hot pursuit of the meaning of that term. In common usage it indicates an aversion for large-scale projects in steelmaking, nuclear power and the like and a concentration on village-scale projects for the Third World, where a little technology can improve life without disrupting it. For example in England the followers of the late Fritz Schumacher (*Small is Beautiful*) have been actively pursuing such interests as windmills, cycle rickshaws and fibre-reinforced cement as a building material—wattle and daub brought up to date.

It is all admirable, but scarcely commensurate with the problems and sometimes a little devious, perhaps, in relation to the declared objectives, because even the modest examples mentioned presuppose the existence of metal-smelting, rubber and cement industries. Running through this conception of appropriate technology is the idea that Indian villages, for example, may gradually enjoy more and more of the blessings of technology, following cautiously a little way in the footsteps of the industrialized nations while trying to preserve the old values and ways of life. Putting my contrasting point of view bluntly, before proceeding to explain it, give them, I say, the highest possible technology—a Santa Claus Machine.

The very term 'appropriate' demands a moral or religious framework of values, but that framework is challenged by the pantheon of 'polar' technologies. The traditional religions have their roots in periods when animal husbandry, cultivable grain, irrigation and bronze swords were the technological extremes, shattering first the Palaeolithic and then the Neolithic order. From the invention of agriculture to the present, 'work and pray' has been the precept for the vast majority of humans. Some religions, notably Hinduism, put more stress on the meditative aspects of life while others, notably Protestantism, emphasize work.

Agnostics and atheists in the sophisticated science-based world have recently been jogging along on Christian precepts while minimizing the supernatural element: Marxism is a case in point, for it matches Christianity in its vows of neighbour-loving and the search for peace. But even as the first vow is being fulfilled in a chilly fashion by social welfare programmes of East and West, the industrialized world is moving steadily towards a *pointless* Armageddon, and amorality in that direction is coupled with alienation, sexual irresponsibility, crime, vandalism, terrorism and the apotheosis of selfishness in personal life. Every anthropologist knows of pagan tribes with more generous and wholesome norms than these. And now the Doomsday Machine, the Santa Claus Machine and the Disembodied Brain present us with decisions far beyond the scope of timeworn codes, while people wanting myths to inspire the quest for Space City look to the cowboys of the Wild West! If we have no better moral compass to steer by, or to say what technological course is 'appropriate' for ourselves, who are we to tell others how to live?

In India, nothing exasperates visiting scientists and engineers more than the discovery of how strongly the ancient Hindu religion still grips that vast country. The caste system stratifies a nominally democratic society, and high-caste Hindus often shrink from soiling their hands in the cause of production, whether agricultural or mechanical. The villagers worship the same assortment of rather disagreeable gods as they have done for millennia and they regard work and privation as punishments for faults in a previous life. The next incarnation can be better, and the yogi sitting under a tree and meditating may contrive to make it so, because spiritual discipline is believed to be the road to personal progress, through the aeons of time. How, the visitor wonders, can you modernize a country like this?

But now ask the question, which of the world's major cultures is best pre-adapted to employing a Santa Claus Machine? Where would there be little grief at the loss of work and no catastrophic disruption of the social order? Where would a readiness to accept unearned gifts be combined with 'voluntary simplicity' and a healthy scepticism about material wealth in the cosmic and social schemes? I have no liking for Hinduism or Yoga but it seems to me the height of folly to try to indoctrinate unwilling Indians with the Protestant ethic of progress through work, at the very time when the West is finding people's desire for work a positive impediment to modernization. So let the Indians keep their peculiar ways, and, while others are agonizing about myths, norms and social systems, they may contrive with Santa Claus Machines to leap directly and painlessly to a bountiful post-industrial society. And as for gollocking—why, you put your feet on the opposite thighs with the soles turned upwards, rest the hands on the knees and look at the tip of your nose . . . Now *there's* 'appropriate technology' for you.

REFERENCES

J D Bernal, *The World, the Flesh and the Devil*, 1929 repub. Indiana U.P., 1969.

N Calder, *The Environment Game*, Secker & Warburg, 1967.

N Calder *Spaceships of the Mind*, BBC/Viking/Penguin, 1978.

N Calder, *Nuclear Nightmares*, BBC/Viking/Penguin, 1979.

N Calder, *The Comet is Coming*, BBC/Viking/Penguin, 1980.

F J Dyson, 'The World, the Flesh and the Devil', Bernal Lecture, Birkbeck College, London, 1972.

F J Dyson, *Disturbing the Universe*, Harper & Row, 1979.

F J Dyson, personal communication, 1981 (for 'Cheap Thrills').

W Morris, *News from Nowhere*, Reeves & Turner, 1891.

J von Neumann, *Collected Works*, Macmillan, 1961–63.

S Nora & A Minc, *The Computerization of Society*, MIT Press, 1980.

G K O'Neill, *The High Frontier*, Morrow, 1977.

G Orwell, *Nineteen Eighty-Four*, Secker & Warburg, 1949.

E F Schumacher, *Small is Beautiful*, Harper & Row, 1973.

K Vonnegut Jr, *Player Piano*, Charles Scribner's Sons, 1952.

H G Wells, *The Island of Doctor Moreau*, Heinemann, 1896.

4

Food and Population: A Time for Reassessment

by Lester R Brown

The world food economy underwent a basic transformation during the seventies. Not only did the world have huge surplus stocks and excess production capacity at the beginning of the decade, but it also appeared that both would be around for a long time to come. Suddenly in 1972 and 1973, they disappeared and the whole world was struggling to make it from one harvest to the next. Global food insecurity was greater than at any time since the war-torn years immediately following World War II.

Although grain stocks were partially rebuilt in the late seventies, the global balance between the supply and demand for food remains delicate. The precariousness of this balance is illustrated by the extreme sensitivity of commodity prices to weather reports. The forecast of rain in western Kansas can send wheat-futures prices down the daily limit on the Chicago Board of Trade. A report that the Indian monsoon has started three weeks later than usual can send wheat prices up the limit. When the balance of supply and demand is so delicate, a crop shortfall in a key producing country can set off a wave of global inflation. In poor countries, where rising food prices can push death rates upward, it can also have a demographic impact.

The great postwar growth in food production sustained a massive increase in world population. But as human numbers move toward five billion the continually expanding demand for food is running up against inevitable constraints. Most of the factors contributing to the transformation of the world food economy are inherent in efforts to expand food production in a world where basic biological systems are under stress, where returns on some agricultural inputs are diminishing and where land is inequitably distributed.

The Past Quarter Century

The third quarter of this century saw unprecedented gains in world food output. Between 1950 and 1975, the world grain harvest nearly doubled, climbing from 685 million tons to 1.35 billion tons.[1] At any other time in history such an advance would have meant more for all. Unfortunately, population growth also expanded at a record rate during this period, increasing by almost two-thirds.

Worldwide, per capita grain production increased some 31 per cent from 251 kilograms (1 kg. = 2.2 lbs.) in 1950 to 328 kilograms in 1971. Despite the return to use of idled US cropland during the seventies, world production in 1977 averaged only 324 kilograms per person. As the seventies unfolded, farmers were hard pressed to keep pace with the growth in human numbers. Fishermen were finding it even more difficult. The world fish catch per capita peaked in 1970, a year before the postwar rise in per capita grain production was interrupted. It fell by 11 per cent, and recovered only gradually, at a far lower rate of growth.[2]

These global food averages conceal wide variations in performance by individual countries. Those governments that have combined sound agricultural and population policies have realized impressive gains in per capita food consumption. Others have managed both so poorly that food production per person has fallen precipitously. Between 1950 and 1975, per capita grain production fell by half in Algeria and by a third in Honduras. During the same period per capita grain production in the Ivory Coast nearly doubled, and in China it rose by more than 20 per cent.[3]

Throughout most of the period since World War II, the world had two major food reserves: stocks of grain held by the principal grain-exporting countries and cropland idled under farm programmes in the United States. Together, grain stockpiles and the US cropland reserve provided security for all Mankind, a cushion against any imaginable food disasters. As recently as early 1972, this dual reserve seemed more than adequate for the foreseeable future, but then the growth in global demand for food began to outstrip production. Adverse weather brought the longer-term deterioration in the food situation into public view. Food reserves disappeared almost overnight. Despite record grain harvests in the United States, the Soviet Union, and India in 1976, and adequate harvests in 1977, reserves for 1978 were still below those held in 1972, when poor harvests in the Soviet Union, India, and several smaller countries wiped out the world's food surplus. Bad weather continued to take its toll all through the 1970s and into the 1980s.

The decision in 1972 by Soviet political leaders to offset crop shortfalls with imports has injected another element of instability into the world food economy. Aside from the additional pressures on exportable grain supplies, the vast year-to-year fluctuations in the Soviet grain harvest sometimes exceed the annual gains in the world grain crop. Wide swings in the size of the Soviet harvest that were once absorbed entirely within the country must now be absorbed elsewhere. The Soviet decision to import may not be irreversible, but neither will it be easily turned around. It has facilitated the expansion of Soviet livestock herds and poultry flocks, which has in turn raised consumer expectations and appetites.

Yet another source of global food insecurity and instability in the mid-seventies was the near-total dependence of the entire world on one region—North America—for its exportable food supplies. Since the Great Plains wheat-growing regions of the two countries are affected by the same climatic cycles, complete reliance on these two countries is even riskier than it first seems.

The high costs of food-price instability take many forms—economic, political, and social. Consumers, particularly the poor, obviously suffer. Most families cannot easily adjust to wide fluctuations in food prices. Nor can producers easily decide how much to plant and how much to invest in agricultural inputs when prices fluctuate constantly. When grain prices soar, livestock and poultry producers get trapped in tight temporary binds that can drive the less financially secure into bankruptcy.

Violent vacillations in food prices complicate economic planning for governments too. Unstable food markets wreak havoc with foreign-exchange budgets, particularly those of countries heavily dependent on food imports. They also undermine efforts to combat inflation. Indeed, soaring food prices contributed heavily to the global double-digit inflation of the mid-seventies.

Food insecurity derives not so much from production failures as from the relentless growth in demand. Virtually all countries with falling per capita food output are those with populations multiplying at the rate of fifteen- to twenty-fold per century. The record global growth in demand for food, for some 30 million additional tons of grain per year in good weather or bad, is fuelled both by the unyielding growth of population and by growing affluence, with the former accounting for two-thirds or more of the annual growth. Each year the world's farmers and fishermen, already straining to feed some 4.5 billion people, must attempt to feed 84 million more people.[4] Each day more than 200,000 new faces appear at the breakfast table.

Since consumption per person remained close to the subsistence level during most of human history, population growth long generated nearly all growth in food demand. Only since World War II has rising affluence become an important factor at the global level. In countries such as West Germany, where population growth has ceased, and in Japan, where population growth is negligible compared with income growth, increases in food consumption derive almost entirely from income rises.

At the opposite end of the spectrum are the poorer countries such as India, in which per capita incomes are rising by a pittance, if at all, and in which population accounts for almost all growth in food consumption. In Brazil, the rapid population and economic growth of the past decade have together created one of the most rapid overall increases in demand ever experienced in any country. Despite its food-production potential, Brazil has become one of the Western Hemisphere's largest cereal importers.

In the poorer countries, the average person can get only about 180 kilograms of grain per year—about a pound per day. With so little to go around, nearly all grain must be consumed directly if minimal energy needs are to be met. But as incomes rise, so do grain-consumption levels. In the wealthier industrial societies such as the United States and the Soviet Union, the average person consumes four-fifths of a ton of grain per year. Of this, only 90 to 140 kilograms is eaten directly as bread, pastries, and breakfast cereals; most is consumed indirectly as meat, milk, and eggs.[5]

In effect, wealth enables individuals to move up the biological food chain. Thus, the average Russian or American uses roughly four times the land, water, and fertilizer used by an Indian, a Columbian, or a Nigerian. (This ratio is not likely to widen appreciably, since the lower limit on consumption is established by the survival level and the upper limit by the human digestive system's capacity to consume animal protein.)

The dominant change in dietary habits since mid-century has been the dramatic increase in the consumption of livestock products among the affluent in both rich and poor countries. This trend has been most pronounced in the United States, where consumption of beef and poultry has more than doubled over the past generation. In the northern tier of industrial countries—stretching eastward from Britain and Ireland and including Scandinavia, Western Europe, Eastern Europe, the Soviet Union, and Japan—dietary patterns compare roughly with those of the United States a generation ago. The demand for livestock products is rising with incomes, but few nations can meet this growth in demand using only indigenous resources. Most must instead rely, at least partly, upon imported livestock products or else import feedgrains and soybeans to produce these products.

Our Eroding Soils

Ever since the beginning of agriculture, the relationship between people and cropland has been a critical one. When land is scarce, people often go hungry. When soils are depleted and crops are poorly nourished, people are often undernourished as well. The soaring world demand for food since mid-century had led to excessive pressures on the more vulnerable soils. This in turn has led to soil degradation and cropland abandonment. Over much of the Earth's surface, the topsoil is only inches deep, usually less than a foot. Any loss from that layer can reduce the soil's innate fertility. Forty years ago, G V Jacks and R O Whyte graphically described the essential role of topsoil: 'Below that thin layer comprising the delicate organism known as the soil is a planet as lifeless as the moon'.[6]

The erosion of soil is an integral part of the natural system. It occurs even when land is in grass or forests. But when land is cleared and planted to crops, the process invariably accelerates. Whenever erosion begins to exceed the natural rate of soil formation, the layer of topsoil becomes thinner, eventually disappearing entirely, leaving only sub-soil or bare rock. Once enough topsoil is lost, the cropland is abandoned. But the gradual loss of topsoil and the slow decline in inherent fertility that precedes abandonment may take years, decades, or even centuries. Although this interim process does not affect the size of the cropland base, it does affect its productivity.

As population pressures mount, cultivation is both intensified and extended onto marginal soils. Some of the techniques designed to raise land productivity in the near term lead to excessive soil loss. In the American Midwest, the intensification of farming has led to the continuous cropping of the corn, thereby eliminating the rotations that traditionally included grass-legume mixtures along with the corn. The transition to continuous cropping has been abetted by cheap nitrogen fertilizers that replaced nitrogen-fixing legumes. While these chemical fertilizers can replace nutrients lost through crop removal, they cannot make up for the loss of topsoil needed to maintain a healthy soil structure.

In other parts of the world, the doubling of demand for food over the past generation has forced farmers onto land that is either too dry or too steep to cultivate and is thus highly vulnerable to erosion. Explosive Third World population growth has forced farmers onto mountainous soils without sufficient time to construct terraces. Once the natural cover is removed from unterraced mountainous land, the topsoil quickly washes into the valley below, silting streams and irrigation reservoirs and canals.

In dryland wheat areas of the world, pressures to reduce the area in fallow could lead to widespread drying up of soils. This proved catastrophic in the US Great Plains during the Dust Bowls of the thirties and in the Virgin Lands of the Soviet Union during the sixties. Except where land can be irrigated, the basic natural constraints on cultivation under low-rainfall conditions cannot be altered substantially.

A summary document prepared for the 1977 UN Conference on Desertification reported that just under one-fifth of the world's cropland is now experiencing a degree of degradation that is intolerable over the long run. The UN report estimated that productivity on this land has now been reduced by an average of 25 per cent.[7]

These broad global estimates become more meaningful when examined at the national level. In the Soviet Union, attempts to regain food self-sufficiency through heavy investments in agriculture are stymied by soils that have lost some of their inherent productivity. In an analysis of the government's agricultural plans Thane Gustafson of Harvard notes that Soviet efforts must reckon with '50 years of neglect [that] have left a legacy of badly damaged soils'.[8]

The Nepalese Government estimates that the country's rivers now annually carry 240 million cubic metres of soil to India. This loss has been described as Nepal's 'most precious export'. In Ethiopia, the deterioration of soils was brought into focus by a drought that culminated in famine in 1974. A foreign ambassador in Addis Ababa described the origin of the problem in graphic terms: 'Ethiopia is quite literally going down the river'. More recently, the US AID Mission reports that 'there is an environmental nightmare unfolding before our eyes . . . It is the result of the acts of millions of Ethiopians struggling for survival: scratching the surface of eroded land and eroding it further; cutting down the trees for warmth and fuel and leaving the country denuded . . . Over one billion—one billion—tons of topsoil flow from Ethiopia's highlands each year'.[9]

A survey by the Soil Conservation Service indicated that 'in 1975, soil losses on cropland amounted to almost three billion tons or an average of about 22 tons per hectare'.[10] The study concluded that if US crop production was to be sustained, soil loss would have to be reduced to 1.5 billion tons annually, one-half today's level. The Council of Agricultural Science and Technology, supported by a consortium of midwestern universities, reported in 1975 that 'a third of all US cropland was suffering soil losses too great to be sustained without a gradual but ultimately disastrous decline in productivity'.

Few efforts have been made to precisely measure the relationship between the cumulative loss of topsoil and the inherent fertility of cropland. Luther Carter writes in *Science* that 'even where the loss of topsoil has begun to reduce the land's natural fertility and productivity the effect is often masked by the positive response to the heavy application of fertilizers and pesticides which keep crop yields relatively high'. The implications are, nonetheless, disturbing. David Pimentel of Cornell University cites three independent studies, all undertaken in the United States, indicating that, other things being equal, corn yields decline by an average of 'four bushels per acre for each inch of topsoil lost from a base of 12 inches of topsoil or less'.[11]

In a world facing an acute shortage of productive cropland, any loss of topsoil should cause concern, for such a loss is essentially irreversible in the short term. Even under normal agricultural conditions—including the heavy use of fertilizers and tillage practices that gradually mix subsoil into topsoil and that incorporate organic matter—creating an inch of new topsoil can take one hundred years; if left to nature, it may take many centuries.

National political leaders and ministers of agriculture are faced with the task of adequately feeding an ever-expanding population without irreparably damaging one of the world's most essential resources—the soil. Mounting demand pressures, whether the subsistence survival efforts of Peruvian peasants or the response of American farmers to market forces, can have the same effect. In a great many countries, efforts to produce more food are now leading to a slow but gradual decline in the inherent fertility of soils.

Conversion of Cropland to Non-Agricultural Uses

The increase in world population and economic activity means land is needed for much more than just the production of food. The

principal non-agricultural needs are urbanization, energy production, and transportation. Each of these sectors is now claiming
cropland in virtually every country.

Wherever national data are available, they usually show the
growth of cities to be a leading source of cropland loss. Within the
United States, cities are consuming cropland at a record rate.
Land-use surveys by the USDA (US Department of Agriculture) in
1967 and 1975 indicated that some 2.51 million hectares of prime
cropland 'were converted to urban and built-up uses' during the
eight-year span. A study of urban encroachment on agricultural
land in Europe (grasslands as well as croplands) from 1960 to 1970
found that West Germany was losing 0.25 per cent of its agricultural
land yearly, or 1 per cent every four years. For France and the
United Kingdom, the comparable figure was 0.18 per cent per year,
or nearly 2 per cent for the decade.[12]

All additions to the world's population require living space,
whether they live in the city or in the countryside. In the Third
World, where land is in critically short supply, cropland is lost each
year to village growth as well as urbanization.

Rivalling the urban sector as a claimant on cropland is the
fast-growing global energy sector. During the final quarter of this
century, as during the third, the consumption of energy is projected
to increase more rapidly than that of food. Like the production of
food, the production of energy requires land. Hydroelectric dams
often inundate vast stretches of rich bottomland; electric generating
plants can cover hundreds of hectares. More often than not, oil
refineries and storage tanks are built on prime farmland along rivers
and coastal plains. Strip-mining of coal and the diversion of
irrigation water to the energy sector both tend to reduce the
cultivated area.

All transport systems require land but some systems use much
more than others. Automobile-centred transport systems are
voracious consumers of land. An enormous amount of US cropland
has been paved over for the automobile. Millions of hectares are
required just to park the nation's 143 million licensed motor
vehicles. But even this is rather small compared with the land
covered by streets, highways, filling stations, and other service
facilities. Moreover, the automobile has encouraged other in-
efficient uses of land, such as urban sprawl.

Just as rising income increases the per capita demand for
cropland, so too it increases the land required for other purposes. In
effect, high income man is a space consumer. All the principal
non-farm uses of land are greater among high-income groups than

they are among those with low incomes.

The amount of cropland that will be paved over, built on, strip-mined, or flooded by a dam by the end of this century is unknown. However, if world population projections materialize, 2.3 billion people will be added between 1975 and the year 2000, a far larger increase than the 1.5 billion added during the preceding 25 years.[13] Given these population projections and the projected gains in income, every non-farm claimant on cropland—urbanization, energy production, transportation—is certain to be greater during the last quarter of this century than during the third.

Yields Rise More Slowly

Direct evidence of the mounting pressures on the global cropland base is seen in accelerating soil erosion, the spread of deserts, and the loss of cropland to non-farm uses. Indirectly, excessive pressures are reflected in falling crop yield. The ancients calculated yield as the ratio of grain produced to that used as seed. For them, the constraining factor was seed-grain itself. As agriculture spread and as more and more of the world's potentially tillable land was

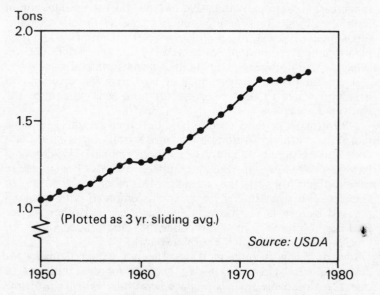

Figure 1. World Grain Yield Per Hectare, 1950-1977

brought under cultivation, the focus shifted from the productivity of
seed to that of land.

From the end of World War II until the early seventies, one of the
most consistent trends in the world economy was the steady rise in
cereal yield per hectare. Between 1950 and 1973, the average
worldwide grain yield per hectare moved steadily upward from just
under 1.04 tons per hectare to 1.77 tons per hectare (1 ha. = 2.47
acres). Beginning in 1974 the trend was interrupted. (See Fig. 1). By
1979–80 it was clear that the global rate of growth of yield per
hectare had slackened from 2.9 per cent per annum in the sixties to
1.7 per cent per annum in the seventies. The US figures were worse,
changing from 3.9 to 0.9 per cent per annum.

Since little new land remains to be opened up to agriculture, this
downturn in yield per hectare has hit the world food economy hard,
contributing to food scarcity and rising food prices. The fall-off
appears to be the product of several factors. The marginal quality of
the once-idled cropland that was returned to production in 1973 and
1974 is perhaps the most crucial factor. In the United States, per
hectare yields of wheat, barley, oats, rye, and rice peaked in 1971;
yields of corn and soybeans peaked in 1972. As of 1977 none had
regained that earlier high.[14] A second factor is the high cost of
energy. The sixfold increase in the cost of petroleum during the
seventies has slowed the growth in the use of energy in agriculture.

A third and closely related factor is the high cost of fertilizer.
Fertilizer prices during the mid-seventies, influenced both by
cyclical trends in the industry and by rising energy costs, soared to
record highs.

A fourth factor influencing the productivity of cropland is a
shrinkage in the world's fallowed area. As world wheat prices rose
during the seventies, the US land in fallow declined from an average
of sixty-five acres for every hundred acres planted in wheat during
the sixties, to thirty-seven acres in 1970.[15] As a result, US wheat
yields have fallen, and severe dust storms reminiscent of those of
the thirties are reappearing in some states.

In tropical and subtropical regions, where fallowing has evolved
as a method of restoring soil fertility, mounting population
pressures are forcing shifting cultivators to shorten the rotation
cycles. As cycles are shortened, land productivity falls.

Diminishing Returns on Fertilizer

The interrupted growth in land productivity gives unwelcome

support to Riccardo's law of diminishing returns. Efforts to expand sharply the global cultivated area have led to a fall in per-hectare yields. So poor is the quality of the new land pressed into service that it has apparently overridden, at least temporarily, the broad-based and continuing efforts by the world's farmers to raise the productivity of their land.

Just as the extension of agriculture onto new land runs up against diminishing returns, so do the development of water resources and the expansion of the use of fertilizer. Most of the world's good cropland is already under the plough, and most of the easy-to-irrigate sites have already been developed. Further expansion in irrigation invariably involves moving up a steeply rising cost curve, either because new dam sites are less desirable or because water tables are falling.

While the application of chemical fertilizer accounted for much of the increase in world food output since mid-century, returns on additional fertilizer use are also beginning to diminish in those areas where its use is heaviest. Crop yields increase predictably with each increment of chemical fertilizer—rapidly at first, then more slowly until they eventually level off.

The shape of the fertilizer-response curve is central to any analysis of future food-production prospects, because the doubling of world grain output since 1950 is due more to the expanded use of commercial fertilizer than to any other factor. Indeed, the contribution of fertilizer may approach that of all other factors combined—improved varieties, expanded cultivated area, expanded irrigated area, improved pest protection, and better farm management.

The earliest data for both world grain production and fertilizer use are those for 1934–38. (See Table 1.) At that time world grain production averaged 651 million tons per year and fertilizer consumption ran about 10 million tons. From then until 1948–52, fertilizer consumption increased by only 4 million tons. After 1950, growth in the cultivated area slowed and fertilizer consumption began to grow by leaps and bounds.

During the fifties, annual fertilizer use increased by 13 million tons, while grain production increased by 130 million tons: each additional million tons of fertilizer increased the grain harvest by 10 million tons. During the early sixties, the response per million tons of fertilizer used declined to 8.2 million tons; during the late sixties it fell further to 7.2 million tons. By the early seventies, each additional million tons of fertilizer yielded only 5.8 million tons of grain.

Table 1
World Grain Production and Fertilizer Use

	World Grain Production (a)	Grain Increment (b)	World Fertilizer Use (c)	Fertilizer Increment (d)	Ratio of (b) to (d) (e)
	MILLION METRIC TONS				
1934–38	651		10		
1948–52	710	59	14	4	14.8
1959–61	840	130	27	13	10.0
1964–66	955	115	41	14	8.2
1969–71	1120	165	64	23	7.2
1974–76	1236	116	84	20	5.8

Source: FAO; USDA.

Clearly, the returns on the use of ever-expanding amounts of fertilizer are diminishing. Barring either a sharp improvement in the capacity of cereals to utilize fertilizer or a sharp rise in food prices relative to fertilizer, the growth in fertilizer use will begin to slow. In fact, it already has tapered off. Ranging from 7 to 9 per cent between 1950 and 1970, the annual growth in world fertilizer use fell below 6 per cent during the seventies.

Improving agricultural practices and breeding more fertilizer-responsive varieties can increase the amount of fertilizer a crop can profitably use; but as application rates rise, such gains become harder to realize. Limits on the amount of water or sunlight, for example, or the limits imposed by photosynthetic efficiency eventually curtail production. Only in countries where application rates are uncommonly low, does the potential for expanding production through the use of fertilizer remain high.

Overgrazing: Eroding the Protein Base

On every continent the area in grass exceeds that planted to crops. The products grown on the 2.5 billion hectares of grassland play an important role in the food, energy, and industrial sectors of the global economy. Grasslands supply protein in a variety of forms, energy in several forms, and numerous raw materials for industry. The ruminants supported by grasslands—beef and dairy cattle, water buffalo, camels, goats, and sheep—supply most of the world's meat and milk. As humanity's demand for protein has risen in step with population and affluence over the past generation, pressures on grasslands have increased markedly.

Besides supplying protein for human consumption, grasslands are a source of energy for agriculture. Just as the firewood from forests provides cooking fuel for close to one-third of humanity, so the roughage from grasslands provides the fuel for cultivating the one-third or more of the world's cropland that is tilled by draft animals. Now that the hope of replacing water buffalo or bullocks with tractors has been deferred in many poor countries because of rising fuel costs, overgrazing both directly threatens the supply of livestock products and indirectly threatens food production by imperiling draft animals.

The one-fifth of the Earth's land surface on which forage for ruminants and other animals is produced is a cornerstone of the global economy. Integral parts of both the world food and the world energy economies, these grasslands and the 2.7 billion domesticated ruminants they support—1.2 billion cattle, 1 billion sheep, 400 million goats and 130 million water buffalo—also represent an essential source of raw materials for industry.[16] Their production potential and their condition directly influence the prospect of feeding our still-expanding population and of further expanding the global economy.

Together, population growth and rising affluence are taxing the world's grasslands at a time when overgrazing is already commonplace. Because the best grasslands are gradually being converted into croplands, most remaining grasslands are either concentrated in arid or semi-arid regions or are located on land that is too steeply sloping to be farmed. As ecosystems, semi-arid and steeply sloping grasslands are among the most fragile, capable of surviving only if grazing is carefully controlled.

In densely populated regions such as Western India, Pakistan, Nepal, northern China, North Africa, the Middle East, and the Andean regions of South America, severe overgrazing has already led to serious erosion. Overgrazing and deforestation brought on by new population pressures have encouraged the Sahara Desert to expand along its southern fringe from Senegal to the Sudan. Unless the desertification process is reversed, Africa, which has the highest birth rate of all the continents, may lose a part of its food-producing capacity.

In India the area available exclusively for grazing in western Rajasthan shrank from thirteen million to eleven million hectares between 1951 and 1961, while the population of cattle, sheep, and goats jumped from 9.4 million to 14.4 million. Chronically overgrazed for several decades, extensive areas of northwest India today appear barren and lifeless—and the livestock population continues to grow.[17]

Even in agriculturally advanced regions, overgrazing is widespread. Recent analyses of the conditions of US grazing lands leave no room for complacency.[18]

Trends in the World Fish Catch

The oceans have long been considered a major potential source of food, but the hope that humans could turn to the oceans for food as pressures on land-based food resources mounted is being shattered. Throughout most of human history there were far more fish in the oceans than we could ever hope to catch. The fish in the seas seemed as plentiful as those in the New Testament Parable. But in the early seventies, as human numbers moved toward four billion, the global appetite for table-grade fish such as salmon and tuna approached and, in some cases, exceeded the regenerative capacity of fisheries. Overfishing led to shrinking stocks and declining catches.

Between 1950 and 1970, fish supplied more and more of the human diet as the technological capacity to exploit oceanic fisheries expanded. During this two-decade span, the catch more than tripled, climbing from 21 to 70 million tons.[19] At nearly 70 million tons in live weight, it averaged some 18 kilograms (1 kilogram equals 2.2 pounds) per person annually, well above the annual yield from the world's beef herds.

At least 90 per cent of the world fish catch comes from the oceanic commons. The remainder is produced in fresh water, mainly in inland lakes and streams. Two-thirds or more of the catch is eaten directly by humans, while the remaining third is consumed indirectly in the form of fishmeal fed to poultry and hogs.[20]

The importance of fish in diets varies widely by country. Among the larger countries, fish figure most prominently in the diets of the Japanese and the Soviet people. Population pressure forced the Japanese to turn to the oceans for animal protein; the fish and rice diet which they evolved has led to an annual fish consumption per person of thirty-two kilograms, the highest of any large country.[21] Soviet consumers now each eat an average of ten kilograms of fish a year, nearly double the American level.[22] In the United States fish comprise an important part of the diet, but direct consumption averages only about six kilograms per capita (compared with about one hundred kilograms of meat and poultry).[23]

World fishing fleets have expanded enormously since World War II. Investment in fishing capacity multiplied several-fold, as the industry adopted sophisticated fishing technologies such as sonar tracking. Between 1950 and 1970, the catch increased by an average of nearly 5 per cent yearly, far outstripping population growth and sharply boosting per capita supplies of marine protein. But in 1970 the trend was abruptly and unexpectedly interrupted. Since then the catch has fluctuated around 70 million tons, clouding the prospects for an ever-bigger catch. Meanwhile, world population growth has led to a 17-per cent decline in the per capita catch and to rising prices for virtually every edible species. Many marine biologists feel that the global catch of table-grade species may be approaching the maximum sustainable limit.

Overfishing, frequently discovered only when the catch begins to decline in a sustained fashion, has become a pervasive global problem. The northwest Atlantic fishing area, extending from Rhode Island northward to the southern coast of Greenland, is a microcosm of world fisheries. The catch of this biologically rich region totalled 1.8 million tons in 1954 and increased steadily until 1968, when it reached 3.9 million tons. It then dropped by 18 per cent to 3.2 million tons in 1970, where it has remained even though the number of countries fishing in the region and investments in fishing capacity have continued to rise.

The catch of several individual species peaked in the late sixties. Fishery experts attribute the declines since then to overfishing. The haddock catch reached a high of 249,000 tons in 1965 and then fell steadily until by 1972 it amounted to only one-seventh of its earlier level. The catches of cod, halibut, and herring peaked in 1968; but all have dropped substantially since then, with declines ranging from 40 per cent for herring to over 90 per cent for halibut.[24]

The decline of the northwest Atlantic fishery is mirrored in the northeast Atlantic, a region that has supplied Europe's tables with fish for centuries. According to an analysis by D H Cushing, overfishing has reduced the catch below the maximum sustainable yield in twenty-seven of the region's thirty fisheries.[25]

Overfishing is not limited to the North Atlantic or to older fisheries. Beginning in the late fifties, Peru's fishing industry expanded spectacularly. By the late sixties, Peru had emerged as the world's leading fishing nation, almost entirely on the strength of its vast offshore anchovy fishery. According to a 1970 UN-sponsored study by an international team of biologists, the maximum sustainable yield of the Peruvian anchovy fishery is roughly 9.5 million tons per year.[26] The catches in 1967, 1968, and 1971 all exceeded this level. In 1972 and 1973 the catch dropped to a few million tons. Since then the Peruvian government has controlled fishing rigorously in an effort to restore the fishery's productivity. So far, these efforts have met with only limited success.

Although some of the potential for extracting food from the sea remains untapped, dramatic growth in the world fish catch of the sort that occurred between 1950 and 1970 looks like a thing of the past. Fish farming has been practised for thousands of years and has been widely discussed for the past decade, yet it still accounts for only a minute share of world fish consumption. Only by turning to unexploited species such as krill, the shrimp-like crustacean found in massive quantities off the coast of Antarctica, will it be possible to markedly expand the world catch in the foreseeable future. As human populations expand further, per-capita supplies of preferred species will likely fall further. Higher prices and growing international competition for available supplies appear inevitable.

As growth in the world catch slows and in some cases declines, the large Soviet and Japanese populations are especially vulnerable. Deprived of oceanic sources of protein, they will likely have to offset declines by importing more feedgrains and soybeans to expand indigenous poultry and livestock production. Taking such a tack will further strain exportable grain supplies. As the world fish catch levels off or drops, pressures on the land are intensifying.

The Protein Bind

The two basic yardsticks for measuring the quality of diets are calories and protein: calories measure the diet quantitatively, protein qualitatively. The several hundred million people who are chronically undernourished suffer from a shortage of calories or protein or both. Since expanding protein supplies adequately became increasingly difficult during the seventies, protein hunger could well worsen in the years ahead.

Most of the world's high protein comes from fish, beef, and soybeans. According to marine biologists, the catch of tablegrade species cannot be markedly expanded beyond current levels. Expanding marine protein supplies thus means turning to 'inferior' species. Similarly, the continuing expansion of the world's cattle herd, which now annually amounts to some forty-one million tons or ten kilograms per person, has already led to extensive over-grazing.[27] Although livestock output can be expanded amply in some countries by improving livestock management, raising productivity of grasslands is difficult, since the world's principal grazing areas are natural or unimproved grasslands in semi-arid regions.

Other important biological constraints impede protein pro-duction in general and beef production in particular. Like the first domesticated cattle, beef cows still give birth to only one calf each year. And since not every cow bears a calf each year even in the best-managed herds, the calving rate is well below 100 per cent. Thus, for every calf that goes into the market cycle at least one cow must be maintained for one full year. Herds could, of course, be sharply expanded if more cattle could be fed on grain in enclosed feedlots. But during the mid-seventies, high grain prices reduced the amount of grain fed to cattle well below what it would otherwise have been. In the seventies roughly one-third of the world's grain harvest was fed to livestock and poultry, and this share may not expand markedly in the years immediately ahead if feed-grain prices remain high.

The third principal source of high-quality protein is soybeans, a crop produced almost entirely by three countries—the United States, Brazil, and China. Between 1950 and 1975, the world soybean harvest nearly quadrupled, rising from sixteen to sixty-one million tons.[28] This growth closely paralleled that of the world fish catch, which climbed from twenty-one million tons in 1950 to seventy million tons in 1970.[29] Like the increase in the fish catch, it also reflects the enormous worldwide appetite for high-quality protein.

Increases in soybean production depend upon the amount of land available for planting, because despite strenuous efforts, none of the three soybean-producing countries has been able to increase per-acre soybean yields significantly. Attempts to raise soybean yields run up against incontrovertible biological facts: legumes fix their own nitrogen and respond only modestly to applications of nitrogen fertilizer. Yields have edged upward only grudgingly. Soybean yields in the United States, for example, have increased by a mere 25 per cent since 1950, a period during which corn yields nearly tripled.[30]

In effect, farmers get more soybeans only by planting more soybeans. From 1950 to 1973, US soybean acreage moved to a new high virtually every year, expanding from seven million hectares to twenty-two million hectares. In 1973, this era of rapid uninterrupted expansion on soybean acreage and supplies was arrested, largely because the idled cropland had vanished.

With one hectare in every six on US farms now planted in soybeans, it is unclear how much more land farmers can shift to soybean production and still satisfy the expanding world demand for other crops, particularly cereals. Yet, while the United States cannot continue to expand soybean acreage as it did from 1950 to 1973, Brazil could substantially expand production.

Unfortunately, in parts of Brazil soybeans also compete with table beans. The surging demand for Brazilian soybeans as livestock feed in Japan, affluent Europe, and the Soviet Union is bidding land away from the production of Brazilian table beans and increasing their price.[31] This in turn aggravates protein hunger among low-income Brazilians for whom they are a staple.

During the sixties, the world price of soybeans was quite stable, hovering around 110 dollars per ton. But since 1973, it has ranged from 220 to 290 dollars per ton.[32] Given the difficulties in expanding the world supply of high-quality protein, strong upward pressure on protein prices seems likely to continue unabated. If the price of soybeans (perhaps the best single indicator of the tightening world protein supply) continues to rise, reducing protein hunger may become even more difficult than it already is.

Growing Dependence on the North American Breadbasket

During the seventies, the list of food-deficit countries lengthened until today it reads like a UN roster, encompassing most of the world. Those countries with significant exportable grain surpluses can be numbered on the fingers of one hand. In the same period dependence on North American food has climbed sharply. The United States and Canada exported 56 million tons of grain in 1970, but by 1976 exports had climbed to 94 million tons (See Table 2). North American farmers now produce a surplus sufficient to feed nearly all of India's 600 million people or half of the Soviet Union's 250 million at their much higher consumption levels.

North America today has a near monopoly of the world's exportable grain supplies, a situation without precedent. The reasons are manifold, but principal among them are rapid

Table 2
The Changing Pattern of World Grain Trade[1]

Region	1934–38	1948–52	1960	1970	1976[2]
	(MILLION TONS)				
North America	+ 5	+23	+39	+56	+94
Latin America	+ 9	+ 1	0	+ 4	− 3
Western Europe	−24	−22	−25	−30	−17
E. Europe and USSR	+ 5	—	0	0	−27
Africa	+ 1	0	− 2	− 5	−10
Asia	+ 2	− 6	−17	−37	−47
Australia and N.Z.	+ 3	+ 3	+ 6	+12	+ 8

[1] Plus sign indicates net exports; minus sign, net imports.
[2] Preliminary estimates of fiscal year data.
Source: Derived from FAO and USDA data and author's estimates.

population growth and agricultural mismanagement in the food-short countries.

The most potent force to reshape global trade patterns in recent decades is population growth. A comparison of population and food trends in North America and Latin America reveals the devastating effect of unfettered growth. As recently as 1950, North America and Latin America had roughly equal populations—163 and 168 million, respectively. But while North America's population growth has slowed markedly since the late fifties, Latin America's has increased explosively. Several larger countries such as Brazil, Mexico, Venezuela, and Peru have population growth rates of 3 per cent or more per year. If the North American population of 1950 had expanded at 3 per cent per year, it would now be 420 million instead of 250 million. Eating at current food-consumption levels, those additional 170 million people would absorb virtually all exportable supplies, leaving North America struggling to feed itself.[33]

Unfortunately, many countries plagued with rapid population growth have managed agriculture poorly. Social forces that have concentrated land holdings in the hands of a few have crowded a majority of the farm population onto a small area of land, or even worse, off the land entirely. Consequently, both land and labour are grossly underutilized. In country after country, the persistence of malnutrition and growing national food deficits is due more to existing social structures than to a lack of productive capacity.

National food deficits have been aggravated by urbanization. When surpluses produced in the countryside are no longer sufficient to feed the swelling urban population, countries must turn to outside sources. Between 1950 and 1975 the urban share of world population, boosted by massive rural-urban migration in the Third World, increased from 29 to 39 per cent. In effect, this record rate of urbanization was made possible by North American food surpluses. Although the United Nations projects a continuation of this trend, with the world becoming 49 per cent urban by the end of the century, the difficulties associated with expanding food production and with generating the requisite surplus in the countryside seem certain to slow this trend.[34] In some countries, urbanization could come to a halt.

While the growth of national food deficits has various causes, its effects—ever-greater pressure on North American food supplies —are always the same. Moreover, they appear to be cumulative. Literally scores of countries have become food importers since World War II, but *not one new country has emerged as a significant cereal exporter during this period*. The worldwide shift of countries outside of North America from export to import status is a well-travelled one-way street.

The extent to which importers rely on outside supplies is also growing. The list of both industrial and developing countries that now import more grain than they produce is lengthening. Among those that now import over half of their grain supply are Japan, Belgium, Switzerland, Saudi Arabia, Lebanon, Libya, Algeria, Senegal, and Venezuela. Other countries rapidly approaching primary dependence on imported foodstuffs include Portugal, Costa Rica, Sri Lanka, South Korea, and Egypt.[35]

The growth in dependence on North American food cannot long continue at the recent rate. Aided by the return of 20 million hectares of idled cropland to production during the mid-seventies, North American farmers nearly doubled their grain exports in ten years. But future gains will not be so easy to realize, and the world should not count on a repeat performance during the next decade.

The international community must at least prepare for the possibility that the food scramble of recent years may not be temporary. Most of the slack appears to have gone out of the world food economy, leaving the entire world in a vulnerable position.

Consequently, the US and Canadian governments could some day find themselves in the uncomfortable position of having to decide who would and would not get North America's extra food in time of scarcity. In effect, the two governments would be operating a global food-rationing programme. Although they have not consciously sought this responsibility, they must now reckon with it.

The Final Quarter Century

During the final quarter of this century, population growth and rising affluence are projected to double world demand for food again as they did during the third quarter. Whether these demand projections will materialize is questionable. Whether farmers and fishermen can double the supply of food is even more questionable. Indeed, the dim prospect for doing so may influence the projected growth in both population and affluence.

Four factors contributed centrally to the near doubling of food output between 1950 and 1975: the spreading use of hybrid corn, the vast expansion of irrigation, the sixfold growth in fertilizer use, and the rapid spread of the high-yielding dwarf wheats and rices. The agricultural use of energy, including the energy embodied in fertilizer and that used for mechanical power, also multiplied rapidly during this period. Numerous other technological advances in both crop and livestock production also contributed.

Maintaining past rates of growth in food output will likely become even more difficult. Net expansion of the cropland base is likely to be even less than the rather modest expansion of the third quarter of this century. Growth in the irrigated area is projected to fall by more than half. The rate of growth in energy use will undoubtedly be far less. The potential for expanding fertilizer use is still substantial in Third World countries; but while the growth rate in these countries is almost certain to fall, the quantitative increase is likely to be quite large.

Constrained by the limits of available land, water, and energy, food production is also subject to biological limits. Whether crop production per hectare or milk production per cow, natural processes eventually conform to the S-shaped growth curve. Crop production per hectare is ultimately limited by the incidence of solar energy. The efficiency with which broilers convert feed into meat is ultimately limited by the physiology and metabolism of the birds themselves.

Selective breeding and improved nutrition by both plants and animals can push up production limits—but only so far. Some of these absolute limits are already being approached in some situations. Corn yields in the United States, wheat yields in Western Europe, and rice yields in Japan may already be well past the inflection point on the S-shaped curve.

As food supplies tightened during the early seventies, confidence in science's power to push back the constraints on food production fast enough to meet growing demands has eroded. Indeed, as Professor Louis Thompson of Iowa State University notes, the backlog of unused agricultural technology is shrinking.[37] Nor is there identifiable technology about to come off the drawing board that can make possible a quantum jump in world food output comparable to that associated with the expansion of chemical fertilizer use or the adoption of hybrid corn. Two possibilities—raising the photosynthetic efficiency of key crops, and the development of cereals which can fix nitrogen—have this potential, but both await fundamental advances in biological engineering.

In any event, considerable unrealized food-production potential (most of it in the Third World) could be tapped using existing agricultural technologies. The obstacles to realizing this food-production potential are not technological but political. Often land productivity in countries with more progressive agriculture systems is two, three, or four times that of countries with less progressive systems. For example, rice yields in Taiwan are four times greater than those in Burma. Similarly, corn yields in the United States are two to four times greater than those in most Latin American countries. With the bulk of the rural population squeezed onto a small fraction of the arable land area, both land and labour are severely underutilized in country after country in Latin America. Then, too, food-price policies that have a pro-urban bias and that fail to provide farmers with sufficient incentive, inhibit agricultural innovation and investment.

The unrealized potential in the poor countries notwithstanding, the conditions under which the world's farmers and fishermen will attempt to expand output during the final quarter of this century are less favourable than the conditions of the past. Whether the world can expand food production is not at issue. How much it will cost to do so and how the cost will relate to the purchasing power of the world's poor are the real questions.

If the rise in food prices that results from rising real costs and scarcity exceeds the growth in purchasing power among the poor, then food consumption among the world's poor will fall. The levelling-off of food production per person in the developing countries since 1971 suggests that it has already begun in some regions, notably in Africa.

A world of cheap food with stable prices, surplus stocks, and a large reserve of idled cropland may now be history. Barring some dramatic increase in the priority given family planning and food production, a future typified by more or less chronic scarcity enlivened only by occasional surpluses of a local and short-lived nature appears to be in store. The steady rise in food-production costs, a rise associated with the employment of marginal land and low-grade water resources, may make global inflation progressively more difficult to manage. At the same time, the international community's failure to respond effectively to crop shortfalls in poor countries may make severe nutritional stress and sporadic rises in death rates more common.

Progress in eliminating hunger and malnutrition is not likely unless available food supplies are distributed more equitably both within and among societies. As the demand for land, water, and energy grows in other sectors, priorities for resource use will have to be established between agriculture and these other sectors. In a world where scarcity threatens to become commonplace and where food remains basic not only to human survival but also to economic and political stability, family planning and food production deserve a higher priority.

REFERENCES

1. Economic Research Service, '26 Years of World Cereal Statistics by Country and Region', mimeographed, US Department of Agriculture, Washington, DC, July 1976.
2. Lester R Brown, Patricia McGrath, and Bruce Stokes, *Twenty-Two Dimensions of the Population Problem*, Worldwatch Paper 5, March 1976.
3. Economic Research Service. *op. cit.*
4. Lester R Brown, *World Population Trends: Signs of Hope, Signs of Stress*, Worldwatch Paper 5, October 1976.
5. *Agricultural Statistics* (Washington, DC: US Department of Agriculture, annual).
6. G V Jacks and R O Whyte, *The Rape of the Earth—A World Survey of Soil Erosion* (London:Faber, 1939).
7. C.A.S.T. study cited in Luther Carter, 'Soil Erosion: The Problem Persists Despite the Billions Spent on It,' *Science*, April 22, 1977; UN Conference on Desertification, 'Economic and Financial Aspects'.
8. Thane Gustafson, 'Transforming Soviet Agriculture: Brezhnev's Gamble on Land Improvement', *Public Policy*, Summer 1979; Jimoh Omo-Fadaka, 'Superdams: The Dreams That Failed', *PHP International*, August 1978.
9. *Master Plan for Power Development and Supply* (Kathmandu: Nepal: His Majesty's Government, with Nippon Koei Company, 1970); Ambassador in Addis Ababa quoted in Jack Shepherd, *The Politics of Starvation* (Washington DC: Carnegie Endowment for International Peace, 1975); US Agency for International Development, 'Fiscal Year 1980 Budget Proposal for Ethiopia', Washington, DC, 1978.
10. Soil Conservation Service, 'Cropland Erosion', US Department of Agriculture, Washington, DC, June 1977.
11. Carter, 'Soil Erosion'; David Pimentel *et al.*, 'Land Degradation: Effects on Food and Energy Resources', *Science*, October 8, 1976.
12. Linda Lee, 'A Perspective on Cropland Availability', US Department of Agriculture, Washington, DC, 1978; European figures from Organisation for Economic Co-operation and Development, *Land Use Policies and Agriculture* (Paris: 1976).
13. Population Division, United Nations Secretariat, *Population by Sex and Age for Regions and Countries, 1950–2000* (New York: 1973).
14. US Department of Agriculture, Foreign Agriculture Circulars FR-1-76, May 1976, and FG-77-77, July 1977.
15. *Agricultural Statistics.*
16. *Production Yearbook 1973* (Rome: Food and Agriculture Organization, 1974).
17. Erik Eckholm, *Losing Ground: Environmental Stress and World Food Prospects* (New York: W W Norton & Company, 1976).
18. *Environmental Quality: Sixth Annual Report* (Washington, DC: Council on Environmental Quality, 1975).
19. *Yearbook of Fishery Statistics* (Rome: Food and Agriculture Organization, annual).
20. Edward Goldberg and Sidney Holt, 'Whither Oceans and Seas?', presented to the Second International Conference on Environmental Future, Reykjavik, Iceland, June 5–11, 1977.

21. Economic Research Service, US Department of Agriculture, private communication.
22. *Ibid.*
23. *Ibid.*
24. *Annual Report*, International Commission for the Northwest Atlantic Fisheries, Dartmouth, Nova Scotia, 1975.
25. D H Cushing, *Nature*, November 25, 1976.
26. Eckholm, *Op. cit.*
27. US Department of Agriculture, Foreign Agriculture Circular FLM-12-77, August 1977.
28. *Agricultural Statistics.*
29. *Yearbook of Fishery Statistics.*
30. *Agricultural Statistics.*
31. Erik Eckholm, *The Picture of Health: Environmental Sources of Disease* (New York. W W Norton & Company, 1977).
32. *International Financial Statistics* (Washington, DC: International Monetary Fund, monthly).
33. Lester R Brown, *The Politics and Responsibility of the North American Breadbasket*, Worldwatch Paper 2, October 1975.
34. Population Division, United Nations Secretariat, 'Trends and Prospects in Urban and Rural Population, 1950–2000, As Assessed in 1973–1974', mimeographed, New York, April 25, 1975.
35. US Department of Agriculture, Foreign Agriculture Circulars FR-1-76, and FG-7-77.
36. Brown, *Politics and Responsibility.*
37. L M Thompson, 'Weather Variability, Climatic Change, and Grain Production', *Science*, May 9, 1975.

5

The Future of the Oceans

by Elisabeth Mann Borgese

To write about the future of the oceans is like writing about the future of eternity. The oceans were there long before life began and they will be there even if life ends. There may be a series of natural and anthropogenic ecocatastrophes: climatic changes, induced by technological imprudence interacting with natural causes; the consequences of a great war with its doomsday machines; petroleum pouring from uncapped wells no one cares any longer to control or exploit; radioactive wastes escaping from corroding canisters dumped on the bottom of the sea. Life might be exterminated over large stretches of the sea, but the oceans would still be there.

There have been ecocatastrophes before, and death reigning over ocean space. Living reefs, the oldest ecological communities on our planet, disappeared for many millions of years at a time and were reborn, destruction alternating with creation, like high tide and low tide. 'I have seen it all perish, again and again,' Brahma said to Vishnu, 'at the end of every cycle. . . . Everything then goes back to the fathomless, wild infinity of the oceans which is covered with utter darkness and is empty of very sign of animate being.'

We may be on the down-beat of extinction now, and what we are doing to ourselves and to our environment, cries to high heaven, as we seem to co-operate with ultimate fate. Yet we need not. The big down-beat belongs to geological time, almost to mythical time, but within its curve there are smaller ups and downs, which belong to human time, or history. Within these limits, evolution is in our own hands. We can stem the tides, change the course of history, act on ourselves in our environment, even though this involves terrifyingly complex social, political, and economic problems, and also collisions of classes, of generations, of races and cultures.

The technological and diplomatic omens are excellent at present: in a troubled world, the oceans are good news.

A trinity of technologies is arousing high expectations for the future. One is aquaculture, the cultivation of marine plants and husbandry of marine animals. Another is ocean mining, the recovery of vast mineral wealth from the oceans, without the disturbance typical of mining operations on land. A third new use of the oceans will be as a source of renewable and 'clean' energy. These I shall describe briefly.

If they were all, the technical possibilities might seem to be just a further checklist of important novelties, to set alongside other options for good or ill, now flowing from technology. These possibilities in the oceans have, though, helped to promote worldwide awareness of the importance of marine resources, for national and global economies. And this awareness has prompted action by the nations of the world, establishing the Law of the Sea, and creating global institutions for managing the oceans for the benefit of all Mankind. To these remarkable political developments, which hold promise for the future extending beyond the particularities of ocean technologies, I shall return later in this chapter.

Food production from the seas could rise rapidly under appropriate management policies, hastening the transformation from hunting to cultivation. We may be witnessing one of the major transitions of *Homo sapiens* brought upon us by a number of convergent factors, including the difficulty of sustaining agricultural growth, coping with a changing climate, and problems of overfishing. The evolution of aquaculture matches the emergence of agriculture ten thousand years ago.

So far from being science fiction, aquaculture has a long prehistory as a well-established art, now being modernized and spreading far beyond the carp ponds of China and oyster beds of Europe. Seaweed culture, too, is traditional, notably in East and South-East Asia; four major species of seaweed have already been domesticated, and Chinese production of seaweed has soared during the past quarter-century. For centuries, the fishermen of Kampuchea brought their catch live to Phnom Penh in ship-shaped floating cages, and fattened the fish for market during the voyage by feeding them kitchen waste. Cage culture became widespread in East and South-East Asia; now it has been taken up and modernized in Europe and the United States.

The use of sewage for nourishing aquatic life is traditional and not without risks to health, but the Woods Hole Oceanographic

Institution has demonstrated the extremely high yields of shell-fish obtainable by using treated sewage as nutrients. In the Woods Hole experiment the aim was polyculture, in a designed system where planktonic algae, seaweed, worms, fish and shellfish were raised together in tanks of sea water. The Japanese go to great lengths to prepare synthetic diets for eels and prawns, analogous to cattle feed. The fry of some fish, mullet for example, are so fastidious in their diet that, so far, they defy attempts to raise them artificially. But the great challenge lies in the oceans, where the natural nutrient elements are quickly exhausted at the surface, but lie unused in extraordinary abundance, in deeper layers of water. The world's fisheries are concentrated where these nutrients well up naturally; in principle they can be raised artificially to fertilize other parts of the oceans.

The protection and manipulation of breeding, in shellfish and fish, is already big business. The United States sends billions of oyster seeds all over the world. Soviet scientists have successfully transplanted fish between their widely separated fisheries and have brought in foreign species. Hybridization of fish helps in their acclimatization, and can also increase productivity or quality. The Japanese even have a fish hospital in Toba Bay, for studying and treating diseases in fish and shellfish, where surgeons carry out operations on anaesthetized fish in the water. But, again, the vast potential dividends from fish lie in the deep oceans. Sea ranching, in which artificially bred fry are released to reinforce the wild stocks, help in the first instance to remedy overfishing; within a hundred years all of the catches of world's fisheries will be subject, in a greater or lesser degree, to such manipulation.

Putting these possibilities together: aquaculture offers the prospect of turning endless blue deserts into croplands. Seaweed and algae, for example, are a largely untappped resource that can be exploited for human food and cattle feed, energy and fertilizer, and a long list of chemical and pharmaceutical products; they can be cultured, selected, genetically improved, and grown anywhere in the ocean, provided there is a suitable infrastructure—a cage, perhaps, or a fence, or a net—not too far from the sunlit surface, and provided that nutrient-rich water is pumped up from the lower levels of the sea. Floating, dynamically positioned nets may cover thousands of acres; the water may be pumped up with simple wave-powered pumps; the nets may be lowered below the turbulence level during storms. The US Navy has carried out feasibility studies off the coast of California, with highly encouraging results.

Seabed mining too has a long prehistory, in coal seams followed outwards from the land, under the sea, and in the dredging of tin and diamonds in shallow offshore waters. From timid experiments eighty years ago, offshore oil drilling has boomed since 1945, with grandiose engineering extending its scope into the Arctic and the stormy North Sea. A new chapter in metal mining was opened with plans to dredge manganese nodules from the deep ocean bed. In these lumps, first discovered a century ago by the British *Challenger* expedition, manganese is only one of the valuable metals they contain: nickel, copper, cobalt and molybdenum are others. The nodules lie under several kilometres of water, and one proposal was to suck them up in liquefied mud, through long tubes extending from the ocean floor to a vessel at the surface. More forward-looking, perhaps, was the French scheme using remote-controlled submersibles to scoop up the nodules and lift them to the surface.

Eclipsing the nodules in importance, at least temporarily, are discoveries made in 1981, with the American manned submersible *Alvin*. On the Galapagos ridge, extending under water from the Galapagos islands in the East Pacific, at only half the depth of the manganese nodules, *Alvin* discovered millions of tons of sulphide ore, rich in iron, copper, silver, cadmium, vanadium, molybdenum, manganese, lead, cobalt and zinc. The leader of the discovery team, Alex Malahoft, called it 'a dramatic turning point' in the history of mining. Similar ore bodies were subsequently found off the western United States, and early estimates suggest that ocean-bed mining and the processing of these sulphide ores would be comparatively cheap.

In an earlier, and geologically related development, the Saudi Arabian and Sudanese governments joined with German mining engineers in experiments in 1979, to raise metal-rich muds from the bottom of the Red Sea. This is a newly growing ocean where hot brine from submarine geysers accumulates in pools on the ocean bed in the midst of the rift. In one such pool, in the Atlantis II Deep, the muds were estimated to contain zinc, copper and silver worth $7 million, at 1980 prices.

Some pioneers in seabed mining have in fact predicted that, in the long run, ocean mining will displace land mining altogether. The consequences, in economic and political terms, would be enormous. Development in non-industrialized countries up to now has been tantalizingly slow, due to the persistence of what might be termed a post-colonial extraction economy, geared to the needs of the industrialized countries, not to those of the mineral exporting developing countries. If mining shifts to the oceans, under a regime in which developing countries participate in the management and in the profits of production, the pace of diversification and industrialization within these countries will necessarily accelerate, and there will be a different division of labour.

In ecological terms, a process would be initiated here too, transforming an extractive, exhaustible system into a cyclic, inexhaustible one: minerals and metals welling up from the interior of the earth, being extracted from the seas, and returned to the seas via the rivers and the atmosphere.

Ocean mining and aquaculture already come together in recent work that points to the importance of aquatic weeds and algae in the process of recycling heavy metals. For instance, the oceans contain billions of tons of uranium, whereas reserves on land are estimated as below three million tons. To extract uranium from the oceans with conventional energy has been too costly in the past. Now experiments are under way to develop hybrid green algae that absorb and accumulate the uranium in concentrations several thousand times that of normal seawater. Mesh containers holding the hybrid algae in 'uranium farms' will be immersed in ocean currents to harvest the uranium.

Another example: the National Aeronautics and Space Administration in the United States has been experimenting with water hyacinth. Water hyacinth has the extraordinary capacity of absorbing, through its roots, heavy metals from industrially polluted waters: mercury, cadmium, nickel and lead, even gold and silver. What is more, this metal can be recovered from the harvested water plants. This can be done by accumulating them in specially designed pits, on a scale that makes extraction economical. Fertilizer and biogas are by-products.

As a source of energy, the potential of the oceans is staggering, even for the supply of non-renewable forms of energy. Half of the world's oil will come from the sea bed during the next 25 years. If nuclear fission energy has any long-term future, uranium and thorium in seawater could in principle 'sustain the estimated 21st-century level of power production for some million years', according to John D Isaacs and Walter R Schmitt, who also point out that lithium and deuterium from the sea, if used in thermonuclear fusion, could 'sustain the power level for the remainder of the life of the solar system'.

The tidal power plant successfully operating at the mouth of the Rance River in northern France is a small token of the renewable and non-polluting modes of energy production from the sea, waiting to be harnessed. Useful tidal energy will be restricted to favoured places where the tidal range is very large, but low-pressure water turbines of the kind developed for this purpose might also tap the energy of ocean currents—for example, from the Gulf Stream where it passes Miami in Florida. Wave energy is more widely available on exposed coasts, and experiments to tap it are under way in Britain, the United States and Japan.

In theory the most prodigious energy-content of the oceans takes the form of differences in salinity between different layers of water, but the technology needed to extract useful energy supplies does not yet exist. On the other hand the temperature difference between warm surface water and cold deep-lying water, amounting to 20° to 25°C in the tropical oceans, can certainly be exploited as an earlier source of energy, as the French first demonstrated three-quarters of a century ago, and as experimental and pilot plants of the 1980's are reconfirming. Because it brings deep, nutrient-rich water to the surface, 'ocean thermal energy conversion', or OTEC, will lend itself to integration with aquaculture, and one use for energy generated in mid-ocean will be to power ocean mining operations. Thus the new ocean technologies reinforce one another.

The new possibilities for the oceans intersect with existing maritime interests, including shipping, where oil pollution is a continual anxiety, and with military uses of the sea, which already include missile-carrying submarines and might in an unregulated future extend to sea-floor missile bases. In November 1967, in one of the most far-sighted and consequential speeches in history, Malta's Ambassador Arvid Pardo put to the United Nations the need to create a legal and institutional framework for ocean management and the multiple, interacting uses of ocean space. In the ensuing fifteen years, the United Nations Conference on the Law of the Sea, the greatest international conference ever convened, laboured on these issues. The Constitution that emerged bears the seed of a new international order.

The oceans are our great laboratory: in dealing with the issues of the law of the sea we deal with food and fibre, minerals and metals, energy, trade, communications, science policy, technology transfer, multinational corporations, disarmament and arms control, development, East-West and South-North confrontations, regional development—the whole range of issues and problems besetting the world community as a whole, and if new and creative solutions for these problems can be proved in the relatively contained ocean environment, they may find other and wider applications later on.

The central theme of the Conference, determining the future of the oceans, was that technological advance and political change, introducing a set of new actors—the developing nations—had made the old maritime order obsolete and dysfunctional. That order was based on the twin concepts of national sovereignty over a narrow strip of territorial sea, and freedom of the seas beyond that. Neither freedom nor sovereignty are adequate to deal with the novel problems of pollution and resource depletion or to forestall conflict and chaos. The new law of the sea transcends the antiquated concept of sovereignty and of freedom with the new and revolutionary concept that ocean space and its resources are *the common heritage of mankind*, which cannot be appropriated by any nation or person but must be managed jointly by all nations, with particular regard for the needs of developing countries.

All nations are nationalistic. But the fact is, in the world in which we are living they can assert their national interests only through international action. Thus the division between 'nationalists' and 'internationalists' really did not play a role at the Conference. Nor did the East-West conflict really determine anything heavily overlaid, as it was, by the North-South division, in which industrialized states, whether Capitalist or Communist, defend the same interests. The North-South division itself was overlaid by several other divisions. One of these is the division between coastal States and the group of 'landlocked and geographically disadvantaged States'. Clearly the coastal States aimed at a maximum expansion of their sovereign rights over ocean space and resources, not brooking any interference from other States, while the disadvantaged States insisted on free access to the sea and some sort of participation in the development of the new wealth of the oceans. The group of disadvantaged States consists of developing—mostly African—States, together with the most conservative members of the EEC, alongside a number of Eastern Europe Socialist countries. The coastal-States group, on the other hand, includes strong States with worldwide naval interests, and weak, developing States, with primary interests in resources. Across the line between coastal and geographically disadvantaged States cuts another line—dividing mineral-exporting from mineral-importing States: the former being interested in maintaining production controls and high prices, the latter, in increased production and lower prices.

The strong, developed coastal States themselves, finally, are torn by internal conflicting interests; for they have the traditional interest in the freedom of the seas to operate their far-flung navies while, at the same time, they need secure rights to deploy their technologies, and they want to protect their coasts against pollution from foreign ships or operations. They have mining lobbies pressing for maximum expansion of national claims, navy lobbies urging freedom of the seas, and fishing lobbies—which, to top it all, are divided among themselves. For instance in the United States, the tuna fishermen of the Pacific needing freedom of the seas for their distant-water operations, while the coastal fishermen of the East seek a wide 'zone' from which to exclude foreign competition. No wonder it was difficult to put the pieces of this multi-dimensional puzzle into place.

In April 1982 in New York, at the eleventh session, the Convention on the Law of the Sea was adopted by 130 states, with 4 voting against it, and 17 abstentions. The chief shadow was that cast by a shift in the position of the United States, which had played a leading part in drafting the Convention and solving apparently intractable problems but which, after a change of administration, declared its wish to re-examine all the emergent concepts. Nevertheless, for those concerned about peace, international equity and the rational control of technology, the Convention on the Law of the Sea is the most remarkable document ever produced.

Its ratification will take several years, but an important interim provision requires 'pioneer investors' in sea-bed mining, whether national enterprises or commercial consortia, to deal with a Preparatory Commission in the spirit of the Law of the Sea. In the longer run, the Convention calls for the creation of an International Tribunal for the Law of the Sea, ruling over the most comprehensive and binding system ever devised for settling international disputes. The Tribunal will have its seat at the old Hanseatic maritime city of Hamburg. Even more significant will be the creation of an International Seabed Authority with its headquarters in Jamaica.

The Seabed Authority will be without precedent among international institutions. The Convention empowers it to generate revenue, to impose international taxation, to bring multinational companies under international control, to plan the use of resources on a global scale, and to protect the marine environment and scientific research. It will hold sway over all resources of the sea-bed beyond the national jurisdiction extending for 200 miles into offshore waters. For such a high-flown concept, there are inevitable snags. In particular, the pace of economic and technological change quickly outdated some of the detailed provisions for the Seabed Authority. Manganese nodules are no longer the prime mineral asset, nor are they likely to be an early source of revenue for the Seabed Authority, as envisaged by the Conference on the Law of the Sea. The newly discovered sulphide deposits were not properly covered in the Convention adopted in April 1982. Nevertheless, when sixty countries have ratified the Convention, the Seabed Authority will come into existence, and will mark a new era in international affairs.

One must not be starry-eyed about it. The rich countries will continue to rule the waves and to exploit the resources of the sea: within what now are their economic zones, and as far out as they care to, into the no-man's land of the High Seas as well as in the economic zones of poorer coastal States. In these zones the rich States and their companies, whether national or transnational, will have made suitable bilateral arrangements, paying rent or royalties. This, however, will not be substantial enough to make any dent in the social and economic status quo. Production, as heretofore, will be geared to the needs and interests of the industrialized countries, not to the needs of the poor, not toward a redistribution of resources, technologies, and skills. If the economic zones of poor coastal States are not exploited by the companies of the rich, they will be under-exploited, for the development of local technological capacity will take a considerable amount of time. The provisions of the Convention emerging from the Law of the Sea Conference are often ambiguous and not to the advantage of poorer coastal States. And who will be able to resist the pressure of the powerful? Nature abhors a vacuum.

The law will last, however, as long as the power structure that created it. There have been national claims over vast ocean expanses in the past: claims more radical even than the present ones. They were staked at the time the nation states came into being and the modern concept of sovereignty took shape: they are repeated at this time when the concepts of sovereignty and ownership are undergoing profound transformations and the age of nation states is drawing to an end—the dusk curiously resembling the dawn. When, in the early sixteenth century, thanks to the enormous advances in nautical and navigational technologies, Portugal and Spain were Super Powers, Portugal claimed sovereignty over the whole Indian Ocean as well as the Atlantic south of Morocco while Spain claimed the Pacific and the Gulf of Mexico. There was no UN at the time, but there was the Papacy, and it issued bulls, as potent as any Convention on the Law of the Sea. In 1493 Pope Alexander VI legitimized the claims of the Super Powers in two papal bulls, which became the basis of the Treaty of

Tordesillas of 1494. But the law lasted as long as the supremacy of the fleets of the Super Powers and the unchallenged prestige of the Papacy. As the British technological revolution got under way, the Portuguese might decayed, the Spanish fleet succumbed, and papal bulls lost their grip on world affairs in the era of ascendant Protestantism, the regime of sovereignty over the oceans gave way to one of freedom of the seas.

Also the nouvelle vague of sovereignty will last as long as the power structure behind it, no longer. What direction and what form the new shift will take is a question obviously far wider than the oceans. Considering the technological imperatives of our age, it cannot take the form of a return to the freedom of the seas. History is likely to move *beyond* the concept of the economic zone, not back from it.

One of the problems developing countries have to face in planning for the management of their economic zones is that of surveillance and enforcement: and the larger the zone, the worse the problem. Rich countries, like the USA, are spending billions of dollars reinforcing their coastguards, acquiring helicopters, linking up with satellite surveillance, installing tracking devices. But what can a poor country do? Expenditures on warships in Third-World countries are rising much more steeply than in the rest of the world. While this development is partially due to the rise of tensions in international affairs in general, it is, undoubtedly, also related to the need to protect the resources in the newly acquired economic zones. What is being spent on warships, however, cannot be spent on fishing fleets, and the arms race directly impinges on the development of the zone.

Developing countries thus would do themselves a great service if they pressed for the internationalization of surveillance and enforcement. Regional surveillance by planes, helicopters and satellites would be cheaper and more effective than national surveillance. Even coastguard continents could be internationalized for regional enforcement purposes. This may be a long-range development and cannot take place everywhere at once, but it would contribute toward making the economic zone a viable part of the new international economic order. It would contribute both to development and disarmament.

The political and technological prospects for the oceans will be served by an integrated approach to development. Only one country, China, has consistently applied this principle, and the results, for land and water uses—flood control, irrigation, agriculture, aquaculture, and navigation, all considered as an integrated system—have been rather spectacular. Suffice it to mention China today produces almost half of the world's total aquaculture harvest, generating food and employment for many millions of people. The oceans are the lakes and rivers of the world community. Water conservancy and management, as the matrix for an integrated system of managing the uses of the oceans, including navigation and communication, aquaculture as a complement of agriculture, ocean mining as a complement of land mining, could over the next decade achieve similarly spectacular results. If so, the future of Man in the oceans could be a lot brighter than his future ashore.

6

Communications in the Year 2000

by Anthony Smith

During the third quarter of the twentieth century United States telephone companies provided one fourth of all new public equity pumped into the American economy. In the single year 1979 three billion dollars worth of public bonds were subscribed in the telephone sector. For the rest of the century telecommunications as a whole will continue to grow at three times the rate of the economy as a whole. It is hardly surprising that this sector of society, with a completely new range of technologies at its disposal, and the entire world waiting for re-equipment, has become wrapped in the most romanticized aura of social prediction. In 1876 Alexander Graham Bell, the inventor of the telephone, predicted that 'some day all the people of the United States will sing the Star Spangled Banner in unison by means of the telephone'. A century later, very similar paradisaical hopes are invested in the new adjuncts of the telephone which will spread throughout developed societies between 1980 and the end of the century, but the current wave of predictions is far more international than patriotic, far more concerned with the resolution of social conflict and environmental threats than with the anticipated triumph of nationhood. Every generation hopes for cheaply acquired gadgetry for solving its profoundest tensions and we learn more about a society perhaps from the hopes it invests in its technology than from the uses to which it actually puts it. Nonetheless, we can be as sure of this as we can of anything, that the most significant new kinds of communications equipment laid down in the last decades of the century will be descendants of the telephone, new devices by which information is 'telecommunicated' from place to place, by which data is processed and distributed in the cause of entertainment, or instruction or administration or in place of specie. The telecommunications boom is our version of the railway boom of the mid-nineteenth century, and the transportation boom of the mid-twentieth.

Our Victorian grandparents would have had very little idea about the kind of people we are if they had been given merely a descriptive account of the communications (and other) technology which we today possess. The telephone, radio and television would have been fairly simple to comprehend as gadgets, but they would not have provided a very clear idea of the real state of mind of the society possessing them. Communications equipment is the equipment which most shapes a culture, and to say something about the role of communications a generation hence one must try to point to some of the cultural wants and needs which the new equipment may come to satisfy, or purport to satisfy.

Every new technology is the expression in physical equipment of new understandings about the working of nature, and these understandings are arrived at generally in response to *ad hoc* interrogations of nature. Technology is thus the expression of the ever-shifting relationship between Mankind and the universe as a whole. Of all the machinery which Mankind devises and exploits in furtherance of the interests of particular groups or societies the machinery of communication comes closest to influencing his nature as a species. When the god Thoth brought Thammuz, King of Thebes, his invention of writing, and declared that this would help the people with their memory, the king replied merely that, on the contrary, it would 'plant forgetfulness in their souls'; every device for communicating information among people exercises a profound influence upon the senses and the operations of the intellect. Society itself is a means for processing information, if looked at in a certain light; class and other hierarchies, governmental and other bureaucratic systems, are all ways by which Mankind circulates information and controls its flow. Harold Innes, the great Canadian pioneer of this line of analysis in the 1940's, pointed out that writing had helped government, or 'empire', to spread by way of administrative organization, beyond the possibility of mere military strength. If we are looking, therefore, at the communications devices of the late century and beyond, they only offer an empty futurism unless we examine them as the counterparts of ideas concerning social, cultural and *moral* development.

The great talking-point of the late 1970's was the microchip. It was presented as a half-vengeful threat to job security at a time when over-manning and recalcitrant trades unionism either was, or seemed to many to be, the cause of social and economic decline in Britain and other countries of the West. The impact of the microchip has been conscientiously exaggerated in the press and on television, and there is evidence of a social motivation behind the exaggeration, at least in so far as a date is put to the expected transformation. We are 'instantly' to do our shopping from armchairs, and cease to write letters any longer; commuting to work is to stop and we shall all open offices in our sitting-rooms; in the cashless society robots will take over all the work still left around, including much of the non-manual labour (that is meant supposedly to make the intellectuals feel as uneasy as the workers). Since the end of the sixties it has been clear that the home is indeed becoming the centre of the social information system, that entertainment, education and general knowledge are becoming domesticized and removed from the sphere of public activity. (That, too, might be a bit of an exaggeration.) A decade after the prediction very little of this process has actually occurred, although many of the necessary devices are now available. A Commissioner of the FCC (US Federal Communications Commission) in 1967 predicted the imminent arrival of a 'home communications centre where a person works, learns and is entertained, and contributes to his society by way of communications techniques we have not yet imagined—incidentally solving commuter traffic jams and much of the air pollution problems in the process'. Ten years or more later, the microchip is evidently to be the chief means by which the vision is to be realized, but even now it has only just begun its progress through the existing institutions and technologies. The prediction taught us more about the special anguish of the 1960's than about the real organization of social change.

The belief that technology is in itself the main determinant of social change is one of the defining characteristics of late twentieth century culture, although Vietnam did much to disturb the complacency of the West about the superior power of technology in warfare, and the resurgence of Islam as a political force has done much to disturb conventional Western thinking about the nature of modernization. The microchip, which was and indeed is to facilitate the great transformation from industrial to post-industrial or 'information' society, is the direct product of certain important tensions within the world and between existing major institutions. The vision we now are being given in the mass media of our society *after* it has been impacted by the chip is heavily influenced by the mood of technological determinism, perhaps the single greatest intellectual fallacy of our time.

When we, therefore, look at the apparently inevitable role of communications technology in the society of the early twenty-first century we must somehow take account of our own doctrinal errors and of the sense of moral frailty which has given rise to the particular vision of a workless endlessly communicating society which is becoming widespread in the early 1980's. The micro-processor is a device which has emerged from the space race. It was essentially an attempt to conclude the Cold War by transferring it to a technological sphere. It has developed its present aura partly because the great corporations which have arisen to dominate the world economy need some non-military zone in which to indulge their intense expansionism; at the same time the deliberate competitiveness which the US government is trying to inject into the multi-national corporations is part of its desire to control them. The entire world is thus being prepared for a commercial war between IBM, Bell, and the German and Japanese giant corpor-ations, in which the prize is the re-equipping of the world with the gadgetry of post-industrial society, when we expect energy resources to be scarce but population very high. The cultural counterpart to the microprocessor is the concept of information as a resource in itself. Perhaps the touchstone of the whole evolution in social communication techniques which we now envisage is the proposition that information can be treated as an autonomous phenomenon abstracted from the processes of mental and industrial production and treated as a physical entity. That, anyway, is axiomatic in any account of post-industrial society and may, in itself, come to be seen in time to be fallacious in its way, or hopelessly misapplied.

We may, however, be permitted to say of society in the year 2000 that it will have passed through a phase in which public investment in information technology will have exceeded or paralleled public investment in energy resources and energy systems; governmental involvement in this area consists largely in the provision of the capacity for tele-communications to take place, that is to say, in cable, microwave and other networks; in putting together, piece by piece, the main branch and local routes through which vast quantities of digitalized information circulates, between govern-ments, companies, universities and people. Secondly, we may suppose that corporations will also have invested in information technology on a scale similar to their investment in energy; they will have acquired the computers and terminal equipment, the instru-ments for sending aural, visual and written communication of which the whole paraphernalia of an 'information society' consists. Thirdly, we must assume that on the domestic level, the devices for leisure and for reducing domestic work will have been attractive enough to induce purchases; each home will have spent as much upon supplying information as on heat and light and transport, and general public awareness of the progressive growth of the information sector will therefore be comparable with public awareness of the role of the energy sector in the 1980's.

In looking at the physical consequences of these three assumed developments, it is, of course, easy to leap into the most fanciful of futurisms. But there are still quite severe problems of technology—of *invention*—to be overcome; for example, a vast proportion of all of the information display devices are still dependent on the cumbersome cathode ray tube; cheap and serviceable as it is for a single domestic television receiver, it is extremely crude and inconvenient as a means for displaying large quantities of written material for use many hours a day, and a cheap substitute is not yet in sight, although many lines of research for new kinds of semiconductor screen are being pursued. There are many other problems of present technological inadequacy which have to be fed into all attempts to predict, and to these must naturally be added the constraints of human inadaptability, particularly when the most powerful, single set of social organizations—the trades unions—have come, in some countries, to fear and resist the changes which go with post-industrial society. In addition, there are, in many places, gaps in available investment in the manufacturing, consumer or governmental sectors, partly as a result of the sheer cost of servicing the existing sunk investment in conventional telecommunications; in other words, some regions and some whole countries will lag behind because they cannot find the way to turn their social capital around in time with the more adaptable economies. For example, until the opening up of the 'information revolution' most of the common carrier work in telecommunications has been undertaken by licensed monopolies, such as Bell, or by public corporations, such as the Post Offices (or PTT's) of Western Europe; these have shouldered an enormous proportion of the total investment in their respective societies' communication needs, because they feared no competition. AT&T has held 50 per cent of the total debt of the telecommunications industry and has, as a matter of policy, subsidized all local telephone calls out of the great profits of its 'long-line' services. Today the latter are subject to tremendous competition from rival corporations which are now moving into the field and into the manufacturing side as well, where AT&T has long played a major role, since it was in a position to order equipment as well as make it. The whole capital structure of AT&T and other such organizations is having to be reorganized, and this in itself will take a decade or more, otherwise all prognostications will be falsified. Computers tend to be written off as investments in five to eight years and traditional telephone exchanges in twenty to thirty years, or even longer. The computerization of switching systems means that quite different rates of write-off must be introduced in organizations where the total investment is often a significant proportion of the total standing capital of a whole society. The book value of a telephone plant has grown far faster than the gross national product in the United States, for example, and the sheer re-structuring which is under way in the early 1980's entails a far greater dependence on available investment capital than is apparent from a mere recital of the gadgetry which is to be developed and circulated. Of course, much of the delay in the spread of cable networks, of domestic computers, of telemail, will be popularly ascribed to the stubborn conservative mulishness of the human beings involved; it would be more accurately ascribed to the extreme difficulty which existing corporations endure in their attempts to exploit a new potential which entails dramatic corporate overhaul. They can see a good thing, but they cannot always locate the resources to grab it and make it theirs, especially when they have to invest far ahead of the actual buying market for the product concerned. In the case of the telecommunications revolution, we may expect that at the end of the change-over period the banking systems of the West will hold a far higher proportion of the total invested capital than they do now, since the PTT's and AT&T's cannot possibly generate themselves from profits the money which will be needed. We shall be living, therefore, when the information society comes, in a world much dominated by banks and perhaps less dominated by governments. But that is merely to illustrate how some of the constraints interact with some of the opportunities which arise in a period of social reconstruction.

Of course, many of the new communication technologies which are today under development are free-standing devices unconnected to the telecommunications networks: there are videodiscs and other equipment which may be purchased and used separately from the expensive computerized networks. Nonetheless, even these are ultimately dependent upon the same industries and techniques of modern telecommunications. They depend upon these for their manufacture, or in the course of their own research and development. We must take as axiomatic, therefore, the universal role of the new electronic common carrier systems and their switchgear in the evolution of the information society.

A reliable, coherent national telecommunications system requires a certain level of social planning or regulation to achieve general compatibility and geographical universality. If, for example, telemail is to replace physical mail, then the networks through which the data passes must be universally laid down within a green area, otherwise society will either have to support two parallel systems or end up with politically unacceptable inequalities of provision. Telecommunications development is rather different from most other kinds of social or economic development in that it can only take place after a degree of overall social prediction and social planning, for it consists of a vast series of interconnections. The creation of a system only arises from national policy in the first place (whether conducted by government or by some other agency) and therefore the whole construction of the industries which use this social resource is greatly dependent upon the machinery of planning and policy-making. Thus telecommunications, for all the freedom of choice which it can provide, as well as the freedom of movement and settlement, tends towards the centralization of planning decisions and perhaps also of social power; of course that does not mean that telecommunications expansion must necessitate a greater role by the state, but it must imply a decision by the state to supervise decisions taken in the private sector. Telecommunications planning has arguably been at the heart of social planning since the 1920's, even though this particular branch of engineering has been extremely adept at self-concealment within national bureaucracies; the extremely powerful measures decided by telephone engineers, telecommunications diplomats and frequency planners, are disguised as 'technical' decisions, dependent upon the will of politicians and electorates. Rather the reverse has been the truth and the financial as well as social and industrial implications of decisions taken in the sphere of telecommunications can sometimes make the investigator wonder whether its engineers have in fact been the real 'unacknowledged legislators' of the century. In the information society of the future, therefore, one might expect that this branch of technology, together with certain other areas, will become more politicized; one may expect electorates to vote and become agitated about networks in the way they do now about nuclear energy or the location of airports and highways.

The telecommunications networks of the future may come to resemble the electricity grid more than the telephone network as it now is. They will consist of a variety of technologies, some physical, such as the new optic fibres and advanced coaxial cables and undersea cables; some invisible, such as the satellite and microwave networks. The last decades of the twentieth century will bring about a kind of layering of national systems, with new techniques coming to intermesh with older ones. In the United States, however, another older concept will still be working itself through, in which different technologies are placed inside different corporations and made to compete. Thus SBS (Satellite Business Systems) will be in full swing after some years of slow establishment; three large companies, Aetna Life Insurance, Comsat and IBM, have joined together to create a message system for large corporations, which will circulate their mail, their telephone calls and their filing systems by bouncing all of them to and from a domestic American satellite. Eventually this system is bound to go international and affect the flow of messages in the private and domestic sector, thereby spreading the competition between IBM and AT&T right across the globe. Within America it will compete with the postal system. By the year 2000 most postal systems, separated from their respective national telephone and data systems, will have become expensive luxuries and sending and receiving physical mail, as opposed to the kind which arrives direct in the home via a special black box, will have become rather like home visits from the doctor or the direct delivery of coal and milk, a slightly archaic luxury.

While North Americans enjoy the benefits of competing mail and message services which are dependent on slightly different technologies, the societies of Western Europe are likely to have hybrid national systems still, the transference from physical to electronic message-sending having not progressed quite as far or as fast as in America. In Europe the new networks will contain a little of all of the new technologies and no one will be certain whether a given invoice or document or newspaper has reached them by satellite or optic fibre or cable; in America each subscriber will be fairly certain which mode has been chosen for the service concerned and this will make for a rather different relationship between consumer and information service.

There will inevitably be a growing gap between the state of provision of communication services in developed and developing societies, in countries of the 'north' and those of the 'south'. The quantities of information available in these rather crudely drawn subdivisions of the globe will vary very greatly. Information *multiplies* in value with usage, unlike most other resources, and therefore, those who have more, so long as they circulate it, get more, and those societies with efficient and coherent national networks will certainly be in a position to exploit their knowledge resources more productively.

Since it will be possible for the entire range of information services, from entertainment, music and the newspaper, to telephone, computer data and business records, to be digitalized, all information will, in essence, be reduced to the same condition and be pumped through the 'bit-stream', that avalanche of 'dots-and-dashes' of which the central core of a society will consist. It will be simpler to charge a given subscriber for the quantity of 'bits' received and transmitted rather than enquire whether the terminal equipment in use happened to be connected to paper, or to a large wall screen or to a musical amplification system. Thus, today, it is cheaper and easier to meter the use of the water supply and the electricity supply rather than calculate the number of baths taken, or separate the lighting requirement from the heating. One may, therefore, expect the basic information system to take the form of a ring-main, with every room in an office or home being fitted with three-pin 'information' sockets linked by cable. Each subscriber will be fitted with a junction box which will separate the subscriber from the system and enable metering to take place, according to overall usage. Naturally, an enormous apparatus of revenue and cost adjustment will have to have been created for the problems of copyright to be dealt with. Books, magazines, tapes, records, video-material, all belong to different kinds of publisher with different kinds of scarcity values, investments, talents employed. Each choice of a service by a subscriber will necessitate a special record being kept either by the individual copyright holder or by specialized revenue-collecting services who will impose special charges and then share them out. Conceivably the network operators could operate this vast system of credit and payment, creating blocks of moving capital similar to those held today by the credit companies. Each system will have to find ways to separate private messages from public information services, since the former will presumably by-pass the special credit agencies and circulate merely at network cost. One can without difficulty foresee something of the mare's nest which will have to be coped with by corporation lawyers in the next twenty years.

An individual equipped with a supply of electricity buys a number of quite separate gadgets and decides which he or she connects to the supply as and when required, from hairdriers to hi-fi's. The information ring-main would be attached to a similar range of equipment offering printed as well as audio-visual products, but these would also require the secondary metering alluded to above. So great a variety of attachments will become available that it is not surprising that these are being seen as the infrastructure of a new form of social organization. So long as societies are able to generate investment for the development of the inter-connecting networks on a high enough scale, and so long as digitalization has progressed far enough through the successive layers of the system and the terminal equipment, one can envisage an integrated information system a generation from now which will be drawn off by each individual user according to the bandwidth, the range of frequencies needed to convey a given message. The PCM (pulse code modulation) network designed in the 1980's for coding and decoding the digital signals at each end of the interconnection would become the branch network of the future, with satellites, cables and microwave providing the great trunk routes. At the local level, however, a completely new concept will have to be evolved and some appropriate network planned, so that digitalized equipment can be used right through the system. This, in the long run, will enable the information society to run extremely cheaply, and for telecommunications truly to displace paper as the common means for disseminating information. The cost will necessarily be very high indeed, but without expenditure at this level, the 'revolution' entailed in the information society will be confined to the central core; for the year 2000 to 'feel' substantially different from 1980 to its average citizen something more than a new range of gadgetry will have to arrive and this must depend on a truly universal, really cheap domestic interconnection system. British Telecom's 'System X' will become widely used in the 1990's, with similar computerized exchanges springing up everywhere.

At the beginning of the 1970's it was calculated that a nationwide video network in the United States would have cost one trillion dollars to construct. At that moment the entire telephone network in America was worth about sixty billion dollars and the gross national product was at the trillion dollar mark. Allowing even for the fact that the cost of building the network is rising below the level of general inflation and that the investment in a national network will enjoy many more immediate revenues in 2000 than in 1970, one has to admit that, along the road, the information society will entail a major thrust of sheer political faith. It is more comparable to competing in the space race than it is to building a transportation system. However, the possession of such a network is the only guarantee that a society will be able fully to exploit the economic potential of its total domestic information. One must, therefore, ask where the benefits are likely to come from, to sustain the high level of administrative determination and imagination which will be necessary?

The one sector of society which will see the most rapid and conspicuous alterations of pace and manner of operation is the information sector itself. Various calculations have been made of the total number of citizens in various societies who are engaged, at a given moment, in the processing of information in all its forms, and, although most estimates are suspect, it is clear that a very large proportion of the workforce of the West—and probably the East, too—is involved in office and educational work and in the administrative work of government and industry. Whether forty, fifty or even sixty per cent of the workforce are involved in supporting information activities, as is variously assessed, is not important. However many there are, one can imagine very easily the social impact of a technological shift which renders it possible to dispense with the physical handling of all text filing and calculation.

The modern office of the 1970's and early 1980's continues to use paper-based information systems, even in organizations where word-processors are most widely used. By the year 2000 one may gauge that the mechanical typewriter, the physical filing system, the photocopying machine and inter-office mail, will all be obsolescent, and quite possibly obsolete. The changeover could come very rapidly, judging by the speed at which the more technology-conscious bureaucracies of the United States went through the preliminary stages in the 1970's. It is thought that a decade would be sufficient for a general transition, as soon as the electronic systems become competitive in price and versatility with manual tech-niques. The mutual dependence of office systems in a given society (and to some extent between societies) means that once the pioneers have established the superior efficiency of a new method, the rest follows very quickly. The pocket calculator is perhaps the exemplar of all such transformations, and that took about five years to turn from luxury to universal necessity.

The electronic 'intelligent' typewriter is the basic device from which the other systems will grow. It will shrink in size to that of a ream of paper, with its display panel growing to the size of a large sheet of paper. Connected to an office ring-main the single typewriter becomes a communicating device, the information added by way of the keyboard. Its inbuilt ability to process text before reproducing it or transmitting it means that it becomes an important labour-saving device. The addition of calculating capacity as well as the ability to receive information through the same ring-main (from outside as well as inside sources) means that the word-processor dramatically alters the function of its operator and reduces many of the copying, carrying and research processes of a normal office.

However, this machine, which is already familiar to a whole

generation of American (but not of European) office workers, has the capacity for many further advances. It could do sales-ledger accounting, stock control and even a little easy market research. It can take and store messages, translating them, if necessary, from one language or alphabet to another, while conducting all the necessary search operations through a company's filing system. It can also be carried fairly easily and can operate as a mobile comprehensive office mechanism. In other words, we are witnessing something quite different from a switch from one technology to another; the new machine performs a much wider range of functions from its predecessor, the typewriter, which in its time (the period from 1890 to 1950) was the key technology of the social transformation of the twentieth century. The typewriter has been associated with the transformation in the role of women from servants to assistants; its electronic substitute will transform the role of men as well as women from executives to administrative communicators. It is hard to imagine the full potential of the word-processor being achieved in an enterprise unit in which roles are ascribed according to sex. Secretaries will remain and might continue to be responsible for those functions where a high volume of text input is needed, but the ability to operate the equipment is most unlikely to be confined in future generations to a single gender. A male unable to operate a word-processor would be like a helpless member of an ancient mandarinate, enveloped in a cocoon of expensive assistance, unable to receive or send messages or even look through his own files. The social, sexual and administrative hierarchies built around mechanical information devices will alter in an age of electronic devices. No doubt new ones will emerge.

Communication between companies will be far more standardized than now; invoices and memoranda will be sent electronically and be generated on standard forms. Urgent messages will be sent instantaneously but the general bulk of filing material, ordering, invoicing, recording will probably use cheap overnight telecommunications rates and be stored at the transmitting end of the communication until the end of office hours. One can envisage the present imbalance between administrative and productive staff being corrected; the number of managers required in a given enterprise will certainly fall, together with the support staff. Some even predict the end of the office as an institution but it is hard to imagine an electronic system replacing the personal contacts of which office communication largely consists. 'Once a thing is put in writing', said Socrates, 'the composition drifts about, getting into the hands of people who have no business with it'. That is no less true today and while one may foresee a shrinking in the size of administration and a transformation in the whole relationship between an administration and the activity being administered, it is difficult to imagine the kind of total dispersal of office staffs which some predict. Tele-conferencing might well reduce the need for physical transportation, especially for those personal contacts which involve a very long journey by several people for a very brief meeting, but the word-processor is hardly likely to lead to the total elimination of collective work within an office. The 'work at home movement' will undoubtedly gather pace over the decades, but is likely to be confined to rather specialized levels of work—post-retirement consultancies, work which involves little interaction with a central office. The peak-hour traffic jams might cease to grow but they are unlikely to disappear.

The microprocessor is inevitably going to produce major alterations in the system of industrial production, at least on the scale of the automation wave of the 1950's and 1960's; but while communication technology has undoubtedly the potential to alter the way in which work is performed, one has to take into account the fact that the factory system of the West has already absorbed an enormous investment in the post-war period, which has already led to a reduction in the amount of work consumed in a given product. Where the administrative/information sector of the economy has been recruiting new workers throughout the century and especially in the last couple of decades, the production sector has been losing workers, relative to the task performed, and so has the agricultural sector. Although these naturally afford opportunities for further economies of manpower, these are likely to be realized only at the price of a greater and more considerable investment than the concomitant savings in the information sector itself. The information revolution will have the paradoxical effect of reducing the percentage of the population employed in the information sector, compared with agriculture and industry.

In the past, the installation of computers in factories, as control systems, has been so expensive that it has been feasible only in the context of complete re-equipment. Today the microcomputer can be added piecemeal to help replace mechanical and electro-mechanical devices. Indeed, one may add computer-power to a single machine or instrument. This should have an important impact on job satisfaction, since computerization in its present phase can be treated as an enhancement of an individual skill rather than as a displacer of a workforce. Although the press and television constantly offer us the spectacle of robot-controlled factories, it is highly unlikely that microprocessors will acquire any of the really subtle range of physical skills which are humanly provided in the advanced factory. The microprocessor is, however, likely to raise the necessary level of skill in the average human worker because it will have the function of supplementing it with the more routine processes. The skill of a trained mechanic consists in the absorption and re-representation of an extraordinarily subtle and complex set of understandings of physical reality; the micro-processor is able to reach towards this assemblage of pieces of half-conscious knowledge only in the crudest way. Of course, where the more familiar kinds of automation have not yet taken place they can now do so with the added advantage of the microchip, but in the factory system as a whole we are unlikely in the 1980's and 1990's to see the disappearance of human skills, where these have already been developed to a high level.

The total number of people actually involved, in the conditions of 1980, in the processes of manufacture, was less than one fifth of the working population, if one excludes supervisory and managerial staff. The microprocessor has, therefore, little scope in this area for making further widespread change. At some point in the 1990's, however, as the re-equipping of offices advances, new concepts for the deploying of artificial intelligence will inevitably be developed, especially in the field of factory control systems. One might see information technology used not so much for the purpose of raising the productivity of labour-time, as for changing the concept of mass production itself. The microprocessor, in the field of information itself, is a great individuator of taste, enabling an individual to explore personal routes through great databases, and select material according to individual choice. One is likely to see control systems in productive industry develop to the point at which manufactured goods are also shaped much more according to individual taste. Of course, it is already possible to multiply the range of styles and colours available, but the pre-ordering of individualized designs is the probable line along which manu-facturing planning will move, and this, more than any other change, is likely to alter the nature of industrial work and the 'feel' of industrial society. It would be one of those easy acts of false futurism to argue that this will itself reduce the alienation entailed in industrial work, by bringing the producer closer to the user, but it might be fair to argue that this facility could help alter the consciousness of mass production workers and abolish the sense of the mass market as a distant de-personalized force. Consumers will, in a sense, become *clients* again.

In the period between 1980 and 2000, however, one must expect a number of social paradoxes to occur in areas where advanced information technology is used in control processes without abolishing the remaining physical slog. A small group of comfortable white-coated technocrats can control the whole of a manufacturing process while primitive methods of truck loading and unloading remain, increasing the gulf between the skilled and unskilled groups of workers. While the highly skilled worker, and to some extent the semi-skilled, will begin to approximate towards the consciousness and function of the pure information worker, the unskilled could easily remain at the bottom of the heap, their role undisturbed by the technological revolution. It is extremely difficult to imagine the robotization of garbage collection although various microprocessor-aided devices might relieve some of the burden. Those tasks which require unremitting physical labour at present, however, are the ones least likely to be eliminated and this is an obvious area of future social discontent. The fact that society contains the knowledge to abolish unpleasant work, as it does, does not mean it is convenient, economic or 'rational' to do so. Hence the tensions.

In the 1960's it was thought that the television receiver would become a kind of central information device situated in the home. The cable and community antenna television (CATV) seemed to offer the major source of belief in the imminent arrival of two-way video communication. Those hopes have largely foundered, partly as a result of sheer cost, partly because the suppliers of cable in those countries in which it is most highly developed (Canada, USA, Belgium) have offered very little in the way of attractive additional material. The cable has become a profitable medium as a supplier of first-run cinema material where the cable head-end has been attached to a domestic satellite sending out video entertainment for Home Box Office or subscription television. That does not constitute an information revolution, however, and the real transformation of home information is likely to come when it is possible to distribute information throughout the home rather than as an adjunct to the ordinary television receiver. For this the ring-main for general information is a pre-requisite or almost a pre-requisite, as is the development of a cheap and improved display system. The one- or two-set home is not able to receive the level of information which in future will be available. Terminals will need to be cheap enough to be distributed in different formats and sizes throughout the home—detachable screen-pads, enlarged high-definition wall-screens, small screens with print-out capability for the newspaper substitutes of the future.

Another of the predictions which have quickly withered has been the computer-controlled home, in which each householder was expected to design his and her own services and self-programme them. There is a great distinction to be noted between those products which can be manipulated at home by expert amateur programmers and those which contain their own programmes. The washing machine, 1980 style, is about as complicated as one can expect domestic equipment to be. Devices which switch themselves on and off will continue to be free-standing affairs, presented by different manufacturers, although capable of being instructed remotely. Thus it might be possible to order music and change it by way of a telephone-attached keypad; it should be possible to order a cooker to switch on or off remotely and for messages to be held, checked and answered according to pre-arranged instructions. But each of these devices is a mild adaptation of its mechanical forebear. As the home develops its own information distribution system, however, perhaps around the turn of the century, the sophistication of such devices will increase. The microprocessor will be hidden from the user and the process of computerization of the home will take place, as it were, by stealth. The simplest keyboard or punch-pad will be the most any citizen will be expected to operate at home, although in the factory and the office far more complex manipulations of information will be regularly conducted.

The range of such programmed devices will inevitably be enormous and each one which enters the home will represent a vast penumbra of altered institutions and social practices. Shopping and choosing goods direct from the home is probably the one single service which will most alter the domestic iife of the individual citizen. It should be possible greatly to extend the service which the British Post Office's Prestel system already offers by which goods advertised on the screen can be ordered through a screen and punch-pad by using a credit-card number. More probably, the number used will be that of a directly-debited bank account where the availability of credit is checked at the precise moment of purchase. Clearly no individual will want to look through the entire variety of goods present on the shelves of a store and equally clearly there will always be ranges of goods which a customer wishes to handle and try on before purchase. It is easy to buy cases of wine electronically since they cannot be opened before purchase, but extremely difficult to buy a suit of clothes electronically.

The business of selling and advertising is bound to be altered by the changed (or additional) methods of electronic purchase. The customer will probably appreciate hard information far more than hard selling when the goods to be acquired are seen only on a screen or in a published catalogue. Already the newspaper industry in North America has gone a long way towards offering the possibility of selective advertising by localizing a great deal of advertising and offering special supplements to selected groups of readers (selected normally according to location of residence.) However, we are likely to see in 2000 a far higher level of advertising selection on the part of the consumer himself while the whole psychology of merchandising is likely to change concomitantly.

It is in the field of entertainment that the most rapid changes will occur. The 'massness' of the mass audience will decline as the profusion of possible choice increases. The optic fibre, used as a method of distributing home entertainment, will offer scores of simultaneous channels rather differently from the multi-channel communities of North America of today. Where today an American viewer chooses between three or four main channels and a variety of secondary material, the future system should make it possible for real competition between the major networks to be inaugurated. Where it is possible to isolate a specialized audience and obtain payment from them, it is possible to eliminate the one great drawback of over-the-air television, the inability of the supplier to discriminate among audiences. If a special charge, however small, could be made for special ranges of programmes—so long as the specialized programme is potentially available to the whole of the mass audience—it becomes possible to finance a much greater range of higher quality material (also of lower quality). The viewer will be able to order his material, therefore, and, of course, to view it at any later moment of his choosing through pre-recording. Over-the-air television will almost certainly remain although the number of channels is not likely to increase very much beyond the level of the 1980's. What will increase is the choice of new and re-run material available through new additional devices.

The late 1970's saw the first experiments in the domestic distribution of text-information. Broadcasting organizations started teletext services in great number and telephone administrations started videotex services in parallel. By the end of the century these will be able to operate on a broader band and will be able to send out still pictures and elaborate advertising and educational material, as well as simple 20-line pages of information. With the arrival of a higher-definition television picture in the 1990's there will be no difficulty in increasing the amount of text material sent out on each page and no difficulty also in obtaining hard-copy of selected material. In those societies with complex ideogrammatic languages, such as Chinese and Japanese, an extraordinary social revolution will accompany these devices, since it has been virtually impossible to type manually in these languages (at least, without very special machines and many years of training). By the year 2000 the Japanese will be able to create text artificially at home by means of a videotex-type service, since keys on a pad can be made to generate specified 'kanji' characters. At the same time the growing sophistication of videotex systems will allow for simple translation and transliteration devices, so that Japanese characters can be reconstituted from messages sent out in English. It is probably also through videotex that the shopping systems, mentioned above, will arrive, although in North America there is likely to be, for several decades, a number of competing and incompatible home-text systems, some modelled on videotex, others built out of large entertainment empires. European societies will have single national systems, converging eventually on a continental shared or mutually compatible system, which can cope with the various alphabets of Europe.

One adjunct of sophisticated home-text systems will almost certainly be direct access to libraries which will gradually have assembled large quantities of material in machine-readable form or in some other computerized mode. Of course the vast backlog of human literature will remain as it is, and fiction will probably continue to be read from paper. But so flexible will the display systems for text have become that it will seem more sensible for ephemeral information to be acquired electronically than physically. Since the display system can be made to have all of the flexibility and mobility of a book or magazine, there exists no argument of convenience and many arguments of cost against maintaining the present cumbersome system. Why supply every home with an enormous set of telephone directories, which largely contain redundant information, when an individual can be supplied with the required nugget of information in a fraction of a second without the physical costs of creating and distributing the whole of a city's telephone numbers? The library of the future will eventually change in nature as it changes in technology. Historically the library evolved as a physical storage system for books, with its research functions developing much later. The librarian was essentially a guardian, although in the present century he has become a sifter and provider of information in addition. With direct electronic access to the written word, the librarian's role becomes more integral to the organization of information and the role becomes more creative since it entails the devising of computer search structures. The library becomes the outward symbol of the new configurations in which information is stored in the computer era. Although the paperless library will almost certainly never arrive, it is out of the modern librarian's function that the new information worker of the future must evolve.

In addition to computer storage and paper storage of information, a general re-apportionment of functions must take place in the next twenty years among the range of published *genres* of information. What is currently seen as a profitable line of information for a reference book or a text book might well end up in electronic mode, accessed nugget by nugget as required rather than presented to the reader in continuous text. Ephemeral information might be better published via videotex or descendant systems rather than on paper. News may well remain for several decades on paper until the raw material and its complex and expensive system of distribution withers away, leaving the newspaper a useful but rather luxury product. However, there are other ways in which the printed page might reach the reader: the videodisc is an excellent and *durable* system of storage, much longer-lasting than the most well produced book, and for archival purposes, including the storage of colour photographs, no technology has hitherto arrived more effective than the videodisc. There are also forms of cassette which hold printed information rather efficiently, but a single disc, even in the prototype stage developed in the late 1970's, can hold the equivalent of 50,000 pages of writing or pictures, every one of them reachable with greater ease than the page of a book. Moreover, the disc is at least as easy and cheap (eventually) to distribute as a newspaper or magazine; in the shorter term, however, the information cassette is more likely to come into widespread use, since the videodisc is not destined to fall greatly in price until the 1990's. The newspaper will also benefit from the advanced satellite, especially in North America, where the transportation of paper itself is a major constricting factor in newspaper economics. Since the 1930's it has been possible to transmit the material of a newspaper page by telephone wire and the home facsimile newspaper has been predicted every few years since World War Two. It could be that the decade of the 1990's will offer the long-awaited opportunity, since at that time the newspaper's negative economics will begin to be outweighed by the new opportunities afforded by computerized technology. Of course, by 2000 hot metal printing will have been eliminated from the newspaper medium entirely and the whole of the content of the newspaper will be created by electronic means in virtually all societies. The extension of the computer's reach onwards from paper in a central printing plant to a printing console in an individual neighbourhood or even individual home will become possible in financial terms. Despite experiments in Japan in the late 1970's virtually all newspaper publishers agree that the home facsimile newspaper or the home computer-set newspaper is not an economic proposition for a further generation. So great is the sunk investment of the newspaper industry—in people as much as plant and capital—that the kind of major overhaul which the home-created newspaper would entail is not possible for many years. The mere computerization of type-setting in the mid-1970's in the United States and elsewhere produced enormous problems (and enormous financial gains) but the further overhaul of the entire distribution system of newspapers must await a decade or two. Nonetheless the year 2000 will see a variety of devices in the average home for receiving written information and the typical *content* of all existing printed and broadcast media will alter significantly as more appropriate means are evolved for dealing with specific kinds of information (videotex, for example, absorbing the more ephemeral 'up-dating' kind of facts). The year 2000 will, therefore, witness a general exchange of kinds of information between media, the establishment of various home and office devices for the display and collection of information, and the start of a wholly new concept in general knowledge—the tailoring of information to individual needs.

In terms of underlying social impact perhaps the greatest change will be the opportunity for individuation, not merely of what a person buys and owns, but what a person *knows*. Where Western democracies have been built upon the broad assumption that the entire electorate has at its disposal the same shared modicum of knowledge about a given society, one might expect the more diversified media systems of the future to suggest that society is more fragmented, not necessarily in an individualistic self-serving sense, but in terms of small groups, fads, fashions. The individual will develop an altered perception of his society. Where a society founded on industrial wealth has aggregated its citizens, gathered them into large markets, large cities, large electorates, one might expect the information society to discover equal economies of scale, more effective markets, more subtle political combinations, in a variety of smaller groups and classes. The organization of factories and cities was constrained (and also facilitated) by the need to house central energy systems, based on coal and oil and electricity. The information society distributes commands across space without difficulty and its energy needs, although very great, do not necessitate the diseconomies which come from the crowding, massing, concentrating of population, industry, entertainment. Technologies, themselves, do not alter societies. Rather they express, as they arrive, the half-understood needs and tendencies of societies. Industrial society brought about the growth of urban population, with all the consequences for social relationships, individual lives and human culture, which are now well understood. Information society will help to express and perhaps alleviate the psychological under-pinnings of the city as a stage in human settlement. Already the city has evolved into a megalopolis, the spreading of concentrated settlement into a broader, more sprawling interconnection of town and country, with the arrival of cheap individual transport. The late twentieth century in most developed societies contained an enormous increase in the demand for second homes, for the switching of careers at mid-life, for the starting of new careers and new educations at the age of retirement. Such patterns of taste are universal in similar societies. The development of the new information technologies is bound to increase the trends towards these forms of invisible transhumance: the city may not disappear, together with its traffic jams, just because of the arrival of the word-processor (as some have predicted), but the psychological acceptance of fixed locations for work and residence, vacation and entertainment, may well evaporate. The city is a state of mind as well as a physical entity and it consists largely of concentric mutually dependent information systems; when the necessity of concentrated location is removed the systems may well remain, but in a looser form.

The question is constantly asked, whether a society whose central highways consist of information rather than industry will be more or less democratic, more or less 'centralized'. That cannot really be answered, since all forms of communication can cause quite contrary and simultaneous effects. The telephone helps dictators to dictate but democratic leaders to confer, militarists to declare war but warriors to make peace. The new communication techniques will undoubtedly turn out to have 'caused' whichever tendency finally sets in; they will really have facilitated the change of direction which society was, in any case, heading for. The society of information grows out of a network, a reticulated pattern of contact, since the nineteenth century telephone has been at its heart. A network is very different in shape from the central pattern of an authoritarian society, whether it be that of ancient monarchies or modern party or military dictatorships. A network spreads itself across large geographic areas just as easily and creates tribal linkages which are not necessarily based upon shared location or physical proximity. It creates its own patterns of trust in which members of a society have to accept orders and advice from people they do not see, but whose capacity or authority is accepted through voice recognition, perhaps aided by paper. The information society must inevitably become one founded on an increasing sense of trust, in which common emergencies can be dealt with through the rapid concentration of and acceptance of authority with a greater sense of shared power prevailing in normal conditions. The information devices which have been referred to—by no means an exhaustive account—simply give some inkling of the kinds of sophistication and differentiation which may just perhaps make the year 2000 able to fulfil more of the ideals of the previous century than that century was able to achieve for itself.

7

Learning at a Distance

by Walter Perry

It would be inappropriate for me, in writing this chapter, to try to deal with those fundamental aspects of the future which will inevitably determine the shape of any educational service. I start, therefore, with a number of premises; and the probability of any of them is no doubt discussed in detail elsewhere in this book. Thus in all that follows I assume

(a) that the world remains free from a nuclear holocaust
(b) that the world production of food is maintained roughly in balance with the world population
(c) that the world remains free of pandemics of pestilence
(d) that the available sources of energy keep pace with controlled demand and that there is a workable system of distributing energy sources fairly between the nations
(e) that in each nation it is possible to achieve a relatively balanced economy.

I wish that I could believe in my assumptions; but in fact I rather think that Malthus is more likely to be a true prophet and that the Four Horsemen of the Apocalypse will ride roughshod over my picture of the future of education. For the moment, however, let us keep their horses stabled and look forward to what the shape of education might be if the stable door stays closed.

The Technology of Education

We have watched, in the last decade, a revolution in the hardware of communications. The silicon chip and the minicomputer have been brought, with incredible rapidity, to a pitch of technical refinement that has opened the door to a host of new developments.

So far, the software has lamentably failed to keep pace with the hardware especially in the wholly unexploited educational market. This is one of the really enormous potential markets; the best-selling books of all time, after the Bible, are mostly school text-books. Yet it is a very difficult market to exploit for it is controlled not by the consumers of education themselves but by academics.

Until Britain's Open University came along to upset the academic applecart it was widely believed that the *only* way anyone could really be educated was to arrange face-to-face encounters with teachers so that 'two minds could rub against each other'. What had been a charming conceit for the elite of the nineteenth century had become an intolerably expensive shibboleth for programmes of mass education in the twentieth, when the Open University showed that people who wanted badly enough to be educated could in fact educate themselves given adequate high quality help through the mass media of communication. The academic world has accepted, as a matter of reason based on evidence, that this is so; but there is still a considerable emotional resistance to its full acceptance. The media that were used by the Open University were the printed book, TV and radio. Those media are, of course, all unidirectional. They provide for no interaction between teacher and student; and the Open University had to provide, in addition, for some such interaction through the postal service, the student sending written work to the tutor for marking and getting back the comments of the tutor on his efforts. This was an interaction with a long delay.

Modern technology has already provided the hardware that is necessary to create an interactive system of communication between teacher and student that has virtually instantaneous feedback. The only thing that prevents the use of such hardware is money. Yet it is probable that entrepreneurial genius will find ways of overcoming even that great stumbling block over the next decade.

The manufacturers of the minicomputer have, of course, been looking anxiously at all potential markets for their product. They have created, in the last year or two, extremely successful markets by developing a range of children's games based on minicomputers; but it may well be that this market will soon be saturated. They have also developed machines that will play chess or bridge and this has provided a further market for exploitation. But the real break-through to the mass adult market will depend, I imagine, on the successful marketing of, first, access to information and, second, training in how to use the information or, in other words, education.

Successful marketing in these two areas depends on brilliant ideas for persuading the public that they need these services; and, on the rapid development of the software needed to offer the services. The great problem is that the development of the software is extremely expensive and financiers need to be assured of the brilliance and, in consequence, the probable success of the marketing ideas before investing the necessary capital in the software.

If we assume that the brilliance and the investment materialize, as I, like the author of the previous chapter, believe they will, we will arrive at a world in which the ordinary man possesses, hires, or is loaned not only a TV and a radio but a whole range of additional machines. He will have a telephone which is connected through a 'modem' to the TV set or to a monitor tube (the Open University has already developed such a modem called 'Cyclops') which will enable him to communicate with a tutor in vision as well as in sound since each will be able to write with a 'light' pen on the TV screen and the image will appear on both screens; the modem will also accept cheap audio cassettes that have been pre-programmed to produce simple images on the screen. Furthermore, he will not only have a minicomputer of his own, he will also be able, by telephone linkage, to plug into a national computer network from which he will be able to obtain access, either to libraries so that he can consult a book by having it appear page by page on his TV screen, or to other sources of up-to-date statistical or other information that he requires. Power is often described as access to information; in this sense the whole population will acquire power; but real power depends also upon the use to which information is put and that calls for skill, knowledge, intellectual ability or wisdom—or all of these. It is the challenge of education to develop them.

Modern neurophysiology has shown that, beyond doubt, the capacity of the human brain to establish connections (synapses) between its cells (neurones) is virtually infinite; but the number of such connections actually made is decidedly limited. If one accepts that memory and the power of rational thought are in some way correlated to the number or quality of the networks of these synaptic connections (which is probable) then it follows that Man has by no means yet reached the limits of his potential intellectual capacity. It is easy to jump unjustifiably from this conclusion to a further one, namely that because of the undeveloped capacity that is latent in everyone, all children are capable of far more intellectual achievement than they exhibit; and that the reason for this failure to achieve lies wholly in the environment. I do not propose to be drawn into the argument about whether such environmental factors are the only determinants of intelligence or whether there are genetic factors that are even more important determinants. Suffice it to say that I am myself persuaded that both have a large part to play in determining the number and quality of the synaptic connections. As educationists we can in any event do nothing to modify genetic determinants; but we can, and should, do all we can to try to make the environment of development approach the ideal. The problem of course is to determine what is that ideal environment. Most people agree that, whatever it may be, it should be made available, as far as possible, to everyone. In other words we should aim not only at an ideal environment; we should also aim at equality of opportunity. Both are unachievable. One cannot compensate for the differences between parents in providing opportunities for their children unless one wholly eliminates the family unit; and even then one must replace it by the creche where the qualities of those adults chosen to look after the children will vary as greatly as do the qualities of parents. But the realization that equality of opportunity is unachievable does not remove our responsibility for trying to achieve it as far as is possible.

In all that I have said I have taken it as axiomatic that 'education is a good thing'. I do not subscribe to the view that society would be happier with less education. Even were it true—which I very much doubt—that the uneducated manual worker of the past was more content with his lot than the semi-educated one of today, the communications explosion has made retreat to such a situation quite impossible. Society will go on being informed, society will go on being concerned about what it is informed about, and society will go on coming to the wrong conclusions and taking the wrong actions about these matters of concern unless we can, by educating each member of society to this limit of his or her capacity, produce a really dramatic change. I see no other way of dealing with the profound impact of the communications explosion.

This leads quite inevitably to the most fundamental question of all, namely 'What is education for?' or 'What are we trying to achieve by our educational programmes?' It seems to me that educational theorists who have tried to answer this question in the last two decades have nearly all framed their answers in terms of satisfying the needs of the members of a modern society. These needs can be variously described as

(i) the need to earn a living—which demands that education should provide some sort of vocational training

(ii) the need to play a role in society—which demands that

education should provide some sort of instruction in the customs and structure of society

(iii) the need to enjoy leisure—which demands that education should develop the creative talents and the skills of the individual

and theorists vary in the extent to which they stress these various needs and vary even more in the ways in which they propose to satisfy them through the educational system.

It seems to me, however, that there is a gap in all this theory, a gap that is the root cause of many of our current problems, a gap that is extremely difficult to fill. There is seldom any mention of educating people to have values. Indeed we have, as a society, torn down and abandoned all the values that formerly provided the principles on which human behaviour in societies was founded. We have, in the Western world, abandoned religious faith except where we have embraced Marxism; we have largely destroyed respect for age and experience in our concentration on the 'rights' of the young; we have eschewed the concepts of empire and of national pride; we have to a large extent disrupted the values of the family as a unit. I am not arguing that we were wrong to abandon all these values; I am, however, arguing strongly that we were wrong to abandon them unless we had something else to put in their place. Those of us, and I was one, who, as adults, embraced humanism as a basis for an ethical code—the Mr. Do-as-you-would-be-done-by philosophy —failed to appreciate that it is a sophisticated concept which cannot easily be taught to young children. It has neither carrot nor whip to attract or compel acceptance. It is essentially based on self-discipline and, before it is accepted as a belief, there is no basis for any imposed discipline. I am quite certain that, intrinsically, all human beings are wholly selfish—the single exception being the unselfishness of parents towards their own children, which is based on the reproductive instinct. Thus to overcome their intrinsic selfishness, people either need a belief that they will benefit in this life or the next, or they need a healthy fear that, if they don't overcome it, they will suffer a penalty in this life or the next. I have no belief whatsoever in any intrinsic human altruism. This is why I believe that Marxism, which promises nothing as a reward and is based wholly on self-discipline, calls for qualities of unselfishness, of 'goodness', that, in the long run, cannot be sustained by human beings; consequently it is ultimately bound to fail as a basis for human societies.

I would therefore answer the fundamental question 'what *should* we be trying to achieve by our educational programmes?' by saying that we aim

(a) to instil a set of values
(b) to develop innate creative talents and skills
(c) to develop intellectual capacity as far as possible
(d) to instil a knowledge of the customs and structure of society
(e) based on all the above to select and train for a vocation

These are the things we *should* be doing. Whether they will commend themselves to our political masters remains to be seen. For the future of education will ultimately depend upon political decisions. This fact is of profound importance. Indeed much sociological theory has been evolved to show that education is shaped by politicians in order to stabilize societies. Thus in capitalist countries, it is said, the educational system is used to condition children to accept the class system that depends upon maintaining the economic differences between masters and men. In communist countries the educational system is used to inculcate in children acceptance of the supreme power of the state and the consequent subjugation of the individual.

The Major Trends in Education in the Future

What then are the main trends that can be discerned in the world patterns of education and that act as pointers to the future change of education?

1. *Homogeneity*
There is a very strong trend, which will almost certainly continue, for the systems of education in different countries to become more homogeneous. There is still a very long way to go. In the USA all children go to school at 6, half of them go on to college, a quarter graduate from college and one in ten continues into postgraduate education. All this adds up to the fact that, on average, the US child will spend no less than 16 years in full-time initial education, emerging to take his or her place in society only at 22+. On the other hand there are still many parts of the world where, on average, a child will spend less than four years in initial education.

Every developing country makes strenuous efforts to increase the literacy of its population, recognizing that this is an essential prerequisite for economic advancement; it is characteristic that amongst the first priorities of each government is a teacher-training programme. The problems that many countries face are truly formidable. I remember being told by the Minister of Education from Delhi that his five-year plan called upon him to create more *new* places in primary schools than all the primary school places in Britain. It was not only an immense task, it was also a very expensive one for a country with chronic economic difficulties.

2. *Escalation of Cost*

The cost of initial education has escalated at an alarming rate in the last two decades in the developed Western world. There are a number of contributory factors:

(i) a growth in the number of children requiring schooling—the 'bulge' in the birth rate

(ii) legislation increasing the period of compulsory schooling

(iii) an increased voluntary tendency to stay at school for longer and go on to higher education

(iv) an increase in the amount of information that is being taught. This follows from the accelerating pace of the acquisition of new knowledge: together with a failure to prune out of the curriculum the less necessary elements

(v) an increased complexity of provision—e.g. TV, science and technology, laboratory experience, language laboratories, sophistication of school music and drama and sport provision etc.

(vi) an increased salary bill—teachers were underpaid but had rewards of status in the community. The latter has been eroded and has led to unionization and large wage demands.

All these causes of increase in real cost (over and above inflation) that have affected the developed world are all the time having increasing effects on developing countries as the trend towards homogeneity continues. Imitation is perhaps the most noticeable feature of educational policies in developing countries. They want to set up systems already tried in the West; and are very suspicious of innovative techniques not yet wholly tried and proven. It was only the fact that the Open University had been proven efficacious in the UK that led to the enormous interest of other countries in its systems.

The escalation of cost that has gone on for many years has, however, flattened off. There has been a realization that it is not possible to go on increasing the proportion of the GNP devoted to education; we could easily end up with a situation where half the population was engaged in teaching the other half and where nothing actually got done. I suggest therefore that this particular trend is beginning to die away and that, in the future, there will be a continued attempt to prune the educational budget by finding cheaper ways of meeting the needs.

3. *The Development of Systems of Distance-Learning*

The development of distance-learning systems, pioneered by the Open University, has been a very striking feature of the last decade all over the world. There are now between 20 and 30 'open universities' or 'open colleges' in existence and more are being founded every year. The reasons for this educational development are varied but amongst the most important are

(i) a desire to harness the mass media of communication to the service of education

(ii) a desire to extend the opportunities of higher (and sometimes of secondary) education to adults who must continue to work and to stay at home

(iii) a desire to reduce the very high costs of higher education.

The success of the OU in accomplishing all three of these objectives has been a major factor in encouraging the creation of other institutions sharing some at least of the same aims.

4. *The Emergence of the Need for Continuing Education*

For several years now people in many countries have come to realize that the pace of acquisition of new knowledge is not only very fast but is accelerating. All sorts of figures are quoted to dramatize the situation; as, for example, the calculation that more new information emerged last year than emerged in the whole of recorded history up to 1900. This sort of statement is easy to make and impossible to prove or disprove; but it indicates well enough the dilemma that we face. It follows that the traditional idea that the initial education that a child is given can be a preparation—and an adequate preparation—for the whole of his or her working life is simply no longer tenable. The average American, it is now stated, changes his career twice and moves house fourteen times during his active life. Much of what he learns at school, college and university will be out-of-date not just before he retires but even before he finishes his initial education. It thus seems sensible to consider whether a period of initial education that *averages* sixteen years is any longer sensible. Clearly education must continue throughout life to provide the updating and retraining that a modern career will demand.

Should we not aim to reduce initial education by eliminating most of the ephemeral information; and by programming the individual for continuing education in his future life? This sounds not only sensible but also easy; it is, of course, extremely difficult.

There are several very cogent reasons for that difficulty:

(i) it is very hard to decide what information is ephemeral. Thus pruning the curriculum is intrinsically difficult. It is therefore easier to add new material and make the period of initial education longer rather than shorter

(ii) there is a real fear of redundancy on the part of those engaged in initial education. They do not realize that they will be needed very badly for programmes of continuing education; or, if they do realize this, they may well consider that it will pose new problems for them so it is tempting to leave things as they are

(iii) there is an enormous vested commercial interest in initial education and consequent resistance to any attempt at reducing its duration.

In these circumstances governments which realize that continuing education is vital pay lip-service to this idea but, faced with the current huge bill for initial education and unable to cut it for the reasons I have given, find it impossible to pay even more for the continuing education they know to be necessary. I think that the next decade will see a break out of this apparent impasse, probably through the use of distance-learning systems.

Conclusions

My picture of the future is therefore one that sees the nations of the world coming closer together in their educational patterns. There will be an increase of initial education in developing countries and a decrease in developed countries. All will provide continuing education on an increasing scale and most of it will be done by distance-learning systems. Schools and colleges will continue to use face-to-face tuition but this will be supplemented by an increasing use of modern technology; and the same technology will be the basis of continuing education. One enormous advantage of distance-learning is that it can readily adapt to the differing capacities of individuals, including, on the one hand, children in need of remedial help and children of abnormally low intelligence, and on the other, gifted children for whom at present no special provision is made.

8

New Economic Policies

by Jan Tinbergen

In periods of crisis the need for a New Economics is often proclaimed. Thus Marx tried to modernize economic thinking in response to the suffering of the masses in industrializing countries. Keynes tried to refresh it, in order to break the deadlock of the Great Depression, when one-third of the industrial workforce was unemployed. When the 1970s brought the world into a new type of crisis, there was, rightly, a call for a New International Economic Order. But do we need another renovation of economic science? I wonder. I think the greater need is that economics and its various messages should be properly understood (c.f. Bombach, 1977–8).

Economic research has shown a high degree of adaptability to the new situation. One feature has been the quantification of economic thinking, so that changes once thought to be qualitative can now be understood as merely a chance in coefficients. Another aspect of the adaptability of economics is recognition of the multi-disciplinary nature of the problems facing Mankind. Economists are prepared to join with other scientists in the many interdisciplinary teams needed to take up the serious challenges of Mankind, and to learn from neighbouring sciences. Psychologists have contributed to a better understanding of consumers and of workers. While educators have been discovering economics, economists have identified education as a major item within the economy. Technologists have aided the development of input-output theory and activity analysis, by which production processes can be better handled by economists. Powerful impulses to growth in understanding have also come from within economics, one example is the accelerated penetration into production processes, leading, for example, to a galaxy of new 'production functions', with implications for our understanding of technological choices.

Biologists have challenged us by specifying ecological bottlenecks and the new scarcities (c.f. Mishan, 1969; Fritsch, 1977).

Mass poverty in developing countries has profoundly changed our thinking on social and institutional aspects (Myrdal, 1970; Adelman, 1977). A wealth of models for different aspects of today's crisis have 'internalized' a series of elements previously thought to be external to economics, but now recognized as part of economic science. This broadening of horizons is not limited to economics, of course, but is a trend in many sciences. One might even say that the border regions in the universe of knowledge, once sparsely populated, have now become territories of overlap explored by interdisciplinary teams.

I have asserted my opinion that we should seek, as citizens, and in our enterprises, governments, and trade unions, better under-standing of economics and many other realms of the mind, rather than a new economic science. We are in need of new economic policies, and this is the theme I propose to elaborate in what follows. I propose first to have a look at the changed situation we are facing in the hope of producing a 'helicopter view' (the term used in management science to characterize the main capability of a manager). Then I shall try to sketch the wider dimensions we need to absorb in our practical decision-making. The remaining sections are intended to be applications of the new attitude needed to the decisions of the entities possessing power now or in the near future, namely: large enterprises, especially transnational ones; trade unions; governments of less-developed countries; governments of developed, mainly Western-type countries; political parties and their superstructures; and finally ourselves, the citizens, who are supposed to control all these institutions. As an economist I have to concede that, as in any science, there is no unanimity on all subjects of economic policy; to say so would be to idealize the situation to no small degree. Yet there remain a sufficient number of messages.

Let me finish this introduction by a few words to my fellow-economists—technical words to illustrate what I meant by asking for more understanding of existing economics rather than new economics. A few illustrations only, chosen at random: the distinction between stable and unstable markets; between tradables and non-tradables; or between short-term and long-term effects; the concept of optimal levels of decision making; and, above all, the concept of a rational international division of labour.

The Changed World Situation

Intellectually we know that the world has always been changing and will go on doing so. But are we aware of the relevant changes below the level of conscious thinking, in the world of the unconscious from which intuitive ideas originate? Are we aware, as Europeans, of where the level of material well-being in Britain now stands—below that of Japan? Of course we should add that the slow rate of growth in Britain may reflect a degree of unconscious wisdom about what we should accustom ourselves to in the coming decades. Are we also sufficiently aware of the fact that France and Germany, too, are only medium-sized nations? Do we yet accept that interdependence has become such a preponderant feature of today's world that the idea of proudly sticking to national decision-making rests on a myth, namely that we can decide ourselves about our future? Nations may be able 'to opt out' of the European Community, but they should not think that by so doing they take their future in their own hands again.

Militarily speaking, the most important power centres today are the USA and the Soviet Union; economically speaking, the USA, Japan and, in a sense, OPEC (Organization of Petroleum Exporting Countries). The People's Republic of China is ideologically powerful. The transnational enterprises, when added together, represent an enormous economic potential, but they are not organized in one institution. The ten top corporations in the USA had, in 1974, total sales of $200 billion (thousand million), but sales are not incomes; so the comparison often made with national incomes of some countries (for instance, the UK in 1974 $201 billion) is misleading. A single transnational enterprise can, though, be powerful in comparison with even a large developing country—but more so before they have set up a factory in such a country than after they have done so. Trade union congresses or confederations command power centres within industrial countries, but not yet on the world stage. Their policies over the last decade have been a substantial cause of inflation, together with the credit creation by the American government, the sudden oil price adjustment and some of the price-setting of Western producers.

Those adjustments of oil prices to the real scarcity of energy constitute a beginning of 'trade unionism' among governments of developing countries, especially because of the degree of solidarity with the Group of 77, that is, the group of non-aligned developing countries. It is on purpose, of course, that I use the phrase 'adjustment', and not 'oil crisis' or similar language. Before the price was raised by OPEC, only experts were aware of the energy dilemmas the world was facing. Although nobody knows the total stock of fossil energy sources available for economic exploitation, even those leading experts who want to avoid the risks of nuclear energy production in its present form seriously doubt the possibility of switching to solar energy without temporary use of nuclear energy (c.f. Wilson, 1977). The shortage of safe energy is one of the so-called 'new scarcities' which characterize the changed world situation. There are at least two more: food, and a clean environment.

The most serious is the food shortage, already keeping at starvation level parts of the world's population, notably in Central Africa and South-East Asia. In the food problem, as in the energy question, expert opinions deviate widely when it comes to judging the situation around the year 2000. Nobody can deny, however, that suffering due to hunger is already part of the situation today. An interesting illustration of diverging opinions on food is available in two English-written, Dutch-produced studies (Buringh, Van Heemst and Staring, 1975 and Buringh and Van Heemst, 1977). The former constitutes an estimate of the 'absolute maximum food production of the world', arriving at thirty times the 1970 production, whereas the latter provides us with 'an estimation of world food production based on labour-oriented agriculture', that is to say, using no fertilizer and tractors. In fact, this second study also contains estimates where the labour-oriented method is applied in less-developed countries and a 'modern' method in developed countries (to put it briefly and therefore not precisely) and it shows us how close we are to the limit of what would seem desirable ecologically—an aspect not dealt with in the first study.

This brings us to the third 'new scarcity', a clean environment (c.f. Hueting, 1980). It is a problem with which parts of the populations of developed countries are faced already, and it is likely to be the motive for which the need to transfer part of national sovereignty will first be accepted by Westerners. The high degree of physical visibility of environmental problems makes it easier to persuade ourselves that certain elements of the changed situation cannot be dealt with adequately without sacrificing some sovereignty to higher levels. What this scarcity has in common with the other two is the lack of precise knowledge about its world-wide extent. Here again, even the experts differ widely in their intuitive guesses. Some recent experience with partial cleaning-up operations supports those optimists who hold that a few per cent of national income will be enough to keep pollution under control. At the other end of the scale of opinions we find worried ecologists who point to recent cases of desertification, overfishing, and the disappearance of a number of plant and animal species, and who stress the uniqueness of some land or sea areas which must not be touched. An excellent recent survey has been offered by Myers (1979), who, as a biologist, took the trouble thoroughly to acquaint himself with economics. The difficulty that these ecologists have with economic optimists such as Herman Kahn (1974) is that the complexity of their problems prevents them offering figures about what part of the Earth's surface must be left untouched, in order to serve as a gene reserve, which indeed we badly need if we want to maintain the yields of our high-yielding varieties of food grains and the like. One wonders whether the study of potential world food production already mentioned (Buringh and Van Heemst, 1977) is not the best type of information we need—but more of it.

The next major element of the changed world situation, in short, is the paradoxical situation known as staflagation. In contra-distinction to cyclical depressions as we knew them (with the Great Depression of the 1930s as the worst of its kind) we now see unemployment accompanied not by falling but by rising prices: stagnation of production and employment, combined with in-flation. The Keynesian remedy against unemployment, namely to raise the demand for goods and services by credit or money creation, now tends to cure unemployment only at the price of more inflation. Hence several years of hesitation in socio-economic policy have brought stagnation to the world at large, including the less-developed countries. What is needed is a temporary wage freeze, so as to re-establish the profit margin needed to resume a moderate rate of growth of total production—a growth rate needed to improve the material position of the really poor of the world. But we need to do other things, in order to let this happen: first, a *quid pro quo* for the sacrifice asked from the workers in developed countries, and secondly, Keynesian spending programmes to neutralize the hoarding by rich oil countries. I shall return to this subject in later sections. The point to be made here is that, after years of hesitation, we cannot continue to tolerate unused production potential in a world with unsatisfied basic needs. The spending programmes should benefit those who are likely to spend the increased incomes quickly. This means that less-developed countries should receive more financial assistance and that public spending, which can be controlled, may be better than induced private spending by tax reduction.

So much for the prevailing situation. It is not enough, though, to look at the present or the short-term trends. Several of the problems mentioned should have made us aware of the need to look ahead over longer periods than politicians accustomed to thinking no further than the next election. Sir Winston Churchill tried to teach us that it is the next generation we have to consider. There are a few gloomy prospects indeed if we try to look ahead. First, military escalations, usually considered, wrongly, not to be the economist's concern. Even the worst economic policy cannot possibly do as much harm as modern warfare. Yet, conforming to the division of labour in this book, I abstain from this subject.

In the more restricted socio-economic realm I see some catastrophes threatening us in the developed countries, if we continue our present international policies or, rather, non-policies. The most concrete example I can offer is that the increased misery of the less-developed countries will spill over, in the form of a steep increase in the so-called illegal migrant workers who will flood our (small) part of the Earth. One symptom is the estimated number of seven million Mexicans who are supposed illegally to work in the United States alongside the comparable number of legal immigrants. In 1977, 1400 Pakistanis attempted to enter one of the small rich Arab oil states; then they were unsuccessful, but will they always be? Shall we always be able to send migrant workers home, at moments we don't need them?

Can we continue to disregard the urgent appeals made by the less-developed countries to help establish a New International Economic Order (NIEO), as first formulated by the Sixth Special Session of the General Assembly of the United Nations in 1974? The resolutions reflected the frustration of the Third World at the attitudes adopted so far by the developed countries—attitudes that had changed little by the Eighth Special Session in 1980. At the root of the very limited success of the UN Conference on Trade and Development (UNCTAD V, Manila 1979) lay some purely economic misunderstandings, including the ignorance of several Western politicians about the difference between stable and unstable (labile) markets. The former, when left to themselves, easily find a new equilibrium, and the latter don't: they show large swings. This is why it is preferable to regulate the unstable markets with the aid of reserve stocks and quota systems, and possibly price floors and ceilings. UNCTAD's proposals about the regulation of raw-material and agricultural markets was perfectly reasonable and the lack of co-operation from the developed countries was unreasonable: their preferences for free markets are senseless in the case of unstable markets and are not even accepted at home.

The highly important report of the Independent Commission on International Development Issues presided over by Willy Brandt, former Chancellor of the German Federal Republic (Brandt et al.,

1980), appeared under the ominous title 'North-South: A Programme for Survival'. The unique feature of this Commission was
that it consisted of experienced politicians, equally divided between
developed and less-developed countries, that were of very different
political persuasions, yet they reached consensus on the Report's
recommendations. Despite its importance, the Brandt Report is
scarcely discussed in the larger industrial nations. This illustrates a
dangerous myopia of today's political leadership, in contra-
distinction to the years when Churchill and Monnet were still with
us.

In the wider field of human behaviour and culture there is a
disquieting downward trend in many places, more particularly in
prosperous parts of the world. Increasing criminality, violence, lack
of concern for others, superficiality, 'human errors' as causes of
accidents, and decreasing care for young children are among the
symptoms. The economic impact shows up in the form of declining
quality of work, increased tax fraud—at widely different levels of
income—and decreasing motivation to extend one's education. In
Western Europe, some of these tendencies may be due to too soft
social policies.

Finally, and less dramatically, we seem to be becoming victims of
the phenomenon of bureaucracy, a way of co-ordinating work done
by others, in spite of increasing doubts about the productivity of
that co-ordination. The precise nature and the possible evils of
bureaucracy have not yet been very clearly identified. An interesting characteristic is the hierarchy with a large number of levels,
where incomes paid depend on the level. It is not very clear what
determines, or what should determine, these levels of pay. Another
striking feature is the growth of bureaucracy in both the public and
the private sector, and in Eastern as well as Western economies.

Widening the Scope of Socio-Economic Policies

If the diagnoses given in the preceding section are more or less
correct, the question is, what changes in socio-economic policies
will constitute adequate answers to the challenge of the changed
world situation—'adequate' in both the qualitative and the
quantitative senses. Quantitative thinking is not a strong point
among most policymakers.

Seeing that one of the main characteristics of the situation is
increased interdependence, one supposes that widening of the
scope of our policies must be an important task. To a few great

thinkers we owe some views that need to be considered.

One vision has been admirably formulated by C F von Weizsäcker who introduced the phrase of 'Weltinnenpolitik': world domestic policy. Important elements of such a policy were pursued by Jean Monnet, the *auctor intellectualis* and the first President of the High Authority of the European Coal and Steel Community, and by Raúl Prebisch, Executive Secretary of the Economic Commission of Latin America, who was also the founding father and first Secretary-General of the United Nations Conference on Trade and Development.

In what fields is the need for wider frameworks already understood, at least in part, by present generations of policymakers and citizens? Environmental policies have already been noted as the best example of increased interdependence, because the world possesses only one atmosphere and one water system. But it is a relatively young example, and policies need time to be conceived, discussed and put into practice. A very old field where interdependence is understood is international trade. And we do observe a movement—albeit irritatingly slow and threatened increasingly by lobbies of weak industries—from free trade within Western Europe to free trade among Western countries, and from there to the wider area of West and South. The recent recession has threatened this wider framework with a return to protectionism being advocated by both employers' and employees' organizations in activities which cannot compete on the world market. Short-sightedness prevails in large sections of the general public. They see the problems of these weak industries—the relatively simple and labour-intensive ones, such as textiles, clothing, leather, shoe-making and woodworking industries. They fail to see that protecting weak industries harms the strong industries. Unless the countries of the Third World can export such simple products to us, they cannot buy advanced products from our strong industries.

Consumer interests have less political influence than producer interests, because a producer is fighting for his very existence, and that cannot be said of a consumer. But we are all consumers of the products of all industries, and producers in only one. By forgetting this we may be driven towards a situation in which we are left with an increasing number of protected industries and a decreasing number of competitive activities. Therefore we should resist protective tendencies, and our power to do so must be strengthened by a better anticyclical policy for smoothing out booms and slumps. As will be explained later, this means, not a better national policy, but a better anticyclical policy for the West as a whole.

This brings us naturally to employment policy, as another example of how the scope of our policies has to be widened. There is a need for more employment—or at the very least more employed people, albeit with less work. The need is world-wide and it is most urgent in the Third World, where there is more unemployment and the life of the unemployed is much worse than in the West.

The greatest single cause of unemployment in the villages of the less-developed countries is population growth, due to better health unmatched by family planning. A lower rate of population growth in less-developed countries is a powerful aid to well-being, as is shown in the few countries where it has been attained: Korea, Taiwan and Singapore. But a lower rate of population growth in developed countries is no less important from the point of view of global ecology: one individual in a developed country consumes far more scarce resources than one individual in a less-developed country. Instead of the Western view defended at the 1974 Bucharest UN Population Conference, namely that population growth should be reduced only in the less-developed countries, population policies should apply to all. Here we have an interesting example of some individuals being wiser than their governments: they apply family planning, and their governments are alarmed.

From the examples given we can see that the widening scope of policies has to take effect both geographically and over time. As a rule long-term interests of groups are more compatible than short-term interests. Not all groups with parallel interests are aware, though, that parallelism can exist, even in the short run. Thus the stabilization of food-grain prices at a relatively high level, necessary for the Third World to attain a higher degree of self-sufficiency in food, as recommended by the 1974 World Food Conference in Rome, is also in the interest of the farmers in the rich continents. Similarly, it is in the interest of Western producers of capital goods that more money be made available to the World Bank Group.

Who will be the actors on the world stage who carry out the new economic policies? Increasingly, and fortunately, the young. Not the noisiest of them, often considered to represent the younger generation, nor the *desperados* who have become victims of drugs, or are too agitationally oriented. Rather one has in mind the young volunteers in many fields, young scientists, young organizers, young employers and others, among whom the generation gap may have some quite constructive consequences. Young scientists and employers, as well as politicians and trade unionists, look out for promising new activities instead of protecting the obsolete ones.

Trans-national Enterprises

As promised, I shall now discuss the new policies in relation to various power groups in today's world. In recent decades trans-national enterprises have shown a quite remarkable expansion, and they constitute a high potential of economic activity, with concentrations of managerial and technological talent. They are regarded with satisfaction by many Western observers, with admiration-cum-fear by their counterparts in the less-developed countries, and with fierce criticism by leftist politicians, for whom they typify Capitalism and Imperialism, and seem to fulfil Marx's prophecy of the concentration of power in fewer and fewer hands.

Trans-national enterprises themselves claim to be the major agents of modernization in the less-developed countries, with regard both to management and to technology. In contrast with governments, trade unions or the average citizen, they are much more effective in co-operation between people from different nations. They know how to avoid the long, roundabout methods of official diplomacy; this they have in common with trans-national professional organizations, but they add to it profitable production processes, training facilities and an international division of labour within their organizations.

All this can be of positive value, provided that trans-national enterprises join with those who study the problems of developing countries in attempting fully to understand these countries' structures and priorities, having regard to the interests of the poorest sections of their populations. Scholars who have specialized in this subject have been forced to change their views in a relatively short period. Initially, say around 1950, their ideas were largely based on socio-economic knowledge about Western countries, which were already developed and had in any case started their development under different conditions and made mistakes that could have been avoided. Now, development experts have to admit, with hindsight, that a considerable portion of the population in developing countries has become worse off, instead of seeing living conditions improved. Experts who have only recently discovered this have to be cautious in any complaints against the trans-national enterprises. The interests of the poor will be better served, however, if trans-national enterprises reconsider some of their policies in the light of the new evidence about progress, or lack of it, so far.

An additional difficulty is the attitude of governments in less-developed countries, which in many cases fail to heed the interests of the poorest half of their peoples. This implies that the optimal attitude of trans-national enterprises would be to take an independent view, not only on their natural tasks, management and technology, but also on how their own attitudes can affect the population's well-being. They might then choose policies which, while maintaining a reasonable level of profits, would best serve the long-term interests of the country, taking into account the social changes that can be expected. Up to a point they have done so in their home countries. Their task, as depicted here, would be eased if all governments also behaved in the interest of their populations at large. Often, however, the government of a developing country serves the interests of big landowners rather than of the poor peasants (c.f. Huizer, 1977). This complicates the situation enormously.

Professional development experts have come to the conclusion that the priorities for the less-developed countries are, in order of importance, greater self-sufficiency in food, the creation of employment, and industrialization. The importance of employment policies is that the poorest in a developing country are the jobless, in a community that cannot afford an unemployment dole. Total employment created by trans-national enterprises is not impressive. One of the reasons is the relatively high investment needed to create a job: an investment per person employed several times higher than what the funds available for investment would permit, if employment of all the jobless were the objective of the country's socio-economic policy. This is why one of the outstanding scholars in the field of development policies, E F Schumacher (1973), stressed the need for small-scale, simple technologies. Some of Mahatma Gandhi's ideas, long ridiculed in some Western circles, may turn out to be more relevant than these Westerners thought. As President of the World Bank Group, Robert S McNamara (1974) drew attention to this aspect of policies for tackling massive poverty.

The critical attitude towards trans-national enterprises has had the beneficial effect that more figures have become available, which may enable all concerned to look for constructive solutions to this complex problem. In this connexion mention should be made of the pilot factory in Utrecht of the Dutch trans-national enterprise Philips Gloeilampenfabriek. Figures of Philips, as well as of Unilever, show that the investment per man employed might be reduced if the general infrastructure of the less-developed countries were improved, to assure continuity of production with smaller working capital. Since improvement of infrastructures is the concern of the World Bank Group, a common task may be identified here.

In developed countries, the activities of large enterprises have become subject to countervailing power (Galbraith, 1952) exerted by the community, usually the national government, and occasionally the multinational economic community. At the world level, the need for such countervailing power has been discussed, and one of the instruments accepted most frequently is a Code of Conduct. Several drafts have been submitted, one by the International Chamber of Commerce, one by the Organization for Economic Co-operation and Development, and one by the United Nations. It seems proper that there be a code with enforceable elements, as recommended by various representatives of the less-developed countries.

All of this is now under discussion. One substantial question is what type of control by the community would be effective without damaging the transfer of useful management and technology from developed to less-developed countries. A permanent and comprehensive system of administrative control might well introduce too many elements of bureaucracy. The form of a Court to which test cases of some importance might be submitted would seem to be a more effective type of countervailing power. The difficulties experienced with price control, for instance, within single countries seem to show that such control is effective only when applied selectively. Lessons can be learned from previous attempts, for example by comparing American and German anti-trust experience. Mention may also be made of a Dutch system, where agreements between firms could either be declared illegal, or be declared compulsory to all firms of some branch of activity, depending on whether the government considered the agreement contrary or favourable to the general interest.

The non-economic hobby of empire-building may lead some enterprises to become larger than is optimal. This general aspect of large enterprises, whether trans-national or national, deserves brief attention, in response to a view expressed by Macrae (1976) and Van den Doel (1971). Very large enterprises may suffer, as stated earlier, from an unnecessarily high degree of bureaucracy. The existing tendency to break them up into federations of smaller units, connected by markets rather than hierarchies, may become stronger. Consideration of such a policy is related to questions of how organization and technology may have to be adapted to the level of education of the work force, in order to optimize productivity and job-satisfaction.

Trade Unions

In the developed countries, labour unions have achieved considerable impact on socio-economic policies and structures. Internationalization has been in progress for a much longer period than we sometimes believe; in fact the creation of the International Labour Office in Geneva after World War I implied the extension of trade union negotiations far beyond national frontiers. The activities of trade unions have shifted into various new directions, very different in centrally planned nations from nations with a market economy, whether pure or 'mixed'. The view expressed in the introduction, that trade union leaders and members might have to understand the economists' messages better than they have so far will now be elaborated.

The circumstances under which trade unions operate in developed and less-developed countries differ considerably, and the discussion will be subdivided accordingly. In developed countries, the main issues include the role played by trade unions in the process of inflation, and the consequences of their attempts to widen their field of activity. The chief thought behind traditional trade unionism is that income distribution in Capitalist and mixed societies is inequitable, and therefore wages must be raised. One message from economic science concerns the difference between the wage rate and the total wage bill of all workers, which is the product of wage rates and volume of employment. Excessive wage demands may endanger employment, especially in countries heavily dependent on foreign trade. The danger of pricing oneself out of the market is far from imaginary, a famous historical case being the diamond cutters in Amsterdam before World War I, who were strongly organized and successful in their wage rate demands, but with the result that diamond cutting moved to Antwerp in Belgium and Hanau in Germany.

In recent years Sweden priced itself out of the international market and the Netherlands were in a similar situation. In the period 1945–1960 Dutch trade unions agreed with economists that the employment component in the total wage bill is important and there was a remarkable acceptance of a cautious wage policy. This policy changed in the early 1960s and between 1963 and, say, 1973 wage rate demands far exceeded the increases in labour productivity. A similar attitude had for long been normal in other countries.

Nevertheless, it is a misunderstanding of some economists and employers' organizations that wage rates should never rise quicker than productivity. If wage rates rise *pari passu* only with productivity, the share of labour in national product would not change. But it can and must be changed if a more equitable income distribution is to be attained. There is, though, a limit to what is possible here, without running into the inflation spiral. Wage rates can rise more quickly than other incomes provided that the relative supply of manual workers diminishes in comparison to the supply of mental workers, by which are meant those with higher intellectual and leadership endowment. In all developed countries the supply of better educated labour has risen more quickly than that of less educated; indeed the supply of the former has risen more quickly than the demand for it. It is by these market changes, a less unequal income distribution becomes possible, step by step, without inflation.

In the last few years union leaders in several countries have shown understanding of this message from economic science. There is a willingness, especially in Germany and the Netherlands, to accept a period of moderation of wage demands, until a necessary minimum of profitability of production has been restored. For the *quid pro quo* for such a wage restraint, unions think of extensions of industrial democracy and profit-sharing. We may add another element, in line with a recent policy in the Netherlands, that consists of applying restraint to high-earning categories, such as salary earners and independent professions (physicians, lawyers, and so on) previously exempt from the collective agreements negotiated for workers in the narrower sense. Supply versus demand in these categories of manpower fully justifies a relative decline of their incomes. I shall return to this subject later, and touch also on the need for solidarity with the unemployed, which also justifies restraint in wage and salary demands. The solution would be simpler if a more active anti-recession policy were pursued.

For trade unions in the less-developed countries, as for transnational enterprises, it can be said that a better understanding of the economic priorities is needed, for arriving at a more rational policy. The really poor in the less-developed countries are many of the peasants and the unemployed, and in any case a far larger part of the population is rural. Those organized in unions are often a very small group of civil servants and highly skilled workers, belonging to the best-paid ten per cent of the labour force. Furthermore, in less-developed countries, the stock of capital goods and land is small in comparison with the number of potential workers. If we want to have employment for all, this can only be attained at very modest wages. These low wages are not some form of dumping, as the International Labour Organization formerly supposed, but simply reflect the state of underdevelopment.

From this diagnosis, two recommendations to international trade union movements follow, and I am happy to note that some understanding for these 'messages' is apparent. The highest priority for the less-developed countries is to create employment. Wage policy must be postponed until there is work for the unemployed. Once nearly full employment has been attained, usually at low wage rates, the time for wage claims will come. That is what happened in Japan, which forty years ago was an underdeveloped country, and is now going on in Hong Kong, where wages are rising. Japan is no longer a threat to Western wage levels and Hong Kong may reach that point in the foreseeable future. Meanwhile, the wish for protection 'against the low wages' of India or Indonesia is to the detriment of people who are much poorer than any unemployed person in the West.

The second priority is to organize the really poor. This means to organize peasants, and agrarian workers, rather than industrial workers. In Western terms it means creating rural co-operatives (c.f. Huizer, 1977). An interesting beginning has been made by the Indian Trade Union Congress, in co-operation with the International Federation of Free Trade Unions. This is a policy of real solidarity.

Governments of Developing Countries

With the ending of colonialism, the governments of the new nations are charged with the difficult task of raising the level of well-being of their populations. Too often, members of small élites in these countries have tended simply to take over the power and the privileges of the former colonial rulers, or to restore the feudal order that prevailed before, or under, colonial rule. Only for a few governments has the well-being of the population at large become the target of policies.

The priorities, as stated before, are a higher degree of self-sufficiency in food, the creation of employment, and industrialization. Generally the economies of less-developed countries are out of balance. In some of the most important ones, there is overpopulation in the sense that, with present technologies, not all of the population willing to work can be employed. This dis-equilibrium makes it impossible to leave the economy to free market forces. A relatively strict development policy is needed, which requires rigorous preparation, usually called a development plan. This plan must be based on a careful selection of the activities to be stimulated.

Planning for development was emphasized at an early stage by Raúl Prebisch, whose Economic Commission for Latin America undertook much research, in order to assist its Latin American member countries in their planning. An interesting report adopted by the 'Club de Dakar' will be very useful to African countries. The Economic and Social Committee for Asia and the Pacific has done similar work for its region. This region happens to have some of the largest developing countries of the non-Communist world (India, Indonesia, Bangladesh and Pakistan) and more initiatives have been taken by these large member countries on their own behalf. Development planning assistance is also given by the specialized agencies of the United Nations, among which the Food and Agriculture Organization and the United Nations Industrial Development Organization play a predominant role, alongside the World Bank Group and the International Monetary Fund, for financial and monetary assistance. In its Lima meeting of 1975, the United Nations Industrial Development Organization formulated the target for the year 2000, that the less-developed countries together should take care of one quarter of world manufacturing activity. Although attaining this target will require a massive effort, it is not impossible, as I have tried to show elsewhere (Tinbergen, 1978).

A number of the less-developed countries now have development plans, at least on paper. Whether these plans are mutually compatible is not yet clear, but the studies needed to find this out are rapidly multiplying. Their results will help national govern-ments to adjust their plans. In some cases it is doubtful whether the most appropriate sectors have been selected for early development, so as to pursue the most urgent targets—the priorities mentioned. In particular, inadequate emphasis may have been laid on the development of agriculture and labour-intensive, small-scale rural industries. A major obstacle to attaining the right emphasis is, however, the protective trade policies of the developed countries.

The New International Economic Order, as formulated by the UN, is the framework needed for international co-operation more equitable than the existing forms. This framework has been formulated so far in qualitative terms, and is in need of quantitative elaboration. One element of the research needed here is the study by Leontief *et al*. (1977). Important additional work is now done by the UN Secretariat's Department of International Economic and Social Affairs (A M Costa c.s).

Assuming that a country has an optimal development plan, one of the important uses to be made of such a plan is to negotiate with trans-national enterprises, willing to invest in the country concerned, in such a way that such investment fits the plan. Clearly the main responsibility here lies with the national government. In this process of negotiation the position of any government can be strengthened by joining a common market of several neighbouring countries. Unfortunately, in most cases we know of, the countries concerned have hardly been able to overcome their own nationalist obstacles better than Western countries (c.f. G Salgado's interesting survey, 1978).

Gradually it has become clear that a general, though negative, recommendation to the governments of less-developed countries is not to copy Western policies and institutions too readily, or the remnants of colonial periods. Different technologies may be needed, while education should be geared to local objectives of development and, among other things, should prepare for high-priority changes in ways of life—in food habits and health care, for instance. Of course, this does not imply that everything originating from the developed countries is wrong. What is required here is a critical choice between what serves and what does not serve the interests of the population at large.

Western Governments

Much of what was said at the outset was implicitly directed at what Western governments should try to understand and to do. Because of their potential in many fields of human activity, and their knowledge and experience, the responsibility of Western nations is high. A mistake made by a Western government is more serious than the same error committed by the government of a young nation. Or, in French: *noblesse oblige*.

The highest priority among the conceivable tasks of the developed countries as a group is to carry out the recommendations of the Brandt Report on North-South relations. The next priority, intimately connected with the first, is to overcome the recession. As I have said, it is intolerable that, in a world with so many poor, part of our production capacity is not used. So stimulating demand is a prime requirement, and this can best be done by instruments of public finance. There is one important condition, of course: costs should not rise and, for some time to come, this means that wages must remain constant so as to let profitability be restored up to a new level of equilibrium, sufficient to induce the investments needed to restore a rate of growth adapted to the new situation, as described earlier. The situation characterized by the 'new scarcities' requires what is nowadays called 'selective' growth, limited, as far as possible, to sectors neither using large quantities of scarce resources nor threatening the environment. Although this sounds attractive it is by no means sufficiently precise to define the path desired, in view of the enormous gaps in information which allow large differences of opinion to persist among experts. Measures to secure the co-operation of the trade unions, by regulation of high salaries and professional fees, have already been noted.

Another objective is to raise or maintain employment by stimulating promising activities. Elsewhere (J Tinbergen *et al.*, 1980), in co-operation with J M den Uyl, J P Pronk and W Kok, I have argued for doubling the volume of research activities by subventioning or paying directly for them. Other possibilities include the production of anti-pollution equipment, the extension of consultancy services (in management, technology, etc) and inter-industrial recycling. Such policies may be called positive restructuring, in contradistinction to protection, which is a form of inertia.

As a third urgent aim for Western policies, I see the revival of European integration. From about 1970 onwards European governments stopped carrying out the Rome Treaty of 1958. If we in Europe want to go on indulging in *Kleinstaaterei* we must be aware of the negative impact it will have on Europe's reputation, already fallen to a very low level. Moreover, the spending policy recommended as an early priority can only be thought of as a common policy, at least at the European, if not the 'trilateral' level (USA, Japan and Western Europe). It is hardly understandable for continental Europe why Britain, with its traditions of efficient world-wide diplomacy, wants to maintain an insular attitude. But in addition it should be understood that monetary integration as organized in the European Monetary System is insufficient as long as it is not combined with financial integration, and that means carrying out the 1970 Werner Report recommendations: that is to say (briefly) arriving, through annual negotiations, at an agreement on a few key figures of each member state's budget. The spending policy should be part and parcel of such an agreement, and this would ease almost every aspect of our present difficulties. A fourth objective is the admission to the Economic Community of countries applying for membership.

All of this would enormously strengthen Europe's position in the North-South dialogue, not shortsightedly but in the interest of medium-term and long-term well-being. To begin with some of the proposals of the less-developed countries on commodity agreements should be favourably considered, together with their reasonable desire to see import restrictions on industrial products reduced: this is not only reasonable, but in our own medium-term interest. The Commission for International Economic Co-operation deserves encouragement, because its two-level system of discussion is much more efficient than the procedures of many international gatherings, with about 150 participating nations.

Among the next few steps are the establishment of some badly needed supranational authorities, to deal, for instance, with the oceans, environmental affairs, energy, and food. Some of these authorities could be the existing inter-governmental institutions, given wider competence. For those nations that still hesitate to assign to such institutions part of their sovereignty there are stepwise reforms available, for instance obligatory mediation in the absence of consensus, and various systems of qualified-majority voting. The question will arise whether Communist-ruled countries are willing to join in the supranational arrangements. Clearly it would be a great advantage if they did but, if not, we can still establish some quasi-world-authorities in which South and West would co-operate.

Political Parties

The new economic policies will have to be carried out by some of the political parties. Our hope must be that their leadership will display enough imagination to give shape, in alternative ways, to the new society for which we are searching, and to carry their membership and the voters with them. Inventiveness is a prime requirement for defining the main features of the new order: inventiveness to translate the basic principles we are striving for, into feasible proposals.

The ways in which political parties operate and are organized, especially for handling international matters, are important matters for consideration. American political parties are baffling and unattractive for Europeans, and a fundamental change in the

American party system is something many Europeans hope for, leading perhaps to the birth of a conservative, a liberal and a radical party, adapted to the American scene.

On the other hand, European political parties are far from ideal. In many countries there are too many of them; the Dutch, for instance, only recently did away with the party against the French Revolution. In Western Europe a trend towards a more rational party structure is now furthered by the existence of a directly elected European Parliament. (It is up to our British friends, when it will become a representative parliament.) Parties in the member countries have organized themselves at a Western European level, with three main groups: 1) Liberals (in the European sense); 2) Social Democrats (socialists in the West-European sense) and 3) an unclear group often called Christian Democrats (in Germany, Austria, Belgium, the Netherlands, Italy) but called by others Conservatives (which in the countries just enumerated is a bad word, although in Germany and Italy they do behave as Conservatives). In the Low Countries it is the Liberals who are more typically conservative. Well, that is their problem; for outsiders the outcome of the ensuing internal debates is interesting, but not vital.

From a world point of view it is more interesting to wonder what the Socialist International will become, now that it has, at last, such active leaders as Kreisky and Palme. Up till now, it was a northwest European club, that failed to seize the considerable opportunities it had, ever since 1950, to become a world movement operating on behalf of the disadvantaged everywhere, without becoming an instrument of intolerant indoctrination. At the moment there is a chance that the Socialist International will unite democratic socialist movements—under various names—in all continents. They are, in the European area, the ones best able to understand a 'trade-unionist' attitude of the less-developed countries. They have the potentiality to push towards a more equitable new international order and to make use of all the new scientific knowledge accumulated since Karl Marx launched the idea of 'scientific socialism'. In the smaller advanced countries—Scandinavia, Canada, Australia, the Low Countries—the desire to show solidarity with the Third World is relatively strong. A strategic role is now taken by the German Social Democrats.

There remains a place for nationalist groups, although by definition it would be difficult for them to establish an International! They can help to maintain cultural diversity, but not, I hope, cultural immobility.

Citizens

Finally, we the citizens are supposed to control all of the institutions dealt with in the preceding sections, although of course we don't. The unit of human life, of thinking and doing, remains the individual. Some are better endowed than others with the ability to innovate; and some are better placed to help carry innovations through. In the end, all programmes, plans, and implementation of plans have to be carried out by citizens. Recent trends in policy recommendations for development rightly stress the role of self-reliance, in all its forms: self-reliant groups of nations, self-reliant nations, down to self-reliant individuals. Development policies should come from the 'grass roots', it is said.

We should not make this another vogue, however, because there are quite a few people who are happiest with a simple, mechanical routine, and there are people who want to be left alone. But it is true (c.f. Bowles and Gintis, 1977) that creativity is favoured neither in education nor on the labour market. A new equilibrium with more creativity is also called for by Macrae (1976). On the other hand the importance of creativity has its limits. When exclusively directed at personal development, without any relevance to the happiness of others, creativity is sterile, and too many who call themselves artists appeal for public support, simply to live a life of their liking. Many branches of art are at a low level of performance today and may later be compared with nineteenth-century architecture—nothing to stand beside Roman, Gothic, Renaissance or even modern architecture around the 1920s and 1930s.

Culture is also at an all-time low when it comes to the care for young, pre-kindergarten children. The relative weight given to the entertainment of considerable numbers of parents is out of balance with the needs of children, clearly identified by child psychologists. More examples could be given: presumably vogues in culture have always existed, but one wonders whether the increased intensity of communication has not amplified the vogues, and the swing from one vogue to the next, at a high price in human happiness. Rightly, therefore, a search for new life-styles is going on, which are meant also to adapt human behaviour to the new scarcities—energy and the clean environment being Western examples. A new life-style should also exhibit a higher degree of long-term thinking, and this implies the avoidance of over-consumption, of the kind which makes itself felt later in life, when the individual is confronted with the consequences of over-indulgence in alcohol or meat. Finally, although I should not give as much emphasis to international solidarity as Myrdal (1970), a bit more of it will be highly welcome.

These few remarks on aspects of welfare, not usually included in economics in the old sense, illustrate what I said at the outset: that economic science, like other sciences, has tried to meet with adjacent fields of study and broaden its traditional content. It still has some messages to all concerned about the present and future world. I hope the messages have been formulated sufficiently clearly; but they are those of one economist, not of all economists.

REFERENCES

I Adelman, *Redistribution Before Growth—A Strategy for Developing Countries*, Institute of Social Studies, 25th Anniversary Conference, The Hague, 1977; Thoughts on the Restructuring of North-South Interaction, Paper read at Bellagio, September 1979 (Conference Paper No. 2).

G Bombach, 'Neue Politische Okonomie', List Forum 9 (1977/8), p.65, p.132.

S Bowles, and H Gintis, *Schooling in Capitalist America*, New York, 1976.

W Brandt, *et al.*, *North-South: A Programme for Survival*, London, 1980.

P Buringh, H D J van Heemst and G J Staring, *Computations of the Absolute Maximum Food Production of the World*, Dept. of Tropical Soil Science, Agr. University, Wageningen, The Netherlands, 1975.

P Buringh, and H D J van Heemst, *An Estimation of World Food Production Based on Labour-Oriented Agriculture*, Centre for World Food Market Research, Wageningen, The Netherlands, 1977.

E Eppler, *Ende oder Wende, Von der Machbarkeit des Notwendigen*, Stuttgart/Berlin, 1975.

B Fritsch, 'Alternative Scenarios of Economic Growth and Energy Requirements —Some Economic and Political Considerations', in: G Bruckmann, ed., *Input-Output Approaches in Global Modeling*, Laxenburg, 1978.

J K Galbraith, *American Capitalism: The Concept of Countervailing Power*, Boston, 1952.

R Hueting, *New Scarcity and Economic Growth*, Amsterdam, 1980.

G Huizer, 'Willen de banken der rijken de "armsten der armen" werkelijk helpen?', Intern. Spectator XXXI (1977), p.757 (Dutch).

K Kahn, *et al.*, 'A Slightly Optimistic World Context for 1975–2000', Hudson Inst. –2146-P, Memo No. 8, November, 1974.

W Leontief, *et al.*, *The Future of the World Economy*, United Nations, New York, 1977.

N Macrea, 'The Management Revolution', The Economist, 25 December, 1976.

R S McNamara, *Honderd landen; twee miljard mensen*, Amsterdam, 1974 (translated from English).

E J Mishan, *Welfare Economics, An Assessment*, Amsterdam, 1969.

N Myers, *The Sinking Ark*, Oxford, New York, 1979.

G Myrdal, *The Challenge of World Poverty*, New York, 1970.

G Salgado Peñaherrera, 'Viable integration and the economic co-operation problems of the developing world', Journal of Development Planning, No. 13 (1978), pp.73–121, United Nations.

E F Schumacher, *Small is Beautiful*, London, 1973.

J Tinbergen, 'Les vingt-cinq pourcents pour le Tiers monde', J Fourastié 40 *Ans de Recherche*, Paris, 1978.

J Tinbergen, *et al. A New World Employment Plan*, The Hague, 1980.

J Van den Doel, *Konvergentie en evolutie*, Assen, 1971 (Dutch).

P Werner, *L'Europe monétaire reconsidérée*, Lausanne, 1977.

C L Wilson, project director, *Energy: Global Perspectives 1985–2000* (MIT), New York, 1977.

9

Growth and the Quality of Life

by Maurice F Strong

Our generation has crossed the threshold of a totally new era in human history. We have now assumed prime responsibility for our own evolution. It is an awesome responsibility thrust upon us by the power which science and technology have placed in our hands; not one to which we have consciously aspired. Nevertheless, we cannot escape it.

The evolution of our species to date has been a product of our interaction with the forces of nature. Our capacity to affect and control these forces has grown immensely, particularly since the Industrial Revolution. But until recently this capacity had its impact primarily at the local and regional levels. Today we have the capacity to affect decisively the basic parameters of the Earth's biosphere on which the survival and well-being of the whole human species depends.

This power is most dramatically manifest in the development of nuclear capability well beyond that which could destroy all human life. Less dramatic, yet perhaps even more difficult to accept, is that the same processes of production and consumption which have produced the wealth of our technological society are now triggering changes in the physical conditions which make it possible for our planet to sustain human life. These conditions are clearly rare, if not unique, in the universe. There is as yet no evidence that they exist in any other part of the universe now within the range of our perception and analysis.

These conditions have existed on Earth for only a relatively brief portion of its total history. The margins which determine the capacity of the Earth's biosphere to support human life are relatively narrow. For example, a two degree change in the average temperature of the Earth would have a devastating effect on its human population. We know that the vast increase in the amount of heat being generated by human activity and the consumption of fossil fuels could affect global climate. We also know that the mounting tide of chemicals we are pouring into the atmosphere, waters and the soil are affecting the chemical composition, not only of these media, but of the food chain and even of the human body itself. Scientists disagree on the precise nature and degree of the risks we face from these phenomena. But there is broad consensus that our activities can affect and are affecting the basic conditions on which the future evolution of our species depends.

We are thus faced with a new set of imperatives. If we now have the capacity to alter decisively the conditions on which the human future depends, it is clear that we must understand and bring under control those activities which will determine the shape of our future. Each human being must determine for himself the mix of ingredients which will provide him with the quality of life to which he aspires. Collectively, we must ensure that the physical conditions, on which the quality of life of the entire human species depends, are maintained.

The activities through which we impinge on the integrity of the Earth's biosphere arise from our individual and collective behaviour. Thus, if we are to secure the integrity of the biosphere there must be a revolution in human attitudes and behaviour as radical and dramatic as that which has occurred in our technological prowess. We require equally drastic changes in the processes and institutions through which we conduct our economic, social and political affairs.

This revolution in attitudes and behaviour must turn its principal focus onto our attitudes towards growth. For it is through the process of growth that the quality of life available to human society in the future will be determined. The main purpose of this essay is to make tne case that the quality of life of future generations of Earthlings depends on radical changes in our concept of growth and our commitment to growth.

It is through the growth process that we create the economic means to meet our social needs, that we affect the physical environment, that we use energy and natural resources, that we create employment and make leisure possible. The drive to growth is the principal determinant of our economic, social and political life. It shapes our educational system, our institutions, our personal life styles. The inflation, unemployment, environmental degradation, social conflicts and economic disparities which now bear in upon us with increasing intensity are not isolated phenomena. They are manifestations of fundamental deficiencies within the growth process which is central to our present economic, social and political systems. It is based on the premise that growth in the purely material sense, in the production and availability of material goods and services, will bring about a corresponding increase in human satisfaction and well-being. The concept of 'Gross National Product' was invented as a means of measuring growth and soon the level of 'Gross National Product' came to be equated with standard of living. The increase in 'Gross National Product' became the central objective of national governments. In practical terms, this has tended to be the case whatever the underlying political ideologies of the governments.

Of course, it has been true up to a point. The explosion of our capacity to produce a multitude of material goods and services which accompanied the Industrial Revolution has brought unprecedented benefits to the peoples of the industrialized world. It has also made it technically possible to improve radically the conditions of life available to the entire human population. Despite this, economic and political barriers continue to prevent the two-thirds of the world's people who live in the developing world from realizing these benefits. Today, the mass market in the industrialized world for whom the mass production was designed has been largely satisfied, if not over-saturated. Most of the unsatisfied needs in industrialized societies today are of a non-material nature which industry rarely searches out as they do not accord with its traditional industrial logic. The remaining large unsatisfied markets for material goods and services are principally in the Third World where people cannot afford them.

But the response of our industrial machine is to expand its markets by creating new wants and new appetites amongst the people who can afford them. We are thus caught in the paradox of having created an industrial system able to meet the basic needs of all the world's people but in fact using it largely to foster further growth in the demand by the wealthy minority for goods and services well beyond what we need or is good for us.

Perhaps worse, this forced new growth is increasingly illusory. Illusory because the industrial-economic system we have inherited aims at the largest possible production of the most simplified goods. Thus competition, which has been vaunted as the essential condition driving our systems to offer greater and greater choice in the market place, has gradually lost that function. In fact, it has been reversed.

The financial need for large production makes innovation into a dangerously expensive risk. To avoid that risk, competition increasingly pits almost identical products against each other in sectors where basic markets have already been established.

The principal differences within that competition are in present-ation and publicity. In other words, this forced growth is not real; it simply offers greater and greater quantities of increasingly similar products—which is to say, of fewer and fewer real products.

This system, like the bicycle, can only maintain its equilibrium when it is moving forward at a sufficient speed. Now that growth has slowed down in most industrial countries, we must deal with the basic weaknesses inherent in the system. One of the most important of these is the parallel increase in the amount of capital and decrease in the amount of labour required to achieve a given unit of production. This in turn means that a disproportionate share of the rewards, and perhaps more importantly, of the power, go to those who control the capital. At the same time there is a reduction in the amount of employment available for a given level of production. And, although those who are employed can be well paid, many of the jobs available to them provide limited opportunities for personal satisfaction. And, for those growing numbers who are not employed, opportunities are limited outside the mainstream of the industrial system either for maintaining their income or employing their time in a satisfying way.

The great backlog of unfulfilled basic needs in the industrialized countries together with the massive reconstruction required following the two world wars of this century gave our industrial system a dynamic momentum which has now receded. There is nothing in prospect that is likely to see this momentum renewed in the foreseeable future. We are now in a transitional period which is almost bound to be more turbulent and difficult than what we have experienced in the past several decades. The pressures on our present economic, social and political systems are bound to escalate. It could well be a period of degeneration for western industrial civilization. But it could also be a period of renewal.

Social degeneration has always been marked in history by overkill through concentration on quantity rather than quality. This was true in ancient Greece where concentration on quality was a sign of the civilization's innate rigor; its subsequent degeneration being marked by encrusting that quality with a plaster-like over-emphasis which eventually dragged the society down.

In seventeenth and eighteenth century France, the decline of the monarchy and its society was first marked by an apparent obsession with quality under Louis XIV. However, this was a false and superficial obsession which was merely the decoration or facade surrounding the court and everything it stood for. There was a very real decline in the actual quality of life during that period as exemplified by the disappearance of adequate sanitation and water supply systems, even in the palaces.

Interestingly enough, the decline of efficient sanitation and water systems has symbolized the decline of societies since before the Greeks. One of the effects of our society's concentration on production has been the abandonment of water systems in the Third World, the pollution of water systems in industrialized countries, the decline in the quality of water available for consumption, especially in urban areas, and a massive growth in the sale of bottled waters which bypass the system.

At the end of a long seige, Athens eventually fell to Sparta because of an epidemic caused by the polluted running water through the city. Medieval Europe's inability or unwillingness to deal with the waste produced by a growing urban population led to an increase in rats which carried the plague which in turn proved so destructive to that society. Degradation of water systems in China in several periods led to disastrous floods, rivers changing routes, agricultural disasters, followed by revolts and the collapse of the empire. Similar circumstances affected the histories of Rome and of Egypt.

The question is not whether pollution, especially water pollution, was caused or produced by degenerating societies. Pollution simply is and always has been one of the signs of societal decline. Following all of the historical precedents, our present pollution problems could point out the degenerative entities now operating in our societies.

We must face the fact that the long period of rapid growth experienced primarily in the industrialized world since the advent of the Industrial Revolution is both unprecedented in history and unsustainable.

Nor can the industrial system developed during this period be patched up to meet the needs for a secure and promising future. Fundamental changes are needed both in this system and in the growth process of which it is the engine. If this period of turbulence is to be one of renewal for our societies, this renewal must be based on a new conception of growth, new attitudes towards the purposes of growth, and a re-structuring of the system of incentives and penalties which motivate the growth process.

Let us examine briefly the consequences of continuing along the growth path followed by the industrialized countries since the Industrial Revolution. The first assumption we must make is that the developing countries will also choose to continue along a similar path. In order for all of the present population of the world to reach a standard of living equivalent to that of the United States in 1970, it would require extraction of some seventy-five times as much iron as is now extracted annually, 100 times as much copper, 200 times as much lead, 75 times as much zinc and 250 times as much tin, and increases of similar orders of magnitude in the production of many other basic resources.

As for energy, such a standard of living would require the equivalent of 7 times as much oil, 8 times as much gas and 9 times as much coal as is now produced annually. All of that at a time when, as an international report by the Workshop on Alternative Energy Strategies pointed out, just keeping up with the growing demands of the more developed world may bring us to a supply gap of 20 million barrels of oil a day equivalent of energy by 1990.

But long before we confront the absolute physical limits of the Earth's supplies of petroleum and other key non-renewable resources, our use of these resources will be limited—in some cases drastically—by the economic, environmental and social costs of extracting and processing them as well as problems of distribution.

While large supplies of some of these materials might theoretically be made available through extraction of the minute quantities which exist in much of the Earth's surface and the oceans, as well as a total commitment to recycling of metals, it is unlikely that the environmental impacts of such a vast increase in industrial activity could be kept within tolerable limits. And it is inconceivable that such levels of industrial activity could be achieved without a degree of political, economic and social mobilization and regimentation which would be incompatible with the maintenance of free societies and the rights of the individual.

And if the industrialized societies should attempt to continue on their present growth paths with little regard for the growth requirements of the developing countries, there is bound to be escalating conflict between the appetites of the rich and the needs of the poor. It is impossible to envisage a secure and prosperous world for either rich or poor under these circumstances. However, our pursuit of present growth patterns would, as I have said, be limited by organizational, institutional and social constraints long before it reached the limits of physical resources. The social costs and economic disparities which we now see as by-products of this kind of growth and the increasing alienation of large sections of the population of industrialized societies make a change in the system inevitable long before these theoretical physical limits have been reached.

In short, the present approach to growth is simply not viable. Basic changes are necessary. They are possible.

'No growth' does not commend itself to any national government today as a viable policy. But no growth will nevertheless be the probable outcome of the policies most governments continue to pursue. The conditioned response to the problems which the present slavish adherence to material growth has produced is to provide more of the same. This is understandable. The prime function of politicians is to manage the issues which are of most immediate importance to their constituents. And today, most political leaders are so overwhelmed by the number and complexity of issues confronting them that they are less and less able to deal with immediate problems effectively, let alone consider seriously the fundamental changes that are necessary to secure the future of their constituents. Industrial societies are on the verge of becoming virtually ungovernable under the present system.

And there is no new body of economic and political theory on which they can construct new political platforms. Both Marxist and Keynesian theories have now been shown to be largely obsolete and no new body of ideas has yet emerged. We desperately need such a new body of ideas—a new synthesis. And they must centre on the need for a new attitude towards growth.

First, we must be clear on the objective of growth. Surely this must be to make possible the greatest number of alternatives for individual choice and self-fulfilment which are compatible with the rights and well-being of society as a whole. This, of course, is easier to conceptualize than to measure. But the difficulties in measuring the non-quantitative elements of growth should not be a serious deterrent to adopting this objective.

We should also accept as the basic parameters for a 'new growth' approach the need:

1. To ensure that every person on the planet has access to the means of providing the basic needs required to ensure a life compatible with human dignity and well-being; and
2. To ensure that our collective activities do not transgress the 'outer limits' of the capacity of the biosphere to sustain human life at acceptable levels.

Within these two parameters, the growth process should be designed to facilitate equal opportunity for all people to pursue an infinite variety of interests, aspirations and life styles.

Conservation must become a key element in the new growth

system. Waste must be reduced to a minimum by redesigning industrial processes and careful planning of plant location to ensure that the residues of one process become the raw materials of another. Technologies for recycling and re-use of materials and abatement of pollution must be integrated into production systems and not merely added on to them. A prime measure of the health of the system will be the degree to which it incorporates effective measures for the preservation of the resource and environmental capital base on which continued development depends.

This is already a practical goal in many areas. For example, steel can be produced from steel scrap with a 75 per cent energy saving over production from iron ore. And aluminium produced from discarded cans conserves 95 per cent of the energy used to produce it from bauxite.

The logical way to measure progress is by the length of time the stock of processed materials is in active use; not by the speed of product turnover. Governments can encourage this in many ways. For example, by offering incentives for recycling facilities and removing or reducing depletion allowances for mining industries.

In many cases, new conservation oriented systems are on the verge of cost breakthroughs. They require major government support. A prime example is the solar industry. The land areas of the world receive some 690 Q (Q=a thousand million kilowatt hours of electric energy) of solar radiation per year after filtering by clouds. In comparison, the world energy production in 1970 was in the area of .24Q or 2,800 times less.

In the late 1970s, the US ERDA (Energy Research and Development Agency) estimated that they expected one kilowatt of photo-electric power at a sunny location to cost about $15,800. But, by 1986, they expect the cost to drop to $1400. At the same time, they expect the cost of electric power generated through nuclear fission to rise in real terms due to more sophisticated safety features and the rising cost of both uranium and waste disposal. By 1986, nuclear power could cost more than solar photo-electric power.

The new growth concept must be rooted in the need to create an effective and functioning world economic system which recognizes that the policies and actions of each nation affect and are affected by the whole system. The growing interdependence of nations requires an increasingly effective international system of institutions and measures for the effective management of the system. This should in no way preclude the development by each nation of the maximum degree of self-reliance. Indeed an interdependent world system is likely to function most effectively when its national components have a significant degree of self-reliance, particularly in their ability to meet the basic needs of their people. This kind of self-reliance should be encouraged and strengthened, with emphasis on the weakest members of the international community. But self-reliance is not autarchy and no nation, however self-reliant, will be able to ensure for its people the maximum security and well-being outside of the world system.

It is in the industrialized societies that the 'new growth' concept will require the most radical changes. It will require a major transition to a less physical kind of growth, relatively less demanding of energy and raw materials. It will be one which is based to an increasing degree on the satisfaction of people's intellectual, moral and spiritual needs and aspirations in such fields as culture, music, art, literature and other forms of individual self-development and fulfilment. These, after all, are the areas in which Man achieves his highest levels of growth in human terms.

At the same time, the industrialized countries must also be prepared to facilitate and support the establishment of most new industrial capacity, particularly that which is resource or labour intensive, in the less developed parts of the world. This, of course, must be done under conditions which enable developing countries to avoid many of the environmental and social costs we have paid for our industrial development.

Fortunately, a new approach to development based on a marriage of economics and ecology has begun to command increasing attention in the developing world. This 'ecodevelopment' is designed to ensure that the precious natural resources of soil, forests, water, plant and animal life in the developing world are exploited in ways which do not destroy the resource bases on which sustained development depends. It is based on making best use of their own skills and labour to produce maximum benefits for their people in harmony with their own culture and value systems. It requires that they have full access to the latest technologies and support for the development of their own scientific and technological capabilities so that technology will serve rather than determine their own growth patterns.

'New growth' will thus require new dimensions of co-operation between industrialized and developing nations. Interdependence, which is now a physical and environmental reality, must become a working reality in economic, social and political terms. There must be a revamping of the present international system of arrangements and institutions to enable them to better support and serve the interests and aspirations of the developing world. The healthy functioning of our interdependent technological society requires the full participation and active co-operation of the two-thirds of the people who live in the developing world and this dictates that we heed their demands for a more just and equitable share of the benefits which this technological civilization makes possible.

The transition to a new growth society has, perhaps, its best analogy in the human body. From the birth of a child to the time it achieves physical maturity, the principal emphasis is on physical growth. Indeed, healthy physical growth and continued physical health are essential pre-conditions to the growth of human personality in its social, cultural, intellectual, moral and spiritual dimensions. Yet growth in these non-physical aspects of human development has only nicely begun at the time that physical maturity is reached. Real growth is still to come. Our industrialized societies are very much like the physically mature human being. For us to continue to pursue purely physical kinds of growth would be as unhealthy and self-destructive to our societies as it would be for an adult person to indulge himself simply to add to his physical dimensions. And it would be just as wrong to say that societies must stop growing when they reach the stage of physical maturity as it would be to say that people stop growing when they stop growing physically.

The real growth of our societies in human terms can still be ahead of us. But it demands that we change our ways and adapt to a more mature kind of growth that is less physically oriented and less demanding of resources and the environment. On the other hand, developing countries are at a much earlier stage of growth in which they must continue to grow in physical terms if they are to meet the needs and aspirations of their people. But they too must emphasize the kinds of physical growth which are healthy and sustainable and provide expanding opportunities for self-expression and fulfilment in human terms for their people.

Technology can be an ally in reducing the physical content of growth. The most advanced technologies today, particularly in the fields of information processing and communication, are moving dramatically in the direction of less material and less energy intensiveness. For example, the same computer capacity which in the 1950's cost several hundred dollars and required a machine that would fill a moderate-sized room is now available for a few dollars on a hand calculator. Similarly, it is technologically feasible to reduce energy consumption by some 50 per cent without significantly impairing present standards of living. And technologies are available to make even further significant reduction in the energy requirements of many production processes. Thus technology can be enlisted to support the drive for achievement of the new growth society.

Similarly, I believe that the public policy levers, which governments can today deploy, are capable of altering the system of incentives and penalties to which our economic life responds. This would be aimed at making it profitable to carry out those activities which are environmentally sound and socially desirable and unprofitable to do those things which impair environmental quality, destroy resources and detract from social goals. We have clearly demonstrated this in fighting or preparing to fight wars. For it is not the operation of the free-market economy which produces the massive market for war materials. That market is created by governments through an act of public policy responding to the belief of their people that their security is at stake.

In fact, the arms industry is the industrial sector to have shown the greatest growth over the last years. In the arms industry, our physical growth oriented society has found its most dependable crutch.

In 1975, the world spent almost $300 billion a year on arms and the developing countries spent more on arms than on health and education together.

What is the meaning of this extraordinary growth in one sector while most others were stagnating or advancing with difficulty? Part of the explanation lies in the fulfilment of the real material needs in the more developed countries. The internal dynamics of the industrial system itself motivate it to create new 'needs'.

Gradually corporations have turned to one of the rare growth areas left. In other words, it is easier for an industry to grow by selling arms than by selling tractors. That growth is not hindered because both the need and the market are artificial. In fact, a warped form of competition is encouraged as nations build up their arsenals. It is a fertile growth market because there are no real limits to demand that is not limited by traditional market factors.

Today the threat to our security through the physical and social imbalances generated by present growth patterns is as great as the threat of nuclear warfare. Indeed, it is even more difficult to deal with because it seems less immediate and less traumatic. The threat of a nuclear war may be averted right up until the moment the button is pushed. But the threat of eco-disaster or economic and social collapse can only be averted by foreseeing it far in advance and acting to prevent it. By the time it is upon us it will be too late.

New growth does not mean a retreat to a more primitive or less desirable standard of life or to a static economy. Indeed, it should be seen as an advance towards a more qualitative, humanly satisfying lifestyle.

Far from being negative to the economy, a commitment to 'new growth' would unleash new and dynamic economic forces and stimulate creativity, innovation and economic activity across a broad front.

If governments can create markets for arms they can surely create markets for other things which society needs but cannot translate into economic demand through the operation of the free market alone.

Also, if expenditures on war materials, which are inherently wasteful whether they are used or not used, can be a major stimulus to the economy, surely expenditures on building better and more liveable cities, improved cultural, educational facilities, recreational areas and opportunities for meaningful leisure, can be just as stimulating to the economy while at the same time adding positively to the real capital stock of our societies.

It is clearly feasible to make the transition to the new growth society. But that does not mean it will be easy. For it requires basic changes in the attitudes, values and expectations of people—in effect a cultural revolution. Governmental action will not be possible unless it is undergirded by this cultural change. It must be a culture that places highest value on quality rather than quantity, on conservation rather than waste, on co-operation above competition. It requires that we learn to applaud and look up to those who adopt lifestyles that are modest in terms of the amount of space they monopolize or the amount of materials and energy they consume; that ostentatious, wasteful and indulgent living become socially reprehensible. The person who drives alone in the city in an over-sized automobile will be scorned, rather than envied. There must be an acute sensitivity to all activities which create risks of damage to our natural heritage or impair the quality of life for others. People of industrialized societies in particular must again nourish their communal values and downgrade their competitive drives.

The transition to the 'new growth' society implies some profound changes in our traditional notions of the distinctions between private and public rights and responsibilities. Here, we must re-think our conceptions of the public and private domains. In a technological society, private acts increasingly affect public interests, and actions taken in the public interest intrude on private interests and rights.

The conditions which determine the optimum balance between individual freedom and collective constraint will be complex and decision-making will not be easy. It will call for a vastly improved method of evaluating the interactions between private and public interests in particular situations, of presenting and disseminating information and of ensuring a maximum degree of citizen participation in decisions which affect them.

There is little evidence at present that we can realistically expect this kind of cultural transition to take place wilfully. The status quo continues to have a powerful grip even on those who concede that such a transition is necessary. We owe a great deal to those people in our societies who are already demonstrating that more qualitative, less materialistic lifestyles can be not only feasible but highly desirable and rewarding. But it is not easy to pursue such lifestyles today even for those who wish to do so. We should encourage and support more experimentation by people in new lifestyles, both within existing communities and by the creation of new communities. If more of the leaders of thought and opinion in our society could themselves adopt such lifestyles, it would have a powerful exemplary effect on the changes in our value system that are needed to make the new growth society possible.

Up to now the human species has changed its ways significantly only after having been chastised by bitter experience. Man's history has been based on repeated cycles of advance, tragedy inflicted by nature or by war, collapse and rebuilding, often for many centuries on a lower level than that which was destroyed.

A sobering thought for those of us in the industrialized world is that the rebuilding rarely takes place on the site of the destroyed societies. The centre and benefits of civilization rarely prosper a second time in the same place. Now that, for the first time in our history, we possess the means of total self-destruction, can we risk repeating these cycles? Even if we could, it is surely doubtful that the wholly unprecedented scale and nature of risks we now face would enable us to have another chance if we were to wait until eco-disaster or economic and social collapse is imminent.

Thus, our generation confronts the ultimate paradox. We have the power to shape our own future and to make possible a better life for the entire human population. But that same power threatens not only the survival of our species, but the survival of those very qualities which give human life its quality and purpose. The key to the future is our ability to control the growth process by which that future is determined. We must become masters of the growth process if we are not to become its victims. Our present growth patterns are debilitating and self-destructive, based as they are largely on greed and unrelenting competition. It is eating away at the body and soul of our society and will destroy its very fabric if we do not bring it under control. A new approach to growth is the only way to secure the more hopeful, promising future which science and technology now make possible. In the final analysis, it is the quality of growth that will determine the quality of life.

10

The Future of Religion

by Ninian Smart

The understanding of worldviews and their analysis is a vital part of thinking about the present and the future state of humankind. Consider how the formation of modern China was carried out under the guidance of a set of ideas, giving special shape to the new China: and consider too how the current change from revolutionary Maoism to a more technocratic ideology is beginning to affect events. Consider how the resurgence of traditional Islam in a form which among other things favours the cult of personality and thus the emergence of the Ayatollah Khomeini as charismatic arbiter of the various revolutions going on in Iran has altered our perspective of the Islamic world. Consider what further Islamic resurgence might portend, from Indonesia and the shores of Australia to the Atlantic rollers which whiten the coast of Western Africa. I said 'worldviews' above, as a more comprehensive term than either religion or ideology. The fact is that belief-systems have two main forms: the more traditional one, in which life on Earth is seen in the light of the Transcendent (God, heaven, nirvana); and the more secular one, in which history and society are interpreted according to primarily secular, non-transcendental principles. To the former category belong Christianity, Islam, Buddhism and other old faiths, though it should also be noted that the contemporary world has seen the emergence of many new religious movements from Synanon and the Unification Church to the ten thousand independent Churches of black Africa. To the second category belong the utilitarianism and social democracy of the West, the various Marxisms and such socialist alternatives as Baathism. Our main concern here is with trying to project the future of the transcendental or religious worldviews, but clearly it is necessary to see them in relation to their secular rivals and companions.

The importance of such an analysis is underlined by the fact that in recent times it has been a fashionable element in the thinking of many educated Westerners, often those wielding great influence and power, to dismiss religious forces as being unimportant and secondary because (in the view of such people) they are irrational. It is always a fallacy to move from normative to empirical judgments, and it is a weakness in the training of many political scientists and economists that they are led to neglect the strong existential power which religious ideas and practices often possess. Thus American policy both in Vietnam and Iran was tardy in coming to terms with the traditional forces which helped to determine the shape of events.

The fact that religions look to the Transcendent and often express themselves in mythic and symbolic terms does not mean that they cannot be subjected to rational analysis: indeed it is an important principle of rationality that one should recognize the power of non-rational powers in the formation of the world and try to understand them, just as in the non-mental world we analyse the non-rational forces of nature. The present state of religions in the world helps us to foresee directions in which they will evolve towards and beyond the year 2000.

As a springboard, then, for our leap into the future let us lay out some of the principal patterns of the early 1980s. Fortunately a certain clarity is beginning to emerge in the configurations of the planetary soul, out of the confusions and conflicts of a turbulent century. Modern conflicts and communications have created in effect a kind of global city, which can be divided very roughly, from the perspective of worldview analysis, into five blocs.

In one bloc is to be found those societies of the Western world which have a largely Christian background and which have become social democracies of one sort or another, from such pioneers as Sweden and New Zealand through the European Community countries to the United States of the New Deal and after. Such societies tend to practise a kind of utilitarian pluralism in which there is space for traditional religion, though Christianity varies in its intensity, from the largely secular society of the Swedes to the more overtly pious and religiously multitudinous United States. In such societies, which some have called post-Christian, but which are perhaps better called trans-Christian, in the sense that they include many Christian elements but also transcend or go beyond them, religion is increasingly considered a matter of private choice. That individualism is encouraged by consumerism, but also has its roots in the radical wing of the Reformation. For it was the Anabaptists and their radical successors (as opposed to the 'magisterial' and establishmentarian Lutherans and Calvinists) who established a clear division between Church and State and between public ideology and private faith. By extension their insistence on personal commitment paved the way for other non-conformist beliefs through to modern Humanism.

One side of Western society is the privatization of belief. By consequence, such societies are pluralistic, and in matters of religion increasingly so in the context of the new global city. Migrants bring other creeds into trans-Christian cultures: Muslims in Bradford and Dusseldorf, Hindus in San Francisco and Birmingham, Sikhs in Montreal and Smethwick, Greek Orthodox in Melbourne and Los Angeles. Moreover culture contact breeds transmissions, so that Wasps can and do follow Zen Buddhism, or Krishna, or Sufism, or Taoist meditation, and so on. Old creeds find a lodgement in new social and cultural settings. At the same time, Western societies are in differing measures secular in the sense that many citizens have a humanist kind of worldview, worked out either explicitly or more implicitly expressed in lack of concern with ideas and rituals directed towards the Transcendent. Thus the majority of people in such countries as Sweden, France, Australia and Britain are not attached to any religious group and do not, except rarely at official or socially significant occasions, participate in worship. Thus in the Western World one can speak of privatization, pluralism and increased secularism.

The second main bloc is the Marxist countries. They are more and more diverse in ideology, but they still retain a similar theory of how to run the State. This implies a fairly rigid establishmentarianism, only now the citizens are required to subscribe to scientific socialism as an ideology rather than a transcendental theology. But the effect is similar: preferment presupposes 'theological' orthodoxy, and alternative worldviews are as far as possible silenced. If a Marxist regime can get away with it, religion is suppressed (as also pluralistic humanism). Thus, religion is more or less fully repressed in Albania, and over a long period was under extreme pressure in China. On the other hand, for various reasons, religion continues to flourish in Poland and Romania, and has a fair degree of life under adversity in Russia and Soviet Central Asia. But Buddhism in particular has suffered greatly under the Marxisms, and institutional religion as it re-emerges from a period of repression may well turn out to be more 'privatized' in the future. But of that, more later. However, much will turn on the relations between the

Marxisms and the transcendental worldviews: this is already apparent in Poland and Central Asia.

The third main bloc within the global city, undergoing fervent change in the early 1980s, is the Islamic arc from Indonesia to Nigeria—virtually unbroken save for the Republic of India, which itself has a substantial Muslim population. Islam has the problem of how to come to terms with the new economic and social forces uncoiled by the world economy and by the crucial role of oil. For Islam cannot easily be privatized (though this, to some extent, is what happens among Muslim migrants in predominantly trans-Christian societies). Its teachings incorporate more than what might be counted as the spiritual: they embrace a detailed system (or set of systems) of law, and this in turn shows that Islam in principle aims at theocracy. On the other hand, both socialism and a kind of liberal modernism have adherents in the Muslim world: socialism as a method of re-ordering society over against the colonialist and capitalist West, the chief region from which the humiliation of the Muslim world emanated in the nineteenth and twentieth centuries: liberal modernism as a way of digesting some of the positive social and scientific values opened up by Western culture. But there is a strong theocratic backlash: in Iran through the Ayatollah, in Pakistan with a new Islamic constitution, in Libya with a new Islamic communitarianism, and so on. How far will such a quest for a theocratic golden age go?

The fourth bloc, more loosely arranged, consists of those old Asian cultures which have not been swamped by the Marxisms—in India, South-East Asia, Taiwan, Korea, Japan. Such societies are much influenced by Buddhism, which entered into the fabric of Hindu society in India, and elsewhere proved more dominant, shaping much of the cultural heritage of such diverse nations as Sri Lanka, Thailand, Burma, Korea and Japan. These old Asian countries are pluralist in ethos, because of the underlying toleration and syncretism of their religious heritage. But also this pluralism has a rather different atmosphere from that of the modern West. The Asian faiths are more ceremonious, contemplative, psychological and magical. Buddhism did not so much directly challenge the religions of the cultures which it permeated, rather it absorbed elements of and helped to modify such traditions as Taoism, Confucianism and Japanese Shinto. It so happens that in varying ways the old Asian traditions have involved themselves in a new interplay with the West, and as we shall see this is one of the most

significant items for the future of religion, so far as it can be
foreseen.

Apart from the blocs we have sketched, there remains a whole
mosaic of smaller cultures, mainly in the world of the South: the
varying and multitudinous ethnic groups of sub-Saharan Africa; the
differing cultures of the clouds of Pacific islands including Papua-
New Guinea and the non-Islamic areas of Indonesia; the varied
cultures of Latin America, now overlaid considerably by Hispanic
values; the smaller groups of the North, such as the Eskimos, other
North American Indians and various Siberian peoples. Such
smaller scale societies of both North and South are largely
Christian, though some retain indigenous 'pagan' beliefs. Most of
these societies are in search of an identity in the face of the strains
which widen the fissures between the traditional past and the
rapidly evolving part-Westernized future. Often new religious
movements, of which there are more than ten thousand in Black
Africa alone, are bridges across these fissures. Sometimes more
traditional Christianity serves; sometimes socialist and Marxist
ideals have a place in these strains and changes.

Of these five blocs, two tend to be more sharply in contradiction
with the rest than are the other three. Islam when taken seriously
rejects much of the West, because of the shape of Islamic law. This
is, at various points, in conflict with the egalitarianism, individualism and political arrangements typical of the West, and where
Islamic nationalism reacts strongly against Western influence the
tension between the two systems is very evident. Equally however,
Islam is in contradiction with atheistic Marxism, and since Marxism
tends to be theocratic in the sense alluded to above, the clash
between the two systems is severe. But it should be noted that Islam
also contradicts both Buddhism and Hinduism, which have typically
suffered at the hands of Islamic power—for they are religions
conceived by Muslims as idolatrous and so rightly to be fought
against. Thus tensions between the religions remain severe in the
Indian subcontinent and in Thailand.

Likewise established Marxisms are, generally speaking, hostile to
both Western democratic values and to traditional religions, and
the Asian religions particularly have, as we have seen, been
especially strongly controlled and attacked.

On the other hand, some countries of the South have found
Marxism attractive, mainly as a means of asserting national identity
against capitalist colonialism. Marxism supplies a theory and
practice of resistance to the North, and at the same time offers a

method of stabilizing power once independence is achieved. But partly because of previous economic ties, the way in which Christianity has permeated the smaller cultures, and because of the attractions of Western-style economic development, much of the South remains closely related to the Western bloc, and, in some regions, increasingly to the old Asian bloc.

It should also be mentioned that it is typical of religious and cultural relationships that new religious movements tend to rise up along the interface between two cultures—for instance across what may be called the White Frontier which runs, so to speak, invisibly between chiefly Western values and influences on the one hand, and the various cultures, which willy-nilly have faced the impact of the West, on the other. But similarly we can see a kind of frontier between East and West, and between elements within the West (scientific humanism, for instance, draws on values from secular society and traditional religion). Across these frontiers also new religious movements spring up. Thus in many parts of the West new Western forms of Buddhism are taking root; new evangelical movements try to deal with the problems of science and faith; new psychologically oriented cults try to use religious ritual in the service of spiritual and psychological rehabilitation; and various new gurus and leaders offer inspiration in the reconstruction of life in community. Thus it is not the case that as religions and cultures meet they simply merge into one another: greater contact does not imply greater unity. For though mergers may in part take place these are new variants on the merging traditions and may be rejected by more conservative adherents of those traditions. So we are seeing in the contemporary world a proliferation of new religious movements, especially along the various frontiers where the older cultures meet and where new forms of social and economic organization impinge upon the old values.

In brief, we may see the world as divided roughly into five religious and ideological blocs. The changes brought about by modern political and economic developments mean too that there is a host of new forms of religion. It is perhaps convenient to stay with our five-bloc analysis and to consider what the future holds in store in each of them: we may then see what it all will amount to globally.

First, the West: here official Christianity, represented by a number of the main denominations, is likely to go much further by the year 2000 in two processes evident today, namely liberalism and ecumenism. By liberalism I mean that the values of a secular society, itself partly produced by the Christian heritage, will have become more deeply embedded in Christian experience and structures. Thus the equality of women will have been thoroughly recognized in most denominations, and Christian social teachings about the family will approximate to humanist ones. On the other hand, such mainstream Christianity in the West will have recovered some of its classical interest in spirituality. The reason is this: that Western culture's utilitarianism and hopeful pursuit of the greatest happiness of the greatest number will have demonstrated a certain hollowness in mundane notions of happiness. This may be much more evident in a society which has created even more leisure and also persistent areas of unemployment. For the Protestant work ethic will lose much of its apparent relevance, and we will be entering on a new and more dramatically critical phase of examining the ingredients of ultimate happiness. Part of that questioning occurred in a confused way in the late sixties. Thus part of the attraction and significance of religion will be found in the contemplative and visionary side. Thus one would expect mainstream Christianity to undergo a much more thorough inversion towards the inner life and the year 2000 may see a whole new dimension of monastic and community life.

This 'retreat into the wilderness' might be seen as part of a transcendental critique of the fruits of utilitarian society. It will be part of what may be described as an increase in the psychologization of Western and indeed much of world religion. For it will be reinforced by the fact that a new general worldview will have evolved which may be described as *romantic monism*.

The weakness of traditional Western rationalism and scientific humanism has been on the whole a restrictive view of human experience, with a tendency to neglect the open and adventurous character of science itself. It has tended to forget that 'there are more things in heaven and earth than were e'er dreamt of in thy philosophy'. But the drive, nevertheless, of modern thought and scientific thinking is towards a certain monism: the dualism of Descartes is undermined, and the thought of a transcendental layer of reality over and above the material world tends to play rather little part in influential thinking about the nature of the world. What emerges and will be more apparent in the future is a new openness to the complexity of the world and a less Procrustean attitude to experience. Religious experience itself will be seen as one of the facets of life to be blended with all the other relevant avenues of access to the world around us. With an increase in awareness of the unitary character of the planet, and the interconnections of living forms, a more favourable view of the visionary side of human existence will contribute to a monism which can have a spiritual dimension. This in turn will mean that religion will be perceived, even more than it is now, as a mode of experiencing reality rather than as a means of access to a separate divine realm.

A more liberal and psychological kind of religion may have, as I have indicated, a prophetic side, in the sense that religious experience itself may serve as a vantage point from which to criticize the shallower side of consumerism.

At the same time ecumenism will have gone far, in that the Christian denominations by 2000 will have effectively become a single federated movement. But the main issue will be how the relationship between Protestantism and the Papacy will be worked out. But characteristically there will have continued a reaction against both liberalism and ecumenism. Thus a continuing important ingredient in Western Christianity will be conservative evangelical faith.

Here it is worth seeing what difference the electronic revolution will make to religion in advanced Western countries. In the early 1980's the present state of television favours a certain rather simple form of preaching, mainly based on straight interpretations of the Bible, and aimed at the viewer sitting, passively, in her or his own home. With two-way communication a greater sense of participation will become possible, and so the possibility of an 'electronic community' will be opened up. This will be of special appeal to those who are less well integrated into actual communities or workplaces around them—the aged, the lonely, the infirm, the unemployed—and this insecure clientele may be increasingly drawn to a warm authoritarian literalistic credo, of which Biblical fundamentalism is the strongest candidate. Thus Western Christianity may bifurcate much more radically into a romantic monist type on the one hand, and an evangelical type on the other hand.

Such religious conservatism will be reinforced over the next thirty years, one suspects, because of continued and more intense social changes. These produce insecurity. Conservative Christianity provides a sense of community, a sense of certainty, and a moral stance that secretly inflates the standing of those who adopt it. Similar motives will be important for the sects: sectarian religion is itself a way of staying in the world, whilst withdrawing from its more menacing and 'sinful' aspects. (One might see a backlash developing within Catholicism, which therefore would be driven in differing directions—towards ecumenism and its own version of romantic monism on the one hand, and towards an authoritarian and more severe style on the other.)

Conservative religion will be an important pressure towards the erosion of the distinction between Church and State which is such a notable feature of American democracy, and which operates less clearly in practice in other Western democracies. This would be a more powerful trend, perhaps exhibited in a religious kind of Macarthyism, if the crumbling structures of Marxism lead to an aggressive spasm out of the USSR. Collective insecurity, issuing in patriotic fervour, often presents an opportunity for a certain type of religious revival.

But Christian ecumenism also spans the divide between North and South. An increasingly vital role in Christian politics will be played by the Churches of Black Africa, and elsewhere in the Southern world. But here, though theology is likely to be more conservative (romantic monism being less congenial in cultures which have less experience of liberal structures of thinking and social relations), the continuance and intensification of economic and social stress will give the Churches a stronger role in reform and social action. Already the signs of this are evident in parts of Latin America. But we shall return to this theme later, in our observation of the new religious movements and their future in the South.

If we turn to the Marxisms, we can see a certain tiredness growing in the ideology, which is relevant to the future of religion. Three factors will increasingly spur the revival of traditional religion, but in a new key, in the Marxist world. One factor is nationalism. Where ethnic identity is partly defined in religious terms, national resentments within the structures of the Marxist regimes will be a stimulus to religious fervour. Thus, Tibet, which has seen a great influx of Han Chinese, is ripe for the next wave of religiosity, over the next twenty or thirty years. The structures of Tibetan Buddhism have been inexorably altered, away from the old feudal arrangements, but the religion will have considerable resurgence in a more privatized and modernized form. Again, Central Asia has an expanding Islamic population, and the turbulences at present apparent in neighbouring areas are a reminder that Islam may itself become a vital rallying point for the Central Asian nationalisms of the Uzbeks, Tadjiks and others. A second reason to expect a revival of religion in the Marxist countries arises from a simple fact: Marxism finds it difficult to create a sense of coping with the existential crises and deeper feelings of people, in the face of death, for instance. This is a problem also for some, though not all, varieties of humanism. Thus one may expect a genuine revival of older forms of religion, especially Christianity and Buddhism, in the Marxist countries. But such religions may well approximate to the romantic monism that I described earlier, for Marxism has been

successful on the whole in imposing a sense of a scientific outlook on
its populations. Thus pre-scientific forms of religion may be used,
but reinterpreted against a background penetrated by materialist
philosophy. Successful also, in a more relaxed atmosphere, will be
the evangelical and other less ecumenical forms of religion, since
rapid urbanization and other changes produce similar insecurities
(hence the relative success of Baptists in missionizing within the
Soviet Union).

A third pointer to the future in the Marxisms is the need in such
societies for some adaptation to the style of the more advanced
technocratic societies, which are run on more open and pluralistic
principles. It may thus be possible for religious groups to re-emerge
in this more open environment. They may, in fact, not be
unwelcome to the regimes, provided that they accept the general
framework of scientific socialism. This probably is easiest in Asia
for Buddhism, because of its inherent isomorphism with modern
cosmology and physics. On the other hand, it is hard to see a role
even in a more relaxed China of the future for the old hierarchic
style of Confucianism. But Neo-Confucian philosophy and Taoist
philosophy may have an appeal to a more educated stratum of the
new society, while the cult of ancestors will be revived in various
forms and contexts as Chinese family solidarity reasserts itself over
the next decades. Thus in the years after 2000 I would foresee a
China which looks much like a revived and modernized imperial
Dynasty.

As Japan becomes more and more concerned with the supplies of
raw materials and energy it will necessarily have to adopt a more
internationalist stance. In regard to this the intellectual and
religious resources of its Buddhist past may prove significant. As
indicated, Buddhism has a harmony with science which gives it a
very modern area, and may be a philosophy which helps to solve the
problems of the emotional split between the past and the evolving
industrial and urban present. One of the most important questions
will be the relationship between Buddhism and Western civilization. Here the *romantic monism* of the new Christianity of the
future will prove itself more easily compatible with the mystical
basis of Buddhist spirituality: for Buddhism too exhibits a kind of
visionary monism, in which the world is seen not merely through the
lens of the scientific intellect but also through the eye of immediate
and fresh experience, made possible by special training techniques.
Thus one may envisage the emergence of a new 'Pacific mind' in
which Western and Eastern themes are woven together, as both
Japan and America (especially California) come to a more mature

appraisal of how the deep resources of tradition can be blended together and put in the service of a new and creative syncretic culture stretching across the Pacific ocean.

Moving round the Asian bloc, to Korea and the Chinese diaspora countries which were all deeply affected in the past by Confucianism and Buddhism, one might expect to see some degree of convergence with the developments in mainland China—perhaps a revival among the educated of Neo-Confucian philosophy, an increased interest in a kind of personal Buddhism, all within the framework of a scientific and technocratic outlook. This may be especially evident in Korea. However it may be noted that for various rather complex reasons Christianity, especially evangelical Christianity, is quite strong in this whole area. Some of the factors leading to the more conservative reaction within the West are operative here also. Thus one can see this cultural area as being fertile ground in the future for evangelical and sectarian religions based wholly or partly on Christianity of a Biblical kind.

South-East Asia represents a different scene. Here mostly Theravada Buddhism in Thailand and Burma provides a counterpoint to the Marxism of Vietnam and its dependent neighbours. Here the future is less easy to diagnose. On the whole the new agricultural revolution will probably mean that Buddhism can avoid the violent uprisings which have decimated neighbouring Buddhist cultures. However it is notable that none of the Theravadin countries have yet made a strong leap towards industrialization and the new entrepreneurial prosperity characterizing the Eastern countries of the Chinese periphery. But there are aspects of South Asian religion, in predominantly Hindu India and Buddhist Sri Lanka, which hold out some significant promise for the future, beyond 2000.

I referred earlier to a new kind of religious 'romantic monism' in the West. There are elements in Eastern culture which favour a new scientifically oriented religious outlook which may be very important for the transition of India into the new industrial revolution. Up to now Hindu ideology has concentrated mainly on undergirding Indian nationalism by a doctrine of all-embracing, pluralist, tolerant religiousness—as evidenced in writings such as those of Swami Vivekananda at the turn of the last century and of Radhakrishnan in the early mid-century (he later became President of India). But in some ways the older religiousness is fading among the newly educated classes of scientifically trained people. Thus the doctrines of karma and rebirth have less hold upon this (for the future) crucial class. Yet, on the other hand, both Hinduism and

Buddhism in differing ways stress the importance of knowledge, and are religions which favour intellectualism. It is not at all surprising that there are large numbers of mathematicians and theoretical physicists produced in the sub-continent, many of them at the present time seduced ambitiously to California and other technologically advanced regions of the Western world. Already there are signs of a new kind of synthesis between traditional religion and modern science. In India it will be less concerned with traditional beliefs such as karma, and more related to a new interpretation of the cosmos and of life. Older ideas of withdrawal from the world will be taken up among the educated as a way of planning one's later years. Hindu traditional spirituality is very well adapted to living in the professional world. I foresee a new more 'rational' modern Hinduism especially attractive to the growing upper crust of technologically and intellectually expert professionals.

But the greatest issue as far as religion in India goes has to do with caste and untouchability. Pressures of population will continue substantially to nullify the effects of greater agricultural and other production. But the great changes in communication will help to generate greater expectations among the poorest classes, and that includes a great proportion of untouchables (Harijans). Already restlessness among them is taking the form of a rejection of traditional Hindu conceptions. It is true that caste loyalties are in some measure reinforced by urbanization and city poverty, because caste provides a framework of mutual help vital for survival. And it is unlikely that so pervasive a social arrangement will disappear rapidly, if at all. Still, one can predict a violent questioning of this aspect of the Hindu way of life. But it would be characteristic of India if this took the form, not so much of a secular questioning, important as Marxist movements are in different areas of the sub-Continent such as Bengal and Kerala, but rather the growth of a new kind of socially oriented sectarian Hinduism. To some extent this is observable outside India where caste has broken down somewhat, as among Indians living in Fiji.

Thus one can see in India the growth of a new monistically-oriented educated class, gaining importance because India is well placed to break through into the new electronic age; and at the same time the evolution of more evangelical forms of Hinduism combining piety with pressures for social reform. However, it is also worth noting that a very large minority within the Republic of India is Muslim: India is one of the major Islamic countries, after Indonesia. The developments I have sketched within the Hindu framework over the next twenty or thirty years will not necessarily be conducive to toleration. Indeed the movements from within the poorer strata are likely to provoke more severe competition between Hindus and Muslims. Thus the sub-Continent as a whole is liable to severe and bloody turbulence during the next three decades. The Islamic backlash will be violent. For one thing Pakistan has to stress Islam as its cement, and the present implementation of an Islamic constitution is but an initial move towards a more militant Pakistan. There, nationalism is inevitably identified with religion. Pakistan has no other theoretical basis. Moreover it is a sort of federation of ethnic groups, liable to fly apart without a strong centre. A military centre is not enough, though it is a logical initial solution to the problem. An ideological centre is needed. (These centres combine interestingly in the symbolism of the 'Islamic bomb' allegedly being hatched within Pakistan.) Thus severe communal viciousness within the Republic of India may well spark Pakistan into action. Such communalism may also give Pakistan and Bangladesh a degree of likemindedness after the bitterness of the past.

In brief one can foresee the Indian sub-Continent as being a major tinderbox of violence in the coming decades. The older pacifist values of Gandhi will have disappeared virtually without trace in this more militant phase of history. There may be the horrors of 1947–8 repeated fifty years later.

Already we have begun to tread upon the territory of the great Islamic bloc which runs in that amazing arc from the eastern wing of Indonesia right across to West Africa. Let us consider what amounts to the main problem for Islam in the evolving global culture in modern times.

Because Islam is, in principle, theocratic and embodies a whole law or *sharia*, and because there are limitations on the reinterpretation of the law since it flows ultimately from the inerrant words of the Koran, it has a strongly cohesive character. But the question of adaptation to new forms of society necessary to and consequent upon modernization then becomes an urgent and difficult one. We have seen some forms of this adaptation. But what of the future? Islam will foreseeably experience a greater polarization than other religions, and one can see the strengthening of forms of conservative Islam, and also of secularization. The two forms of conservative Islam are likely to be, what may be called, militant traditionalism and evangelical Islam. Militant traditionalism has arrived in Iran, though it may be that Iran in fact will end up with a more moderate kind of Islamic socialism (socialism being significant not so much because of the need to reorganize society, but because it is a mechanism of keeping out foreign influence). But one can foresee the growth in the next decades of a conservative reaction against reform and socialist regimes. Thus Syria and Iraq are especially prone to right-wing Islamic revolution. Moreover, the uneasy symbiosis practised by the oil-rich states to the south between a rather formalistic adherence to Islamic principles (as interpreted by the Wahhabis in Saudi Arabia) and the exploitation of Western technocracy is unstable. A more fervent Islamic backlash against Western influence is predictable, especially as the oil states tend to import poor workers from Islamic states to service their economic miracle. These are ripe for a mixture of piety and resentment. So it is unlikely that the oil states will escape a new kind of Islamic militancy.

This may in fact be reinforced by the phenomenon which I have dubbed evangelical Islam. The division between public law (often semi-Westernized) and private religion and family life which characterizes reform Islam, as seen in countries such as Egypt, is conducive to piety encouraged by brotherhoods and societies. Islam would breed such a 'moral majority' within the ambience of insecurity, already produced by rapid social change and the contiguity of foreign values.

At the opposite extreme are forms of worldly secularism and ideological secularism. Thus, a Westernized middle-class may substantially turn its back on Islam much as many educated Westerners have turned their back on and are hostile to older Christian values. Sometimes this turning away has been more ideological, as with Turkey after Kemal Ataturk, and among the Baathists, but it is doubtful whether worldly secularism has an easy place in the Islamic future. The difficulty lies in the fact that the changes which will occur in the Islamic belt in the next three decades—which may, at least in the Middle East and Africa, entail greater prosperity and industrialization—will provide the milieu among the poorer classes for increased conservativism in religion; a more evangelical atmosphere. But a 'worldly liberalism' among the bureaucratic and technocratic classes would scarcely live easily with this, and might increase social tensions. This is specially so because cosmopolitanism brings home foreign influence; and national sentiment and feelings of inferiority towards the more dynamic non-Islamic civilization of the West will stimulate Islamic reaction against such influence. So a polarization within Islamic societies is likely. Nor can Islam easily provide the framework of that 'romantic monism' which unites religion and science, and provides a new kind of spiritual humanism.

But one element within Islam, namely the Sufi orders, does have potential in this direction and might provide a synthesis which might, to some degree, soften the polarities. For Sufism with its outer conformity and inward freedom suggests ways of viewing the world in harmony with the scientific outlook. It has some affinities with contemplative Hinduism and Christian mysticism, even Buddhism. It has a more tolerant outlook. So one may see in the future a real revival of this meditative and more spiritual kind of Islam. By a paradox, the most intensely pious and religious of movements may prove the one which finds it easiest to adapt to the new global situation.

Thus I foresee a period of polarization and tension within Islam, one that may play a role in actual warfare in the Indian sub-Continent; and one that will probably herald a long period of rather more rigidly Islamic governments in a number of countries. The internal tensions may well lead to a new Islamic revolutionary chaos in the oil states.

And what of Israel? The question poses a problem of course about the future of the Middle East. But it also poses a question about the future role and structure of Judaism. Judaism has, mainly as a result of the tragic events in Europe before and during World War II, ceased to have the same place in European culture and life that it once had. The centre of gravity in Judaism has shifted to the United States. There it has had a wonderful cultural flowering. But it is coming to the end of an era. Secularized Jews, traditional and reform Jews alike, have been preoccupied with Israel in the decades since the War. Israel became the icon of Jewish identity and the fulfilment of many religious hopes. But partial peace in the Middle East, worries about the religious significance of an increasingly secular State that sometimes in its policies fails to embody the ideals which were invested in it, and the passage of time, have led to a realization that the main future of Judaism is largely independent of events in Israel. Israel itself has ironically ceased to be a truly Jewish State because, inevitably, it has absorbed the pluralistic character of Western social democracy. If it is Jewish it is so in an ethnic sense (that is, the ruling group is). Moreover the future of Israel has to be founded on a pluralistic acceptance of differing Islamic and Arab values in its midst, or in contiguity with it. Though, of course, always invested with great emotion by the Jewish world population, Israel, because of its situation, will cease to be a strongly determining factor in the evolution of the Jewish religion itself.

Judaism is a religion of practice: without it the religion inevitably begins to blend with Unitarianism and liberal Protestantism. Reform Judaism has played a noble role in American society, but can it of itself have such a vigorous future? It belongs to a more classically rational age. Already signs of a more romantic Judaism, more in line with the 'romantic monism' I have outlined, can be seen; a new version of older Kabbalistic and Hassidic or mystical forms of Judaism is emerging. It will, I think, have a stronger future beyond Reform Judaism, and will serve as a possible ideology for scientifically educated Jews: Einstein had something of this spirit. At the same time such 'romantic monism' is adapted to a revival of Jewish practice, for it can give a new meaning to older rites. At the same time Orthodoxy and Conservative Judaism are likely to maintain vigour, since Judaism poses to Jews a strong question of identity. But clearly many more Jews are likely to merge into the wider world of secular liberalism, so that the religion will go into the future with a continual process of winnowing. But its role will remain essentially as a light to the Gentiles, meaning in particular the Western world; in short Judaism will be increasingly identified with Western-style pluralism.

If we now turn to the South, what here can be predicted? An important question relates to secular ideologies. So though Marxism may be crumbling somewhat in the North, it will still continue to have an analytic and emotional appeal in the South. On the other hand, Western pluralism, at least as institutionalized in democratic forms, has less appeal in situations of ethnic tension and amid the problems of ethnic identity. Out of the mosaic of new religious movements in Black Africa one can foresee emerging the drive towards a more universal black messianism which can overcome some of the traditional divisions while giving Blacks a greater sense of dignity and effectiveness in confrontation with the still powerful and intellectually fertile White culture with which they inevitably will be in increased contact. Thus, one might foresee a continued development of mainstream ecumenical Christianity, more friendly to Northern values, and a harsher and more vibrant Black Christianity which has a new kind of theology and succeeds in expressing a sense of the numinous Power which vibrates through so much of traditional African religions. All this may be reinforced by the fact that in the next two or three decades the gap between North and South in terms of prosperity and technical sophistication may widen. Also, Islam may continue to increase its appeal in sub-Saharan Africa, despite older tensions with the Arab world over slavery.

Latin America represents a different scene, partly because prevalent Catholicism may encourage a greater turn towards Marxism, as in parts of Europe. Religiously, this may help to reinforce forms of revolutionary and liberation Christianity, since the Church is one of the few major forces capable of allying itself meaningfully with the poor. The opening up of Brazil and other rich regions may help to fuel new evangelical forms of Christianity, both among the Indian populations and among other sections of the urban and rural poor. Latin America will be fertile ground for a new wave of Messianic movements.

In Oceania and among the smaller ethnic groups of the Pacific various factors will moderate reactions to social change and so prevent too violent changes in religion. But it can be foreseen that the indigenization of Christianity will proceed much further, as smaller ethnic groups reach back towards their pre-Christian identity.

One may also, however, perceive in the South as elsewhere a growing cosmopolitanism. Thus old Asian religions, notably Buddhism, which have never hitherto spread far beyond the Equator, will have greater opportunities of establishing themselves on a modest basis in the world of the South.

But the forces for assimilation towards a very powerful global Northern culture will remain strong. If, especially in the Pacific region, a new pluralism and a syncretistic romantic monism become part of the fabric of advanced industrial culture, then this vibrant material and spiritual culture will have a strong magnetism for those who are moving towards assimilation and turning their backs upon the older indigenous patterns. In some measure Hawaii may be a harbinger of the future—essentially American but incorporating old Asian and Polynesian motifs.

Let us then try to sketch in the scene that might greet us religiously in the first decade or so of the 2000s, assuming that a global war has not obliterated a large part of the Northern hemisphere. First, in the trans-Christian world of the technologically advanced and plural West, many liberal folk may be reaching towards a romantic monism—a spiritual outlook which plays down the transcendent and mythic elements of religion, but stresses the vital character of religious experience and the need to criticize shallow consumerism and a restrictive materialism. Such a religiosity will have a largely Christian flavour, but may well incorporate Eastern elements. In any case in cosmopolitan societies, every religion will become a choosable denomination rather than an overarching way of life. But at the same time social changes will continue to fuel insecurity which in turn will produce a considerable evangelical and conservative backlash.

Something analogous will be brewing as the Marxist societies relax and begin ideologically to disintegrate. And an analogous conservative reaction will occur within the Islamic world, which will be increasingly polarized between Westernized and pluralistic secularism, with a move to restore ancient ethnic and religious pride. Similarly, Hindu India will experience new turbulences arising from aggressive and evangelical-style Hindu movements which help to express and cope with the frustrations of rising expectations and urban poverty. From the side of East Asia, especially Japan, a parallel ideology to the romantic monism of the West will evolve, beginning, however, from traditional Asian elements but grafting on aspects of Western humanism.

In the South we can expect that mainstream Christianity will still have a vivid role to play, and Northern ecumenical Christianity may be much more than it is now affected by ideas stemming from the South. But new religious movements will express a new sense of Africanness, while in Latin America new styles of Messianism are likely to appear.

But the spirit (or if you prefer the non-rational) bloweth where it listeth. Who could have predicted Islam in 590 CE? Since the globe is forming into a huge international society not altogether unlike the world of the Roman Empire, it is ripe for a new religion to emerge which may help to give it a new shape. One can safely predict that the number of new sects and movements will have greatly multiplied by 2010. But hidden among them may be one or two which might take the globe by storm.

But such a religion would have to make sense of science as well as the emotions. So far as one can see, the kind of religious monism I have alluded to is the one most capable of doing this. But as human history shows, the non-rational impulses towards hope and new identity in periods of crisis and change often express themselves irrationally: the non-rational is forever bifurcating towards romanticism on the one hand and a stormy irrationality on the other. Both forces will be very evident in our future.

11

Ideologies and Political Parties
in a Changing World

by Silviu Brucan

Although ideological forms are relatively autonomous in society and acquire in each country national traits, world politics marks the various stages of ideological confrontation with certain particular features that vary according to the evolution of predominant issues and conflicts.

In the post-war years when the Cold War was prevailing in world affairs the ideological struggle reached so high a tension that a showdown between the two contending camps seemed inevitable. The extension of social revolution in Eastern Europe and the Holy Alliance of 'containment' and 'roll-back' policies initiated by the US dominated the scene of bitter confrontation.

A new period followed as the political situation in Europe was stabilized; with the emergence of tens of new states under the ruins of colonial empires, the centre of gravity of revolution shifted to the developing continents. Since all this coincided with the extended economic boom of the fifties and sixties in the West, a neo-capitalist euphoria sprung out extolling the virtues of 'affluent society' and 'stable democracy', while Daniel Bell and Raymond Aron were triumphantly proclaiming the 'end of ideology'. Central capitalism of the West seemed to have resolved its explosive social problems.

Actually, whereas during the Cold War class-ideological motivations were prevalent in international relations, in the new period national differences and strategic interests of great powers went to the forefront of world politics with ideological considerations receding into the background. In this ambiance the advent of the Third World as a new political fact projected nationalism as a powerful motive force on the international scene.

In May 1968 the social upheaval in France opened up a long period of instability, crises and social convulsions in the West blowing up the myth of 'industrial peace' and the claim that the class struggle and the ideologies underlying it had faded out. The monetary crisis of 1971 with the shake-up of the dollar and the energy crisis that ensued compounded the instability turning it into a worldwide global phenomenon. The emergence of OPEC as a new type of power was heralding a new stage in the North-South conflict in which the Third World was telling the rest of the world that it was no longer satisfied with playing a marginal role in international affairs. In Eastern Europe as well as in China, Communism was faced with problems of its own, the solution of which could no longer be found in the classical texts or in previous experience.

It is in this general context that I propose to examine the state of political ideology and parties in the world of the 1980s.

I. Ideology in National and International Politics

In the post-war years, the habit of presenting international politics as a clash between opposite ideological camps was favoured greatly by politicians and writers on both sides of the 'Iron Curtain'. To American advocates of the 'protracted conflict' theory, the Cold War and the resulting nuclear race were ascribable to a sinister Communist master plan of political, military, and psychological warfare unceasingly directed against the Free World and aimed at world domination. Seemingly disparate events in widely separated parts of the world were intimately linked in a sophisticated conspiracy scheme that could be easily traced back to Moscow and/or Peking. One author concluded that the war in Vietnam, the attempted coup in Indonesia, and the disorders in Bolivia, Colombia, Ecuador, and Guatemala, were all part of a plan masterminded by Mao Tse-tung and Ho Chi Minh for a 'tri-continental war' against the Free World.[1]

In the East, the structure of dogmatic theory was strikingly similar—only the villain was different. Conflicts and disorder throughout the world were attributed to the class struggle strategy and since war is rooted in the Capitalist system and particularly in its paramount power, the centre of counter-revolution was identified as Washington DC.

There is an explanation for this striking similarity. Polarization of social forces always produces simplified ideological images. Indeed, the greater the social polarization, the simpler the ideological model. At the peak of the Cold War, Western bourgeois politicians depicted the 'totalitarian police state' of the East, while the other side spoke of 'rotten decadent Capitalism'. Each system was described as being doomed to disintegrate or to collapse shortly.

The very nature of the class struggle explains this phenomenon. After all, ideology is indispensable to any class or social group striving for a goal. However great the false image it conveys, it is ideology that makes men act together, fight together, resist together, hold on to power together. *Without ideology as a catalyst, there is no large-scale social action.* And because of this specific function, the intensity of ideological confrontation grows with the polarization of the social forces involved. In the Cold War years when the very existence of Capitalism in Europe was at stake, the ideological exchange was extremely virulent. However, in the sixties when class conflict slipped into the background and national difference took hold, the ideological tensions diminished and bourgeois writers jumped to the conclusion that the ideological era was over.

Those who had become used to the bipolar image of a world divided by ideology now stand baffled and perplexed before recent developments. President de Gaulle started protesting 'American hegemony' in the West while the harsh Sino-Soviet polemics broke out in the East, soon after Soviet and American experts were drafting jointly the test-ban and non-proliferation treaties both rejected by France and China on the grounds that they were designed to ensure nuclear strategic monopoly for the Super Powers; in the Indo-Pakistani war of 1971 and in the war in Angola (1976), the US and Communist China ganged on one side of the fence while the USSR stood firmly on the other. One can hardly explain those bizarre constellations in terms of class and ideologies that go with them.

What is the theoretical thrust of all these developments?

The basic reason why the dynamics of international relations differ from that of the class struggle must be sought in the distinct role played by *nations* in world politics. Indeed, though nations are made up of classes and other social groups with clashing interests, once they are consolidated as nation-states and largely integrated (owing to their common language, territory, economy, culture or religion) nations acquire a *drive of their own* in international politics that cannot be identified with any of their component classes or groups. Once again, the behaviour of the whole differs from that of its parts particularly since the whole is exposed outwardly to different conditions. Apparently, while the class struggle remains the motor of society's development, and classes in conflict tend to solicit support abroad (e.g. the factions in Lebanon), they do not always extend straight ahead to their ideological comrades because in international politics they enter a different sphere where other forces are at work. Indeed, since nations are great or small, mighty or weak, rich or poor, developed or underdeveloped, such discrepancies and gaps generate a type of conflict (and co-operation) that is utterly distinct from the interclass conflict triggered by contradictions in the mode of production and in the social structure.

Hence, the role of ideology itself in international politics is different from that within society. The reason simply stated is that while in society class struggle is the overriding factor of politics, in the international environment it is not.

Therefore, political initiatives, compromises, and understandings between ideologically conflicting parties that are almost unthinkable in society, prove perfectly feasible at the international level. Thus, we have witnessed a series of agreements in foreign policy that could hardly be replicated domestically.

A classic illustration is the famous Molotov-Ribbentrop Pact of 1939 between Nazi Germany and the Soviet Union. Today this applies to summit meetings and agreements between the US and the USSR and China. The kind of understanding that was possible between Nixon and Brezhnev is inconceivable say between Nixon and Gus Hall, or for that matter between Brezhnev and academician Sakharov.

II. The Vertical Ideological Competition

1. Methodologically, therefore, one must deal with ideology at two levels of analysis—the *national* and the *world* level. As we already noticed, there is a constant interaction between the two, though each one has its own logic.

Since we have seen how ideology works at the world level, let us now focus on the internal environment, on what I call the *vertical* competition, i.e. within society.

In the first world (West), whereas during the Cold War societies were polarized with almost everybody fighting either for or against communism, in the following decades of economic boom most political parties and forces converged toward the *centre*—the pivot of stability. Whatever the names of the parties or coalitions competing for the massive pool of votes at the centre, the dominant politico-ideological creed throughout the North Atlantic world was *social-democracy*. Traditional bourgeois parties were reluctant to acknowledge it as such, choosing to cover it up under the large label of liberalism, particularly in the US where middle America was jittery about 'creeping socialism'. The welfare-state lies at the heart of social-democratic politics showing more than anything else the viability of its belief that Capitalism can be 'improved' by gradual reform. A whole generation has espoused it—in the US by democrats and republicans alike—in Western Europe by Labour and Conservative parties, by Gaullists and Christian Democrats, by Catholics, Protestants, and Dutch Calvinists, not to mention Socialist and Social-Democratic parties.

Characteristic of that period is that the old-style bourgeois party of individual representation as well as the mass-integration party, product of an age with harder class lines and sharp denominational structures, have both transformed themselves into a *catchall people's party*, according to the formulae of a perceptive analyst.[2] The main purpose was electoral success and since the bulk of votes at the centre was rather heterogeneous both in terms of class and denomination, one had to drop every doctrinal identification that could deter segments of a potentially wide clientele. Bourgeois parties began to display a social conscience while socialist parties dropped Marx and the class struggle slogan from their programme.

A happy combination of technological revolution and Keynesian economics stimulated massive investments and unprecedented growth based on cheap oil and other raw materials from the South. This provided the economic base for the 'stable democracy' of the multiparty system. The conviction arose that the interests of corporate capitalism and of multinationals can best be served by such a political system. It was so decided and eventually applied in all twenty-four member states of the OECD (Organization for Economic Co-operational Development).

However, as the crisis broke out and the dominant metaphor of the seventies became *stagflation*, the political assumption of social democracy turned out to be as fallacious as its economic one. The political spokesmen of the welfare state began losing ground everywhere. In Britain, Labour's social democratic right was beset by its left wing; in the US the old Roosevelt coalition disintegrated and suffered a major electoral defeat. Even in Scandinavia the social democratic hegemony of the last forty years seems to have been broken. Such exceptions as Helmut Schmidt and Bruno Kreisky survived, as most observers agree, owing to their out-standing leadership merits rather than to their parties which were equally affected by the current eclipse of social-democracy.

Apparently, social-democracy and liberalism could no longer

provide solutions to the pressing problems of late Capitalism. Both were good at doing incremental reforms but were utterly inadequate when structural changes were required.

The years of expansion and growth that provided the means to subsidize the welfare state were gone. And so, *the massive vote at the centre dispersed throughout the political spectrum, producing a fragmentation of political interests and multiplication of parties claiming sectorial or regional constituencies.*

Hence the ideological competition became far more complex than the clear-cut antagonistic model of the past opposing the Right and the Left. The time of two grand ideologies originating in the basic contradiction between the bourgeoisie and the proletariat was over. The fragmentation of political interests and the diversification of voting patterns produced a much more intricate ideological picture. In France, for example, the Socialist Party became ideologically divided into three factions, while the governing coalition experienced recurring ideological clashes. The same thing could be said about the three major labour unions which very seldom succeeded in joining forces for united action at a time when stagflation systematically cut into the purchasing power of the working men.

As a result, industrial countries are now often governed by *political coalitions* whose heterogeneous ideological composition and lack of political consensus can hardly provide effective government to cope with the crises piling up. Even Ronald Reagan's celebrated landslide victory brought into the White House a 'minority president': because of the poor turnout, he got no more than 27 per cent of the American electoral vote! In France Mitterand is presiding over an uneasy coalition with the Communists while in West Germany, the Free Democrats switched from the alliance with the Social Democratic Party to the one with the Christian Democratic Party. In Britain, the Labour Party is so beleaguered by internal strife and challenged by the new coalition between Social Democrats and Liberals that it has little chance of regaining power. As for the Netherlands, Belgium, and Scandinavian countries, the small political parties forming the government clash with each other most of the time.

Small wonder that the Trilateral Commission has reached the conclusion that the West is confronted with what Professor Huntington calls a 'crisis of democracy'—a line that has been strongly pursued in recent years by the *new right* and the *neo-conservatives*.

What is the basis of this shift in the social structure of industrial countries? In a study on *Poverty and Inequality in Common Market Countries* we are told that the top 10 per cent earn about 30 per cent of all income earned whereas the bottom 30 per cent earn a mere 10 per cent.[3] In the US in the mid-seventies, according to the Census Bureau, the top 1 per cent of American families earned more than $50,000 annually, while at the bottom 35 per cent of families could not enjoy a decent life in American terms. In other words, the structure of inequality built into the Capitalist system has successfully survived the era of 'general prosperity'. Only the middle-income groups are doing a little better today than before the post-war economic miracle—conclude the authors of the EEC study. In a sharp critique of this book, Ralf Dahrendorf questions the assumption that this is an undesirable or unbearable state of affairs and he asks rhetorically: 'Are there not important differences between the qualitative inequalities of the lord and his serfs and the quantitative inequalities of a professional and a working class?'[4] There is a hitch in Professor Dahrendorf's equations. When he deals with the feudal system he opposes its two social poles—the lord and his serfs—whereas when he deals with present-day society the North pole is missing. The one at the top of the top ten, namely the industrial lord of today, is discreetly replaced by the professional, a trick that makes the inequality of Capitalism look less striking. The point, however, is that even the middle-income groups who were doing a little better are now badly affected by inflation and this is what worries the ideologues of Capitalism. Surely, it is preferable that the middle people turn to the right rather than left?

Neoconservatism is the modern ideology of the American right. In recent years, a group of academics and writers who used to call themselves liberals have veered sharply off to the right and aggregated around two journals: *The Public Interest* edited by Irving Kristol and Nathan Glazer, and *Commentary* edited by Norman Podhoretz. Though the views of this group are not uniform, they seem to be united by their anti-communism, their dislike of government intervention in social welfare, of egalitarianism and populist movements, and of course of detente with the Soviet Union. Fifteen years after members of the group had announced the end of ideology, the whole group is now proclaiming the imminent death of liberalism and warning that the decline of Western civilization will follow shortly, of course, if their demands for change in policy are not met.

Actually, they all appear to have been traumatized by the sixties which they perceive as a period of agitation and violence that threatened to destroy the institutions, the universities and the public order. They view the two principal demands of the sixties— for extensive *participation* of the masses and for greater social and economic *equality*—as having made it nearly impossible to govern the US. In his programmatic work *Twilight of Authority*, Robert Nisbet describes America as radically corrupted in its culture and values and deranged in its institutions. He surveys the scene and pronounces it to be a desolate one, with the littered remains of authority, political community, family, religion, moral values, and culture. Presiding over this wasteland is the giant political apparatus of the modern state; part war machine, part welfare apparatus, complete bureaucracy. Greased by the lust for power and stimulated by corruption, it produces conquest abroad and dispenses material benefits at home. Nisbet's dream is an idyllic America that existed after the Civil War. There was no Leviathan-state and localism and pluralism flourished. The values of family, work, and the 'sacred' were respected. Political parties were models of virtue and ideological fervour, and 'our wars were proper ones'.[5]

Nisbet blames the left, the intellectuals or 'political clerisy', for warfare, welfare, and Watergate. His avowed predilection is for an *authoritarian* regime to revive a curious assortment of elements: ethnic nationalism, fundamentalist religion, the commune, kinship and localism, and what he calls the 'still enigmatic role of the multinational corporations'. Tradition rather than law should rule.

I insisted on this neoconservative manifesto merely to point out the ingredients this ideology is made of. Ethnic revival is strongly emphasized, for, as Daniel Bell puts it, ethnicity is a strategic preference for those who could choose another group (classes, for instance) as a means to get into power.[6] One reviewer explained: 'If you slice the cake into ethnic pieces, classes become less visible. And neoconservatives would choose anything that makes people forget about classes and class struggle'. In addition, Daniel Moynihan launched an all-out attack against the Third World demand for a new international economic order, rejecting the accusation that the present order is exploitative and designed to preserve the economic domination of the West. The neoconservative warrior retorted that poverty is the fault of the poor and that the under-developed nations are merely ganging up on the US to extort the wealth it has legitimately acquired as an efficient producer. It is time, therefore, for the US to move into opposition, to forget the lessons of Vietnam and get tough with the rest of the world. Getting the message, Professor Robert Tucker published an article in the same *Commentary* detailing his plan for an American invasion of the Persian Gulf to reassert control over the oil reserves.

With such prestigious contributions neoconservatism may now claim a well-rounded politico-ideological programme. Since the medieval melancholy of Nisbet could create some confusion as to their economic choice, Irving Kristol decided to dispel any mis-understanding and entitled his book *Two Cheers for Capitalism*.[7]

Indeed, to be a force in the real world an ideology requires some class or movement whose interests and objectives make them a natural carrier, a historical agent. The tragedy of this group is that its activities look like an operation egghead. The aspiration to be literate, elegant and graceful in style, erudite and sophisticated in content, has alienated the neoconservatives from the masters they are so eager to serve and whose support is so essential to their whole enterprise—the *American businessmen*. It is a traditionless class which is committed to continuous innovation, technological change, and to everything that makes money. Its mode of action is rational decision-making, its ethic is enshrined in cost-benefit analysis, its politics is efficient administration.

Struggling desperately to find their ideological roots, American conservatives have passionately adopted Edmund Burke, the guru of anti-revolutionary politics. However, Burke's stubborn defence of feudal values, including inherited privilege, a traditional ruling class, political power based on landed property, a cosy intimacy between Church and State, might make sense in a society like England's where reminders of the past lingered on, but sounds fairly hollow in a society with no feudal past like America.

The aggressive activists of the 'New Right' who believe in organization and fund-raising rather than in theorizing stand a better chance to influence American politics. Most analysts feel that Ronald Reagan owes much to the rightist organizations for their support. Unlike the neoconservatives, the New Right operates at the grassroots, organizing meetings, mailing letters, raising funds, and mobilizing votes. Most of them are one-issue groups like the 50,000 members Eagle Forum fighting the equal rights amendment to the Constitution. Other groups oppose homosexual rights, abortion, etc. The opportunity to contest the treaty with Panama about the future of the Panama Canal was a boon to the New Right; many senators voted against it under the pressure of such organiz-ations. Liberal senators like Frank Church were defeated because of their support of abortion.

The new right organizations do not fit a neat sociological package; they appeal to a mass audience that is mixed in religion, social class, and geography. Social issues are often reduced to single

defects of character; leaders are strong or soft. They say the old
American pieties of God, Family, and Country are in danger; they
must be defended against the enemy. The slogans are simple and
effective (homosexuals cause Communism, *or* give America back
its mothers). But the membership is growing and with money
pouring in it tells us something about the political culture of
America.

Since the US is the leader of the West, one wonders how much
this will affect ideological and political developments in Western
Europe. As we have already seen, the social setting is different in
many ways; the political representation of classes has a strong
tradition while political culture could hardly encourage the models
of the US new right to be imported as such.

Though the left in the US does not enjoy either similar
aggregation of academics and writers or massively financed
publications and organizations, there is a process of radicalization
with an increasing impact in the universities and in the large sections
that made up the Roosevelt coalition.

At a time when so many authors are riding the wave of the right it
is symptomatic that Heilbroner should entitle his book *Business
Civilization in Decline*,[8] Harrington *The Twilight of Capitalism*,[9]
and a scholar of Barry Commoner's reputation should write a book
in which he argues that the time has come to see the defects of the
Capitalist economic system in the US from the perspective of a
socialist alternative, and to discuss the relative merits of Capitalism
and socialism.[10] That's swimming upstream with a vengeance, but
the message of these books will make its way for it says that the
current stagflation reflects a deep structural fault in the system that
in turn reflects the corporate domination of US economy. The way
out of the crisis is neither in the revival of old pieties nor in Milton
Friedman's nineteenth century *laissez faire* liberalism.

2. The Second World (East) is going its own way though not as
insulated from the global economic crisis as one used to think over
here. The recent events in Poland have highlighted the kind of
problems Eastern European countries are facing today and brought
to the fore the need to re-examine some of the political and
ideological assumptions on which these societies have been built. In
China such re-examination is already in progress.

Eastern Europe appears to have reached a critical stage in its
strategy of rapid industrialization based on regular allocation of a
large portion of national income to development, most of it going to
heavy industry and very little to the consumer sector and agri-

culture. The asymmetrical structure of East-West trade and the privileged position of Western currencies in financial transactions have resulted in heavy debts to Western banks, compelling Eastern countries to spend billions of dollars just on debt servicing. On top of that, poor grain harvests, particularly in the USSR and Poland, have forced the spending of large sums on food imports.

Gone are the years of spectacular economic growth that made the USSR the world's second-ranking economic power and enabled the Eastern European nations to achieve for three decades a growth rate almost twice as high as that in the capitalist countries. Despite higher investment ratios, recent years have been marred by a slowdown in economic expansion. As a result, the previous steady rise in living standards has halted; wages barely keep up with prices, while there are various shortages, particularly of meat and other foodstuffs—though Hungary and Bulgaria are notable exceptions, achieving substantial surpluses in their agricultural trade balances.

In the analysis of this situation, my starting point is that development comes first, socialism only afterwards. Hence, the major transformations that have taken place since 1917 in Russia, and subsequently all over Eastern Europe, can be described more accurately using the concept of *development strategy* on a non-Capitalist path rather than that of socialism, which is a post-Capitalist and implicitly post-industrial society. For industrialization belongs historically to the capitalist era—it is the Western bourgeoisie that formulated the theory of industrialization and invented the ways and means to implement it.

To define the state created in Russia, the class-theoretical criterion is not enough; one has to consider also the mode of capital accumulation indispensable to build industry. For to accumulate capital by appropriating the surplus produced by labour and the peasant sector has become the primary function of the state. The harsh political climate of the class struggle, the civil war and foreign intervention of imperialist states, were equally effective in shaping the form of the state and determining its other functions. Thus, an apparent dichotomy developed between the class content and socialist ideology of the state and the form of law and state equally determined by functions essentially bourgeois. While Marx and Lenin anticipated the 'dialectical puzzle' of the revolution having to preserve in the early stage 'not only the bourgeois law but even the bourgeois state—without the bourgeoisie', they never thought of the consequences upon the new state of an extended period of capital accumulation with its inner contradictions in a class-society and its international stimuli and constraints in a world economy in which central capitalism holds a commanding position. Actually industrialism comes into conflict with socialist ideology however much the Communist party is struggling to mitigate this conflict by socialist indoctrination.

Furthermore, massive industrialization is bringing with it tighter integration of national economies into the world economic system and subjecting them to the latter's laws and fluctuations to which Eastern European countries must adapt. Equally obvious is that modern technology and large-scale production have finally outgrown such old methods in industrial management as administrative fiat and shock-labour. To cope with these problems new managerial concepts and techniques are required.

Hungary was the first to break new ground with its sweeping economic reforms giving local managers a greater say in investment, production, and price decisions while the government maintained control over the economy through a series of credit, price, wage and foreign trade 'regulators'. In a nutshell, the plan is regulating the macrostructure while the market is regulating the microstructure. In agriculture, massive investments, strong material incentives and market freedom have resulted in a soaring production of food without precedent in that part of the world. However, in the USSR and other Eastern countries the actual implementation of new management concepts encounters political resistance and ideological bias. Two major issues have emerged as basic prerequisites for such a change: *decentralization* of decision-making, and the will to use *economic means* instead of administrative means and ideological emulation. As we will see shortly, the two are in fact closely interrelated. Ideology and power are the crux of the matter.

Here, one is reminded that whereas Lenin, and later Bukharin, emphasized that the co-operatives should be based on marketing, buying and credit, and argued that only through the struggle in the marketplace would socialist agriculture defeat private competition and create a higher productivity, Stalin carried a policy dominated by his impatient drive towards rapid and forced collectivization, his fanatical belief in administrative fiat and the mobilization of the party on the 'agricultural front'. To this day, the party must organize campaigns every season to determine the peasants to sow, weed and harvest. The old Stalinist suspicion of economic means and incentives (Stalin used to label them 'capitalist devices') has turned into a strong ideological bias embedded in the whole politico-bureaucratic structure of the state and the party.

Thus, the political system that was set up to deal with the

enormous task of industrializing and modernizing a huge backward country in a hostile international environment has now become the single greatest barrier in the way of an industrial society that is now ripe for a transition to socialism. Apparently a conflict has grown between the emerging socio-economic system and the old political structures; the latter appear too rigid, over-centralized and anachronistic to be able to lead the necessary process of change. In political terms also, an educated working-class with its huge army of competent engineers, scientists and administrative cadres demand to participate in decisions that are still concentrated at the top.

The Communist party is required to change accordingly. It has evolved from the Leninist organization of 'revolutionary professionals' into a mass-party with all political initiative monopolized in the Politburo. To retain its leading role in society, the party must now democratize its structures and methods so as to get a real political input from the working-class as a whole.

3. Most of the conditions described earlier as having influenced the development strategy in Eastern Europe also apply to the Third World countries. For they start from backwardness and under-development and are bound to industrialize and modernize their economy under adverse conditions dictated by the dominant position of central capitalism in the world economy and by its economic and technological advance. Such basic co-ordinates are essential for the understanding of the ideological and political developments in the Third World.

To begin with, political parties in the modern sense of the notion are historically related to development. Indeed, political parties emerge whenever the activities of a political system reach a certain degree of complexity or whenever the notion of political power comes to include the idea that the mass public must participate or be controlled.[11] Placed in the context of the North-South system and the division of labour underlying it between the rich industrial metropolis of the North, and the peripheries in the South specializing in agriculture and raw materials, the ideological forms and political movements in the latter have been strongly influenced by the task of national liberation, and after independence, by the political economy of state-building and development. In Africa and other backward regions, the problem of national integration—of asserting and legitimizing the priority of the nation-state over tribal and traditional loyalties—acquired enormous urgency. Such paramount goals have been complemented—sometimes compounded—by demands for social justice and agrarian reform with the view to getting a more equitable distribution of society's wealth, and the desire for greater social and economic opportunities even before substantial economic growth has occurred. The surplus of wealth which made it possible for the Western bourgeoisie to partly satisfy the demands of the working class without substantial reduction of the income of upper classes is absent in the Third World. This is why the whole ideological setting in the developing nations is so different in many ways from the European theatre, starting with the social structure which can be hardly defined in classical Marxist terms. The main ideological confrontation in this part of the world revolves chiefly around the strategy of development and more specifically around the question: Who benefits from What?

To mention but one typical example of Capitalist development—the Brazilian 'miracle of growth'—in an impressive spurt from 1969 to 1974, Brazil's per capita output increased by a third to $1500 whilst the income gap among Brazilians still widened. In 1960 the affluent 5 per cent accounted for 35 per cent of the wealth and the lower 50 per cent for only 14 per cent. By 1976, the division of wealth between these groups was 39 per cent and 12 per cent.[12]

In nations adopting a non-capitalist strategy of development, the basic elements have a characteristic relationship. High rates of investment and capital accumulation imply a fast tempo of industrialization and urbanization. That in turn means wider planning, of social as well as economic development, and tighter protection against external pressures, including those of multinational companies. In the end, the state becomes more authoritarian, to control the whole programme and get things done. But this is not necessarily a matter of ideology: the same forces are at work in fast-developing countries that have followed the capitalist path, and have produced authoritarian states in Taiwan and South Korea, for example.

A final point here. The commanding economic position of central Capitalism is significantly strengthened by the diffusion of its culture and civilization. We live in a world in which the Western model (chiefly made in the USA) sets the pace and calls the tune. Starting with accessible items of clothing (e.g. blue jeans), continuing to jazz, pop music, dances, movies and TV serials, all through the cult of automobile and the philosophy of growth; the whole Western lifestyle has spread all over the world as a fellow-traveller of industrialism and modernization. From the moment a nation starts industrializing it gets caught in the whirlwind of the system. The nation then struggles desperately to escape the politico-ideological side-effects of that pressure. The cultural revolution in China and the Islamic revival in Iran, each in its own way, represent daring and stubborn attempts to resist the domineering model of the West. They also illustrate the tragedy of such ventures in the absence of an adequate economico-techno-logical base upon which to build a modern alternative to that model. Lacking such a base, post-revolutionary societies (including Eastern Europe) resort, instead, to the past to secure a cultural identity. Old folk music, dances and even costumes are revived on a large scale.

In Iran's case this is only part of the story. For we are dealing here with a radical populist and anti-imperialist revolution with a very distinct character. Khomeini has tried to build an Islamic state based on a symbiosis of religion and politics to be run by the Mullah Fundamentalist Party as a power centre of the Islamic world radiating an ideology of its own. Indeed, ideology never appears in a pure form in domestic or international politics. Ideology always mingles with power: it serves to get hold of power and once in power the political carriers, i.e. parties, of a particular ideology, uses the power base to consolidate its position and expand it. Great powers are very good at that: they project their power abroad to 'make the world safe for democracy', or 'to save socialism'. Thus, it is not fortuitous that throughout history the great religions or ideologies with universal vocation have centred around a power base. Ideologies are then moulded according to the particular interests of the power centre.

However, Khomeini has not succeeded in building a strong power base for his Islamic doctrine. Iran itself is beset by internal strife and power struggles, and no real economic and social programme has been formulated to consolidate the revolution. Actually, the Islamic world is fragmented and divided as never before: its subdivisions are asserting their ethnocultural peculi-arities, radical nationalist regimes are clashing with monarchical conservative ones, local variations and legacies of earlier civiliz-ations are resurrected for the occasion. The war between Iraq and Iran is an extreme form of such manifestations and the alignments shaping up behind the two belligerents define with greater strength the divisions within the Islamic world.

III. Foreseeable Political and Ideological Developments

Since I have dealt elsewhere[13] with political forecasting and future world modelling let me briefly resume my own approach. I began with the assumption that modern technology and productive forces are driving people, things and processes toward a shrinking world, compelling its subsystems, particularly nation-states, to regulate the various activities that transcend national borders and eventually to integrate into larger units than the nation-state.

Yet, because of social cleavages inside societies and rivalries among nations, the drive of modern technology does not operate as a one-directional sweep, but as *a dual and contradictory motion*. The effect is a dialectical interplay between the factors that create division and conflict and those that create cohesion and integration. The best illustration of this is the vagarious history of the EEC, where moments of elation about political union have been followed by discordant decisions of individual members on monetary policies and imports threatening even the basic customs union.

Accordingly, I expect the process of integration to be marked by progress and regression, advances and setbacks, and to proceed in stages. It is my assumption that geographical and ecological factors as well as ideological ones will determine the process to proceed first on a *regional* basis.

Western Europe is the principal regional unit taking shape within the First World. New political and ideological developments in that region may come from a variable that seemed dormant, namely *social change*. At a time of economic turmoil with high unemployment and inflation compounded by an apparent inability of governments to overcome the crisis, large sections of the population get disenchanted with the system and are ready for a change. Whether the political parties of the Left will be able to unite and turn these conditions into a real change of guard is still an open question.

In a regional system dominated by NATO under US command and by the EEC, both committed to the preservation of Capitalism, a new regime would come up against horrendous pressures and constraints. The regional system is so tight that neither Italy nor France could isolate themselves to build 'socialism in one country'. Eurocommunism, though innovative in its internal strategy, has not yet faced up to this issue.

This is not to say that social change in the West is no longer a practical proposition. It simply means that in a tight interdependent system like Western Europe, conditions for a successful revolution must be ripe not only internally but also externally. The task of the anti-systemic forces is to change both the politico-economic fabric of society and the structure of the regional system. It logically follows that political parties and ideologies would have to adapt to the new situation.

In the Second World, the only region with a geographically focused pattern of interaction among its members resulting in a systemic mode of co-operation is Eastern Europe. As I already mentioned earlier, significant changes will have to take place in order to secure the smooth functioning of a socialist society.

However, Eastern Europe is a regional system dominated by the Warsaw Treaty and the CMEA (Council for Mutual Economic Assistance), both committed to the preservation of the existing structure of power. Events in Czechoslovakia in 1968 and more recently in Poland have clearly shown that in Eastern Europe also the state is embedded in a regional structure of power which resists change. This will have its own impact on the political system and its ideology throughout the whole region.

A striking similarity is apparent in both regional systems of Europe: structural societal changes require transformations in both the form of the state and in the regional structure of power of which the state is a part. This will affect not only the vertical ideological competition inside societies but also the East-West level of ideological confrontation.

REFERENCES

1. Stephen T Possony, 'Mao's Strategic Initiative of 1965 and the US Response'. *Orbis* II (Spring 1967): 159.
2. Otto Kirchheimer, 'The Transformation of the Western European Party Systems' in *Political Parties and Political Development*, Eds. Joseph La-Palombara and Myron Weiner. Princeton Un. Press, 1966.
3. *Poverty and Inequality in Common Market Countries*, Eds. Vic George and Roger Lawson. Routledge 1980.
4. R. Dahrendorf, 'Social Policy'. *London Review of Books*. 3–16 July 1980.
5. Robert Nisbet, *Twilight of Authority*, Oxford Un. Press, 1975.
6. Nathan Glazer and Daniel P Moynihan, *Beyond the Melting Pot*, MIT Press, Cambridge, 1975.
7. Irving Kristol, *Two Cheers for Capitalism*. Basic Books, New York, 1977.
8. Robert L Heilbroner, *Business Civilization in Decline*, Norton, New York, 1976.
9. Michael Harrington, *The Twilight of Capitalism*. Simon & Schuster, New York, 1976.
10. Barry Commoner, *The Poverty of Power*, Alfred Knopf, New York, 1976.
11. *Political Parties and Political Development*, Eds. Joseph LaPalombara and Myron Wiener. Princeton Un. Press, p.3.
12. Editorial, *International Herald Tribune*, 14 July, 1980.
13. Silviu Brucan, *The Dialectic of World Politics*, Free Press-Macmillan, New York, 1978.

Silviu Brucan, *The Dissolution of Power*, Knopf, 1971.

12

The Political Map of the Future

by Shridath S Ramphal

It was probably always true that no generation could draw the political map of the future with assurance; but, perhaps, never so true as it is now. As Man's life span on the planet unfolded and the memory bank of human experience grew, there developed, it is true, a capacity to look into the future through the prism of the past. Long familiarity with old certitudes served to justify at least a cautious prediction of political patterns. Much of that has changed. Most of these certitudes have gone and the pace of change has quickened. The past may be no longer as safe a guide to the future. To a rather special degree, the one great certainty of the future is its uncertainty.

There is increasing acknowledgement that the post-war period, say 1945 to 1975, was an era in itself, and that the last quarter of the twentieth century marks a new time in human affairs. There is a widely shared consciousness that we live in a time of transition; that our world is already no longer the world into which we were born and will be even more significantly different at the turn of the century. What kind of world it will be is less clear; but it is my central thesis that the future will depend essentially on what Man in all his infinite variety but his inseparable humanity is able to agree on; that agreement rather than imposition, negotiation rather than dict-ation, are the particular ways by which the political map of the future will be drawn. Those of us who prepared the Brandt Report (North-South: A Programme for Survival) declared: 'We are looking for a world based less on power and status, more on justice and contract; less discretionary, more governed by fair and open rules.' That is the world our map may well depict: a more genuine society of nations—unless, in a mood of senseless determinism, we first destroy ourselves.

Post-war technology has evolved many aids to map-making, but none, perhaps, more useful than the ascent into space. For the first time a decade ago Man saw the planet as we had for half a millennium known it to be, one whole—confirming visually a view of the world previously known only to the mind. Although the automatic camera has now travelled millions of miles farther than its maker, the most illuminating moments in the space odyssey have occurred when Man himself has been at the controls of his machines and looked down upon his planet. What he has seen has profound implications, not just for real map-makers, but for any who would contemplate the political cartography of the future.

The human journey into space affected mortals in differing ways. 'The vision of earth rise seen by human beings standing on the moon had its impact', Barbara Ward has written; and she continued: 'Planet Earth is a small place'. Small the Earth undeniably is to the astronaut's eye, to the satellite sending back weather pictures of the planet, and to the miracle machines of modern communications which have brought into focus the global village. Yet, as striking from space as the world's smallness is its wholeness, its integral character. When Man walked on the moon and looked upon the world, what he saw was oneness. 'Earth rise' was an image of unity; and now satellites daily confirm how small and vulnerable, but essentially how whole, the planet is—how the clouds and storms and gases that assail it take no notice of the separateness we sustain below, almost in defiance of nature.

This wholeness of our global society must be, I believe, the dominant assumption of future political realities, whether or not it finds expression in the kind of formal relationships that show up on the political maps. Even today, in our politically disparate world of customs posts and passports, a frontier is increasingly an expression of contiguity no less than of separation; borders are crossed by trade, by transport, and above all by people, playing their part in the ever deepening process of human integration. Robert Frost reminded us that 'Heaven gives its glimpses only to those not in a position to look too close'. Perhaps Earth-bound Man is too close to discern his oneness. We talk of 'balkanization' in pejorative terms—the axiomatic nonsense of a fragmented society, but we live with a 'balkanized' world that so contradicts the glimpse from space. Yet there are glimpses of our one world here in our confused present.

We have lived for so long in a world of separate worlds that we find it hard to admit, sometimes even to recognize, the oneness of our world. Over the millennia, our separatism fed on differences of tribe and race, of language and religion; it fed on divisions of class; it fed on human aggrandisement and lust for power; it fed on an adversary system which our model of the nation state moulded and our concept of sovereignty sustained. It might almost be said that separatism, disunity, antipathy even, was Man's natural condition. And yet, over the centuries, we have been moving away from our primitive instincts, our loyalties evolving from family to tribe to nation to region—always towards a sense of oneness, an awareness of belonging to steadily enlarging groups. Each stage marked an advance from smaller and narrower separate worlds.

Certainly setbacks occurred; progress comes only from un-remitting effort, and we must not fall prey to doctrines of its inevitability. Thus, the enlightenment that brought reform to Western societies stopped at national frontiers: the rights of Man were denied their reach to all the human race, and still too often are—witness Southern Africa, where the ramparts of the 'Broederbond' remain to be breached. Yet, elsewhere, the empires have been almost entirely dismantled. The surge of philosophical, religious, political doctrines which had developed from the ancient Greeks onwards could not be checked; it continued to sweep Man on to visions of a nobler, broader future. And, as the world turned in terror from the scourge of war in 1945, the image of one world already glimpsed with the League of Nations in the early twenties came into clearer focus; and it was in that image that the United Nations was conceived.

Between the image and reality, it is true, fell the shadow of the past—the shadow of power which made some more equal than others even under the Charter; the shadow of dominion that lingered in its political, and even more so, its economic cast. But it is perhaps our new awareness of the limits of power in relations between nations, and indeed within them, which signals most clearly that the old times, and with them the old worlds, have gone. In the nuclear age, we have reached the threshold of absolute power only to find that across it lies oblivion. The ultimate sanction is to destroy not just the enemy's world, but one's own as well; it is, indeed, all one. The threat of 'mutual assured destruction' (how apt its acronym 'MAD' is!)—the possibility of eliminating life on this planet—has actually become the shaky cornerstone of human co-existence. In its name, the Super Powers have made and hold in store enough nuclear weapons to guarantee such a unified human fate, and are engaged in a race to produce even more. As we view their confrontations with increasing alarm, it is well to recall the warning of Calgacus to his fellow-Britons on the eve of the Battle of Grampians—a warning about the Roman 'Super Power' almost exactly nineteen hundred years ago—which Byron later put more lyrically:

> Mark where their carnage and their conquest cease,
> They make a solitude and call it peace.

And other desolations threaten. The air we breathe is not ours alone; the seas that wash our shores wash other shores as well. Like the common clay of our soil and bodies, all are one. So by our separate abuse of the environment we have made our oceans a dirty communal pond and our atmosphere a polluted universal sky. And now we reach beyond the atmosphere to litter outer space with debris, and weapons, that threaten a destiny we only dimly understand—save that it will finally make no distinction between nations or among people.

That question of survival is affected by our numbers as much as anything else. At the beginning of this century, our planet had less than two billion people; today it supports four and a half billion; on present trends, it will have to sustain about six and a half billion by the end of the century; the increase alone over the next twenty years will be more than the world's total population eighty years ago. Nine-tenths of that increase will be in the Third World—because of, rather than despite, poverty. We add to the world a million people every five days, and face the prospect of a planet of fifteen billion in the twenty-first century. The one thing constant is our 'only one earth'. We need desperately to come to terms with its realities if we are to optimize our prospects of making it secure and habitable for all. On an over-populated planet, as in an over-populated city, there is no insulated world, no sanctuary, no final refuge from the terror of 'a box of matches'. Already a swollen tide of refugees warns us that human misery cannot be quarantined. We cannot disinfect the global environment of the contagion of mass starvation; and, even if we could, who would want to share such a world inoculated against itself?

When Abraham Lincoln said of his United States threatened with disunity that it could not 'endure permanently half-slave half-free', he was talking of more than social or economic disparities, he was talking of the limits of immorality within oneness. So it is with our planet. More than a century after Lincoln, are we going to decide differently? Perhaps to answer as in Brecht's satirical *Threepenny Opera*:

> Some in light and some in darkness
> That's the kind of world we mean.

Those you see are in the light part.
Those in darkness don't get seen.

It is principally in the economic domain that the real lessons of oneness are to be learned; because it is here that we have flirted most with the illusion of several worlds. Interdependence may have become a code word meaning all things to all men; but it aptly reflects the proposition that the world economy is so interlocked that all nations and all people—to different degrees, it is true—have become dependent on each other. How valid is this? How relevant to the political map of the future?

The post-war period has seen unprecedented technological change and economic growth, intensifying the breadth and depth of economic interaction between countries. There has been a phenomenal expansion in trade and in the movement of capital, tourism, technology and information across international frontiers. Many national economies have grown fast by any historical standard; international economic linkages have grown faster still. For most of the post-war period the growth in international trade has grown twice as fast as world output; the result: increasing global integration and internationalization of national economies. Linkages have grown particularly fast among the industrialized countries; but the developing countries and the centrally planned economies have also been significantly involved in what is a global process.

The developing countries are the weaker, less resilient elements within the world economy. It is perhaps not surprising, therefore, that the case against interdependence sometimes summons in its support the statement of Professor Sir Arthur Lewis (in 1979 happily honoured with the Nobel Prize for his work in development economics) that 'if Africa, Asia and Latin America sank beneath the sea tomorrow, this would scarcely much affect the present or future affluence of Europe or North America'. Arthur Lewis made that statement in 1969. I am not sure that in saying so he was intending to testify against the interdependent character of the world economy. He has more recently referred to the obverse—that the Third World's 'potential for growth would be unaffected even if all the developed countries were to sink under the sea'.

The real point, however, is not whether the rich can survive if the poor cease to exist or the poor if the rich were no more, but whether rich and poor can survive together if things go on as they are. The postulate of interdependence is not the inability to survive in isolation, but the need of each other in the context of co-existence—the context we face today: co-existence in one world.

What are some of the implications of that co-existence? Nearly ten years after the first significant oil price increase—a shock to the world economic system which the West insisted on describing as a 'crisis', but which history is already confirming as a necessary catalyst for beneficial change—ten years on it is almost trite to observe that the OPEC (Organization of Petroleum Exporting Countries) countries have become a powerful factor in the world economy. There are still some who harbour the illusion that this is a passing aberration that need not permanently change the status quo. Fortunately, there are others who know better and see the need to adjust to the new realities.

But other groups in the Third World have also had a significant impact on the world economy. The newly industrializing countries (the NICs), from Brazil to Korea, from Singapore to Mexico, have become major exporters of manufactured goods to the industrialized countries and increasingly to the developing countries as well. And they and some other middle-income countries have become substantial participants in the Euro-currency markets, their borrowing greatly helping to sustain the exports of the industrialized countries.

Meanwhile, in the traditional areas of trade and the supply of raw materials, the dependence of Northern economies on the Third World has become substantial in special areas—more substantial than revealed by overall figures. Northern trade with the developing countries has been growing faster than trade between the developed countries. In the case of Japan, now the most dynamic industrial economy, dependence on Third World markets is approaching fifty per cent. Significantly, it is the economy least affected by the recession. The extent to which Third World imports helped to sustain the industrial economies during the seventies and in fact prevented a much deeper recession is now well documented; it was the equivalent, OECD has acknowledged, of some 900,000 jobs in industrialized countries every year during 1973 to 1977.

On raw material imports, while only about twenty per cent now emanate from the Third World, for certain commodities, some of strategic value, Northern dependence is much higher; it is higher also for some countries—like many in Europe and Japan—whose dependence ratios for some minerals exceed sixty-five per cent. The projections are that even the United States, with abundant raw materials of its own, will by 1985 be looking abroad for more than one-half of its supplies of nine basic raw materials. This is not to imply that Third World producers of commodities other than oil have the same economic power as the oil-producers. It suggests, however, that it is illusory and dangerous, to believe that these factors of economic interdependence are not central elements of what we now readily describe, but often without awareness of its full implications, as 'the global economy'—the economy of one world.

But if these linkages spell out the message of interdependence, its real lessons are taught by the crisis that now faces the world economy—an interdependent world economy. In 1980 the Brandt Report said that 'the world community faces much greater dangers than at any time since the Second World War'. Events have all too clearly confirmed this prognosis; there is less of the criticism that we were unduly pessimistic. The long expected recovery is still not here—the depth and stubbornness of the recession pointing, as we suggested, to complex and fundamental causes calling for structural changes in the international economic systems, and confirming our view that the self-interest of nations can now only be effectively pursued through taking account of mutual interests.

Protectionism provides a striking example of the fact that we ignore at our peril the interdependent character of our world economy. It is well established that because of prevailing linkages protectionism forfeits many more jobs than it secures; that emerging out of the fight against inflation it in the end fuels inflation itself. Few governments would dissent from this; for most, 'free-trade' is quintessential doctrine. Yet protectionism is on the march. Half a century after the events of the thirties it should have been self-evident that at the end of that road lies damnation; that there must be an international dimension to the battle against inflation. The World Economic Conference in 1933—chaired in London by Ramsay Macdonald and attended even then by sixty-four countries—came too late to assist in averting the depression, and was too half-hearted to arrest economic disorder. Must that history of myopia and tardiness be repeated in the eighties?

But protectionism is not the only danger that arises from our failure to acknowledge the mutual needs of all countries and their mutual interest that those needs be met. The dangers in the financial and monetary fields, and particularly in relation to international debt, are simply staggering. At the end of 1980 the total outstanding debt of developing countries was $456 billion, of which $373 billion was owed by oil importing countries. About $300 billion of that debt is owed to private sources, largely the commercial banks, and about two-thirds of this amount—$200 billion—has been raised at floating rates of interest. Loans from the commercial banks carry relatively short maturities—about seven to ten years. The combination of very high interest rates and short maturities has now imposed crushing debt service burdens on the borrowing countries. On the $200 billion raised at floating rates, a one per cent rise in the interest rates increases interest charges by $2 billion; and new borrowing at the higher rates adds a further burden. There has been a fall in interest rates but this provides only a slight amelioration and may only be a respite.

The debt service payments of developing countries are now $92 billion a year. They are rising, and rising as a proportion of foreign exchange earnings. In 1973, 14 per cent of export earnings went to repay debt; the debt service ratio today is 20 per cent, and it is rising. For some countries it has reached frightening levels. For 1980, of developing countries for which figures are available, eleven had a debt service ratio exceeding 20 per cent. For six of them it was already between 25 and 30 per cent.

These developments are as worrying to creditors as to debtors, and worrying as well to the rest of the international community— testimony that the self-interest of nations demands taking account of mutual interests. It is ironic that it should be in Poland that the crisis has first struck; that this major bailing out by Western governments has had to be applied to Eastern ideological opponents—not Southern friends.

But Poland may be only the tip of the iceberg. While borrowing needs are increasing—to repay debt and meet deficits—borrowing capacity is declining. By the end of 1980, before the advent of high interest rates, twenty-six countries faced repayment difficulties; their aggregate arrears were already $6.4 billion. And the problem, inevitably, is not only declining capacity to borrow, but increasing reluctance to lend as many banks find themselves heavily exposed to a small number of developing countries.

Once again, merely defensive responses and a lack of global management could produce a cycle of disaster. There could well be a gradual seizing-up of the international credit system. Current trends cannot continue without precipitating a crisis either through default by a major borrower and the domino effect of default on the whole international credit system or through intolerable burdens of adjustment imposed on the weakest economies in the absence of international support for their minimal financing needs. Clearly, the current situation has been aggravated by inadequacies in international economic co-operation, by an ineffective inter- national system which seems to stand helpless while the world economy drifts into increasing distress. It is now virtually the case that the private banks—not governments—are managing the global financial system. Is there a single country in which since the 1930s this has been acceptable at the national level? Can the world afford the attendant risks?

The Brandt Report has alerted the international community to these and the many other risks that it faces at the beginning of the '80s. The greatest compliment paid the Report is that it has called forth critical commentaries; and there are elements of validity in many of them which can help to strengthen its overall thrust. Neither singly nor together, however, do they shake its central message—the message of mutual interest in change: 'We are convinced that there are gains for all in a new order of international economic relations and hope for humanity in achieving them'. Perhaps that is the answer to the paradox of 'popular acclaim and academic attack'—its enthusiastic welcome by people and its sometimes angry rejection by academics. Its message, it seems, has reached a wider public whose intuition tells them of its truth, whose instinct for survival warns them of approaching danger long before their economists can confirm it, or their leaders dare acknowledge.

This dual reaction is both reassuring and a cause for concern. Reassuring over time because it recalls a long history of struggle against conventional wisdom—a history which confirms that today's heresy is often tomorrow's orthodoxy. So it may be with 'Brandt'. If it is, it would be essentially because we sought to articulate the collective vision of the many thinkers whose views we considered —people like the the late Barbara Ward, who memorably once declared:

> We dare not forget the really poor who are the great majority, because prosperity, like peace, is indivisible.

The vision of our Report may not yet have gained the general acceptance of governments, or of academics, but it is perhaps even more important that it has struck a chord of assonance in the hearts and minds of people in many lands.

But there remains the dimension of concern—the damage that any unyielding conventional wisdom inflicts on human society when it denies passage to a new truth. No one has put this better than Ivan Head, President of Canada's International Development Research Centre, when he addressed the American Association for the Advancement of Science:

> The denial by the Catholic Church for 200 years of the true nature of the solar system did not cause the earth or the other planets to pause for one second in their revolutions about the sun. The

denial did, however, suffocate scientific enquiry in the vast realm of Catholicism for two centuries and gave an opportunity to the Protestant nations to gain a predominant position in scientific endeavours . . .

The Catholic Church survived its lengthy blindness towards the solar system: one cannot be certain that the industrialised nations can survive their apparent blindness toward the international economic system.

Therein lies the present danger—made greater by the fact that when we now speak of 'survival', realism dictates that we speak in universal terms.

Interdependence is not new. What is new is the intensity and variety of the economic relationships that have emerged in the post-war era and the actual recognition, in many quarters, of the elements of mutual interest in them. And what is new, as a result, is that we have lost the option of ignoring our interdependent state—of ignoring the reality that we have become one world.

All this is a positive gain. That the world has become more interdependent must not be seen as a process of decline and fall. It should be a source of reassurance as we contemplate the political map of the future and the future of the world. Responsive to the practicalities of interdependence, we must move from a system of international relations characterized by reliance on force and fear to one based on co-operation and mutual benefit. In doing so we will almost certainly find that we have also moved towards a more peaceful world, not because we have avoided conflict, but because the realities of interdependence, what Sartre called 'the infinite unity of (man's) mutual needs', provide incentives for the resolution of conflict otherwise than by return to force and threat.

How palpable today those mutual needs! How obvious the need for a global coalition of survival to rescue our world society—our one society—from collapsing into economic chaos or sliding to self-destruction! And how inter-linked those dual fates: as concern for national security drives up military spending which produces massive budget deficits which sustain high interest rates which deepen the recession which threatens widespread economic collapse, creating new centres of instability and tension and heightening still further the national security concerns with which we started.

Because we are one world—one inseparable humanity—we will feel trapped by our interdependence so long as we indulge the illusion that we are sovereign states with unbridled choices, masters of our own destiny, responsible only for the interests of our societies, insulated from the fate of others—in short, dependent on no one, accountable to no one, responsive to no interests but our own. We need release from these myths. The way out of the imagined 'trap of interdependence' is simply to recognize that the door opens outwards.

The concomitant of interdependence is co-operation between nations and between people; recognition that we need to better co-ordinate our conduct, and make more progress towards global management of human affairs. And here the ghosts of entrenched nationalisms rise up—in North and South, in East and West—to frighten us; they scare us away from a sharing of power even though it responds to power's changed realities; they scare us from trimming the edges of sovereignty though we know that its contours have long been wearing away; they scare us—especially our political leaders—from admitting that solutions to the problems of our one world cannot all be found in any one fragment of it, that national philosophies, national doctrines, national action cannot by themselves provide all the answers.

Why are we still so blinkered by nationalism in the era of interdependence? Why do we remain shut up behind our 'narrow domestic walls' when all our senses tell us that there is no safety within them? One answer is that to win elections politicians feel compelled to promise better economic times; and to develop and project political machismo they convince their electorate (and sometimes even themselves) that by their own unaided efforts, by the infallibility of their economic philosophy and its resolute translation through domestic policy, they can deliver those better times. To admit the inhibiting relevance of the global factor is somehow to admit to being less than effective or to imply that the ideological platform may be flawed.

These are unnecessary burdens of self-sufficiency that politicians assume. But it is now a significant if sad political reality that current management of the democratic process is all too frequently leading it to work against internationalism. This is so not only in the North; even in the South, where external constraints on development are so manifest, ideologues of one kind or another tend to look askance at the external dimension. This partly explains the curious point of contact between ideologues in the North who disparage the North-South dialogue and those in the South who call for 'de-linking' from the global system. But the global factor does not go away because it is ignored; it operates instead to invalidate the strictly domestic approach to better economic times and to defer them still further. It remains the determinant of the future.

The international community, in this time of transition, is wandering without a sense of direction. We have lost our intellectual bearings as the certitudes of the post-war era have one by one disappeared. We need urgently a new intellectual framework for the internationalism of the eighties and beyond; but it is slow in emerging. Even as the war was ending, indeed long before the end was in sight, Keynes and White were laying intellectual foundations for the economic internationalism of the post-war era. What wisdoms are to guide our vision of the world economy in the end years of the century?

The world has changed since 1945—changed because of 1945. That was in part the achievement of the institutions and systems established in the post-war period. But in changing the world they stand in need of adjustment themselves. All is not well, in particular, with the United Nations system which in too many areas has become ritualistic and inbred and increasingly technocratic. All are to blame—East and West, North and South—for the image of endless, tedious, tiresome and ultimately self-defeating dialogue that the UN system has come to personify. As a result, the United Nations is in danger of losing its support among the world's people; for it cannot hold their faith if it ceases to inspire.

But the United Nations is not something apart; it is governments that have allowed it—even encouraged it—to grow apart. It has been a convenient stage on which to act out national performances; but these are played so often—and by all countries—that they become charades, masking even the few really genuine roles. All countries know that they need the United Nations and that if they continue to assist its decline every country will be poorer. Yet they show little sign of being ready to strengthen it. Here again we need a new vision, a renewed sense of purpose, a fresh contouring of the concept of world order if the political map of the future is to be responsive to the changing circumstances of our time.

This is not to imply that the United Nations should be filled with ambition for a quasi supra-national role. It has to work with its members and through them, carrying them with it to the highest reaches of peace and understanding to which its Charter commits it. Ritchie Calder once issued the wise corrective that

when we are critical and sometimes disenchanted by the short-comings of the United Nations, we are forgetting that it is not a supranational but an international body, dependent on the loyalty, the input of high-quality personnel, the financial and material resources, the judgement and the experience of member states. Nothing short of that can serve.

The UN needs to become more consciously a chamber for consensus and less an arena of conflict. It must somehow move away from a combative and adversary spirit to one inspired by a more genuine search for the agreement which is attainable; but mindful always that 'a man's reach should exceed his grasp, or what's a heaven for?'

Above all, the United Nations must recapture the faith of its constituency among the world's people. A generation ago young people in particular looked to the United Nations as the embodiment of all that was noblest in international endeavour. We need more practical reminders that it still is, so that as the world's people become more committed they will in turn help their governments to return to belief in the United Nations as an institution through which they can work collectively to find the accommodations they must make for survival. The United Nations will be a pale reflection of Man's highest hopes if it is misused, or so misuses itself, that nations, and more especially the major nations, see it negatively as something that must be endured rather than positively as deserving their constant and practical support.

Nor need our internationalism see the United Nations as the sole agency for the promotion of peace and understanding. The practical politics of our time will continue to require supplementation of the efforts of the United Nations in many ways, both in the political and the economic sphere. There are some things that member states can do between themselves in advancing the goals of the United Nations itself. The United Nations is not diminished by that effort. It is not diminished by disarmament negotiations between the Super Powers; it was not diminished by Cancun; it was not diminished by Commonwealth successes in Zimbabwe; it will not be diminished if the efforts of the Western Contact Group working in tandem with the United Nations were to bring freedom to Namibia. Indeed, it is our responsibility to find all possible ways to harness the highest potential that lies within the international community to help in fulfilling for Mankind the objectives of the Charter. We can do so through innovation, creativity and a breadth of outlook more impressed with reaching worthy goals than with the virtues of the trodden path. All these are part of the new spirit of internationalism for which our world society yearns. Wherein, then, lies hope for the future?

Some hope lies in the new processes of summitry that are

evolving. Three summits in 1981—Ottawa, Melbourne and Cancun—could have marked a new beginning. It is certainly the Commonwealth's experience that the ambience of a political discussion at the summit can produce results otherwise beyond grasp. The 'risks' of summitry are mostly feared by those who guard the status quo. Those risks bear no relationship to the gains for all that even so modest an achievement as a new climate for consensus constitutes. Summitry is not a cure for all the world's ills. It is not guaranteed to remove all impediments to progress. It has limits no less than strengths.

But in all times of crisis it is the political actors who must play the leading roles. The trade-offs involved are ones that only political leaders can make and the political will required to sustain them is more likely to be attained collectively rather than in isolation. The leaders are the only actors with licence to change the lines and with them the style and meaning of the play. There is a greater prospect that they will be changed through a process of personal encounter that enlarges understanding, builds confidence and reinforces political will. We shall have to give this political process at the summit greater and greater opportunity—using it always with circumspection but not merely out of despair. The lesson of Cancun is not that summitry does not work, but that we have to work harder at making it work effectively.

And hope lies also in our capacity to find a way out of the maze in which suspicion, misunderstanding and real conflicts of interest from time to time entrap human society—once we allow ourselves to be guided by the twin beacons of principle and practicality, never veering so far in the direction of one as to lose the other. My own experience has confirmed for me how real is this potential for consensus and how rich can be the returns for all elements of the international community if we develop it with imagination, creativity and, above all, a sense of purpose.

The Lomé Convention for example, concluded in 1975 between the enlarged Community of Europe and what were then forty-six states of Francophone and English-speaking Africa, the Caribbean and the Pacific, established the framework of a new and promising economic relationship that 10 years earlier would have been regarded as highly improbable even by all its participants.

In a wholly different field, with principle and practicality as the guide, and working always in harmony with member govern-ments—with Britain, with the African Frontline States and with other Commonwealth countries—it was possible for the Commonwealth to bring to an end a conflict which had plagued not just Africa and the Commonwealth but the wider international community for more than a decade and which threatened the eruption of a racial crisis not only in Southern Africa but much further afield. Within two years between the Lusaka (1979) and Melbourne (1981) Heads of Government Meetings a war had ended, a new state had been born, a nation was in the making, and at Melbourne, around the Commonwealth table, Margaret Thatcher and Robert Mugabe could sit down as equals, not only without bitterness but with mutual respect.

And that capacity for consensus extends even to areas in which nations feel threatened by change. The Brandt Commission brought together under Willy Brandt, a true internationalist, men and women from nearly every sector of our world society, with different backgrounds, different talents, different perceptions of the past and, in the beginning perhaps, even different visions of the future. We worked at issues that had divided the international community through what was then already six years of unprofitable dialogue. Yet we found it possible, guided by these same beacons of principle and practicality, to develop a convergence of view on where we were as a human society, on where we had to go and how we might get there.

Convergence does not come without compromise; but compromise itself guided by principle and practicality is not a sign of weakness. It takes great strength to be able to reach the higher middle ground. The Brandt Report is now read in over twenty languages and with the greatest enthusiasm by younger people. Herein lies perhaps the greatest area of hope. The world's people know that the human race is able to do better; they are conscious that there must be higher purposes and nobler pursuits to which societies must aim; from whatever regions they come they are looking for a vision of the future that they can share in good conscience with the rest of the human race. They may yet have to lead their leaders to a new internationalism for the interdependent world that a younger generation seems to understand more intuitively than their leaders.

As the concept of the one world comes to signify more clearly a single human community rather than a coterie of states, we shall better understand the need to trim the edges of sovereignty, to move away from an adversary system of international politics and to reconcile our national loyalties without global obligations. These perceptions must begin to inform our conduct, for, in the end, human interdependence is not a matter of dialectics, but of destiny. How we respond to it is the great challenge of our time. The nature and quality of that response will be the quintessential determinants of the political map of the future.

REFERENCES

Alastair Buchan, *The End of the Post-War Era*, Weidenfeld and Nicolson, 1974.

Régis Debray, *Revolution in the Revolution*, Penguin Books, 1968.

Dag Hammarskjold, *Markings*, Alfred Knopf, New York, 1974.

Roger D Hansen and Contributors, *US Foreign Policy and the Third World: Agenda 1982*, Overseas Development Council, Washington (annually).

Chandra S Hardy, *Rescheduling Developing Country Debts, 1956–81: Lessons and Recommendations*, Monograph No 15, Overseas Development Council, Washington, June 1982.

Shridath Ramphal, *One World to Share: Selected Speeches of the Commonwealth Secretary-General*, Hutchinson Benham, 1979.

Ruth L Sivard, *World Military and Social Expenditures*, World Priorities Inc, Leesburg, Virginia, 1981.

Jan Tinbergen ed, *RIO: Reshaping the International Order*, Dutton, New York, 1976.

Barbara Ward, *Progress for a Small Planet*, Penguin Books, 1979.

Barbara Ward and René Dubos, *Only One Earth*, Penguin Books, 1972.

The Common Fund (Commonwealth Expert Group Report, 'The Campbell Report'), Commonwealth Secretariat, 1978.

Common Security: A Programme for Disarmament (Report of the Independent Commission on Disarmament and Security Issues under the Chairmanship of Olaf Palme, 'The Palme Report'), Pan Books, 1982.

Commonwealth Declarations, Commonwealth Secretariat, 1981.

North-South: A Programme for Survival (The Report of the Independent Commission on International Development Issues under the Chairmanship of Willy Brandt, 'The Brandt Report'), Pan Books, 1980.

Partners in Tomorrow: Strategies for a New International Economic Order (essays presented to Jan Tinbergen), Dutton, New York, 1978.

Protectionism: Threat to International Order (Commonwealth Expert Group Report, 'The Cairncross Report'), Commonwealth Secretariat, 1982.

Towards a New International Economic Order (Commonwealth Expert Group Report, 'The McIntyre Report'), Commonwealth Secretariat, 1976.

World Development Report, World Bank, Washington (annually).

The World Economic Crisis (Commonwealth Expert Group Report, 'The Arndt Report'), Commonwealth Secretariat, 1980.

Index

aboriginal peoples 22
abortion 184
acceleration of change 10, 12–13,
  16–19
Adams, Henry 8, 10–13, 16
Adelman, I 122
advertising, future 105–6
Africa 207–8; food supply 66–7;
  national integration 188; religion
  158, 162, 166, 173
agricultural civilizations 23–6
agricultural technology 75
Albania, religion 160
algae, and uranium 83
Algeria, grain stocks 55
altruism 116
Alvin expedition 82
Amsterdam, diamonds 133
Anabaptists 159
Anderson, Sir John 6
Anti-Comet Battery possibility 33,
  42–3
Antwerp, diamonds 133
appropriate technology 50–2
aquaculture 80–1, 83, 84, 88, 89
arms race 8, 154–5, 196;
  Doomsday Machine 34–6
Aron, Raymond 176
Asian religion 161, 166–8, 174, 175
AT&T 94, 95
Atlantic fisheries 68
Atomic Age 1
atomic bomb 5–6
atomic energy, peaceful use 8,
  124, 151

Attlee, Clement 5, 6
authoritarianism 183
automation, industrial 36, 37,
  102–3

Baathism 158, 171
banks, and world finance 201
Belgium 140, 181
belief-systems 158; privatization
  160; transmissions 160, 163
Bell, Alexander Graham 90
Bell, Daniel 176, 183
Bernal, J D 33, 40, 44
Big Brother Machine possibility
  33, 48–9
Biotechnology Age 1; Green
  Machine 38–9
birth rates *see* fertility rates
bit-stream 98
Black Christianity 173
Bombach, G 121
borrowing, international 200–1
bourgeois political parties 180
Bowles, S 141
Brahma 79
brain: capability 114;
  transplanted 43–4
Brandt Commission Report 126–7,
  137, 194, 200, 202, 208
Brandt, Willy 208
Brazil: food consumption 57; food
  production 71; growth 189, 199;
  population 72; religion 174
Brecht, Berthold 197

British Telecom 'System X' 99
Bronowski, Jacob 5
Buddhism 158, 160, 161, 162, 163, 166, 167, 168, 169, 174
Bukharin, N I 187
Bulgaria 186
bureaucracy 127
Buringh, P 124, 125
Burke, Edmund 184
business: class 184; communication in 101–2
Byron, George Gordon, Lord 196–7

cable television 104
Calgacus 196
Calvinists 160
Canada, food exports 71
Cancun summit 206, 207
capitalism 191; evils of 178, 181, 182, 185; reform of 180; successful 176, 189
Carter, Luther 60
cathode ray tube 94
Catholicism 165, 174, 202–3
cereals see grain
Challenger expedition 82
change: acceleration of 10, 12–13, 16–19; and technology 92; see also technological change
Cheap Thrills Machine possibility 33, 44–5
children, needs 141
China 123, 158, 185, 190; grain stocks 55; ocean development 88–9; religion 160, 167
Chisholm Brock 4
Christiantiy 51, 158, 159–60, 163–6, 167, 174, 175
Church and State 160, 166
Church, Frank 184
Churchill, Sir Winston 6, 126, 127
citizens, economic role 141–2
class struggle 177, 178, 183
climate, changing 144–5
Climate Regulator possibility 33, 39–40, 50

Club de Dakar 136
coalition governments 181
co-existence 198–9
Cold War, and ideology 176, 177, 178, 179
colonies, liberation 2, 135
comet: progress as, 8–9; collision with 42–3
Commoner, Barry 185
Commonwealth 206, 207–8
communications equipment 91, 94, 100–3, 105, 114; see also telecommunication
Communism see Marxism
competition 146–7
compromise 208
Computer-Communications Age 1
computers in education 112, 113–14; see also microprocessors
Confucianism 161, 167, 168
conservation 150–1, 155, 197
conservatism, new 182–5
conspiracy, Communist 177
consumer interests 128
convergence 208
cosmic rays 46
cosmopolitanism 174
Council of Agricultural Science and Technology 60
Council for Mutual Economic Assistance (CMEA) 192
creativity 141
crops: and fertilizer 63–7; and soil 58–60; yields 62–3
Cuba crisis (1962) 7
Cushing D H 68
Cyclops modem 114
Czechoslovakia 192

Dahrendorf, Ralf 182
data banks 49
Davy, Sir Humphry 26
death see mortality
debt, international 200–1
degeneration, social 147–8
demand, stimulation of 146

democracy: crisis of 181;
  theoretical 27
depression, economic 121, 125; see
  also recession
desertification 59, 66–7, 124
despair and protest 27–8
developing countries, see Third
  World
diamond cutting industry 133
dietary habits 57–8, 67–8, 69, 141
digitalization of information
  services 97–8, 99
dinosaurs, extinction 43
discovery, acceleration of 16–19
Disembodied Brain possibility 33,
  43–4, 45, 51
distance-learning 119, 120
Doel, J Van den 132
Doomsday Machine possibility 33,
  34–6, 41, 51
Dyson, Freeman J 33, 41

Eagle Forum 184
earnings: inequality of 182; policy
  125, 133–4, 135, 138
Earth, full exploitation of 42
East, the: economic conditions
  185–6; ideologies 185–8, 192
ecodevelopment 152
economics: adaptability 121; new
  121, 122; social policies 127–42
ecumenism 163, 165–6, 175
Eden, Anthony 5
education: continuing 119–20; cost
  118–19, 120; distance-learning
  119, 120; future trends 117–20;
  homogeneity 117–18; interaction
  in 113, 120; purpose of 115–17;
  technology of 112–14, 120
Einstein, A 173
emotional satisfaction 44–5
employment: policies 129; social
  aspects of 37–8; see also
  unemployment
Encke comet 42
energy sources 40, 66, 123–4;
  conservation 150–1, 155; costs
  63, 123–4; and land use 61, 62,
  66; and living standards 149;
  ocean as 80, 83–4
entertainment, future 106
environment: clean 124–5, 144–5;
  conservation 150–1, 197
equality 183
Ethiopia, soil erosion 59
ethnic revival 183
Europe: earnings 182; integration
  138–9; political parties 139–40;
  population growth 26
European Monetary System 138
European Parliament 140
evolution 14–15, 16, 24, 144

facsimile newspaper 108, 109
factories, computerized 102–3, 104
farming, abolition of 39
fertility: control 28; rate 25, 28; see
  also population growth
fertilizer and food supply 63–5,
finance, international 200–2
fish stocks 55, 67–9, 81
Food and Agriculture
  Organization (FAO) 3, 5, 136
food supply 4–5, 74–6, 124; and
  demand 54, 56, 58, 74, 75–6;
  and diet 57–8, 67–8; and
  population growth 54, 55, 56–7,
  72–3, 74, 76; prices 54, 56, 70,
  75–6, 129; rationing 74; surplus
  54, 73; from USA 70–4
forecasting, technological 31–2;
  polar approach 32–4
France: energy sources 83–4; land
  use 61; political parties 181;
  social conditions 147–8
Franklin, Benjamin 19
free trade 128, 200
Friedman, Milton 185
Fritsch, B 121
Frost, Robert 195
Futurology 10, 13, 14

Galapagos mining 82
Galbraith, J K 132

Galilei, Galileo 26
games, electronic 113
Gandhi, Mahatma 131, 170
Ganges Water Machine 39
Gaulle, President Charles de 178
Gibbs, Josiah Willard 10, 12
Gintis, H 141
Giscard d'Estaing, President
    Valery 181
Glazer, Nathan 182
grain stocks 54, 55; consumption
    57; imports 73; prices 70, 129;
    surplus 73; yield 63–7, 75
grazing land 65–7
Greece, Ancient 147, 148
Green Machine possibility 33,
    38–9, 48, 50
Gross National Product, concept
    of, 146
growth 198; cessation of 150;
    concept of 145–6, 152, 156–7;
    and conflict 149; cultural
    revolution 155–6; illusory 146,
    147; new policies 150–7;
    objective of 150; real 153; and
    technology 153–4, 198
Gustafson, Thane 59

Hall, Gus 179
Hanau, diamonds 133
Harrington, Michael 185
Hawaii 174
Head, Ivan 202
Heemst, H D J van 124, 125
Heilbroner, Robert L 185
Hinduism 51–2, 162, 168–9, 175
Hiroshima 6
history, acceleration of 20, 29
home: computers 105; facsimile
    newspapers 108, 109; work from
    92, 102
Homo sapiens 21, 22, 80
Honduras, grain stocks 55
Hong Kong, wages 135
Hot Line 7
Hueting, R 124

Huizer, G 131, 135
Humanism 160, 164, 175
Hungary 186, 187
hunger 124
hunting and food-gathering
    peoples 21–3
Huntington, Professor 181
Huxley, Aldous 44
Huxley, Julian 5
hydrogen bomb 7

ideology: conflict of 176, 178, 181;
    Eastern 185–8, 192; function of
    178; nations, role 178–9; power
    base 190; Third World 188–90;
    vertical competition 179–90,
    192; Western 179–85, 189–90,
    191; world analysis 176–9
India: agriculture 66, 67;
    appropriate development 51–2;
    caste 169; education 118; food
    consumption 57; Ganges Water
    Machine 39; grain stocks 55;
    religion 161, 162, 168–70, 175;
    wages 135
individualisation of knowledge 109
individualism: and
    microprocessors 103; and
    religion 159–60
industrial society 26–9, 146, 147,
    148, 152, 186, 187;
    newly-industrialized countries
    (NIC) 199; social change 181–2
inequality 182
inertia, concept of 26
information systems 91, 114;
    digitalization 97–8; domestic 98,
    104, 105; electronic 100; future
    development 47–8, 49, 100–3;
    153; public investment in 93;
    ring-main 98, 104; text
    information 106–9
Innes, Harold 91
institutions, social and political
    23–4, 25, 26, 27
integration, international 191

interdependence 123, 127–8,
  138–9, 151–2, 152–3, 195–6,
  197–8, 200, 203–4, 208
Inter-Governmental Consultative
  Organization 4
International Chamber of
  Commerce 132
International Labour Office 133
International Labour Organization
  (ILO) 3, 135
International Monetary Fund 4
International Postal Union 4
International Seabed Authority
  86, 87
International Telecommunications
  Union 4
International Tribunal for the Law
  of the Sea 86
Iran 158, 159, 161, 170, 190
Iraq 171
Iron Curtain 177
Isaacs, John D 83
Islam 92, 158, 161, 162, 170–2,
  173, 175, 190
Israel, religion 172–3
Ivory Coast, grain stocks 55

Jacks, G V 58
Japan 123; fish farming 81; food
  consumption 57, 67–8, 69;
  religion 161, 167, 175;
  text-information 107; wage rates
  135
Jonestown massacre 35
Jouvenel, Bertrand de 24
Judaism 172–3

Kahn, Herman 125
Keynes, John Maynard 27, 121,
  125, 150, 180, 205
Khomeini, Ayatollah 158, 190
Khrushchev, Nikita 7
knowledge: objective 19, 20, 28,
  30; and religion 169; see also
  information
Kok, W 138
Korea: industry 199; religion 161,
  168

Kreisky, Bruno 140, 180
Kristol, Irving 182, 184

land: fertilizer 63–5; and food
  supply 58–67; grazing 65–7; soil
  58–60; use 60–2, 72–3; yields
  62–3
Latin America: Economic
  Commission for 136; population
  72; religion 162, 166, 174, 175
law, and oceans 80, 84–8
Lenin, V I 186, 187
Leontief, W 137
Lewis, Sir Arthur 198
liberalism 140, 163–4, 171, 180,
  182
libraries 107–8, 114
Libya 161
life expectancy 26
life-style: new 141, 156; Western
  189
Lincoln, Abraham 28, 197
literacy 117–18
livestock products 57–8, 70
living standards 149
loans, international 200–1
local cultures 48
Lomé Convention (1975) 207
Louis XIV, King of France 147
Lusaka summit meeting 208
Lutherans 160

Macdonald, Ramsay 200
Macmillan, Harold 2
McNamara, Robert S 131
Macrae, N 132, 141
Malahoft, Alex 82
Malthus, Thomas 26, 112
managerial groups, East and West
  27
manganese 82, 86
Manhattan Project 6
markets, Third World 199
Marx, Karl 121, 130, 140, 180, 186
Marxism 150, 158, 162–3, 168,
  173, 174, 175; changing 188,
  191; conspiracy 177; evils of 178;

problems of 177, 187; and religion 160, 166–7, 173, 175; values 51
Massachusetts Institute of Technology, Project Icarus 43
Maxwell, James Clerk 10
meat production 70
medical engineering 43–4
Melbourne summit 207, 208
messianism 173, 175
metallic muds 82
Mexico: industry 199; population 72
microchip 91–2, 112
microprocessors 93, 102–3, 104, 105
Minc, A 37
minicomputers in education 112, 113–14
mining, seabed 80, 81–3, 89
Mishan, E J 121
modems 114
Molotov, V M 179
monism 164, 165, 166, 167, 168, 169, 171, 173, 174, 175
Monnet, Jean 127, 128
Morris, William 38
mortality: prevention 4, 28; rate 25, 26, 28
Moynihan, Daniel 183
Mugabe, Robert 208
multi-national corporations 180; competition 93; control of 132; economic policies 130–3, 137; power 123, 132
multi-party system 180
Myres, N 125
Myrdal, G 122, 142

nationalism 104; and religion 166
nations, role 178–9
needs, material 146, 147; social 115–6, 152
neoconservatism 182–4
Nepal, soil erosion 59m 67
Netherlands: political parties 140, 181; wages 133

networks 96–7, 98–9, 110–11, 114
Neumann, J von 36
New International Economic Order 121, 126, 136, 183
newspapers 108–9
New Zealand, religion 159
Nisbet, Robert 183, 184
Nixon, President Richard 179
Non-Proliferation Treaty 8
Nora, S 37
North Atlantic Treaty Organization (NATO) 35, 191
North Sea drilling 82
nuclear bomb: control 7–8; development 6, 144
nuclear energy 8, 124, 151
nuclear war, probability 35, 154, 196

objective knowledge 19, 20, 28, 30
ocean thermal energy conversion (OTEC) 84
oceans: aquaculture 80–1, 83, 84, 88, 89; durability 79; as energy source 80, 83–4; and food 67–9, 80–1; law of 80, 84–8; mining 80, 81–3, 89; sovereignty 87–8; surveillance 88
office work 100–3
oil supplies 82, 83, 123; prices 123–4, 199
O'Neill, Gerard 40, 41
Open University 113, 114, 118, 119
optimism 9
Organization for Economic Co-operation and Development 132, 180, 199
Organization of Petroleum Exporting Countires (OPEC) 123, 177, 199
Orr, John Boyd 4–5
Orwell, George 48

Pacific, religions 162, 167–8, 174
Pakistan 161, 170
Palme, Olof 140

Panama 184
paper, elimination of 99, 100, 108, 109
Pardo, Arvid 84
participation 183
Peru: fisheries 69; population 72
Pimental, David 60
pleasure, achievement of 44–5
pluralistic societies 159–60, 161, 173, 174
Podhoretz, Norman 182
Poland 186, 192; economics 201; politics 185; religion 160–1
polar approach to forecasting 32–4
political parties 188; *catchall people's party* 180; coalitions 181; economic policies 139–40; fragmentation 181; and growth 150; and religion 166
pollution, environmental 124–5, 144–5, 148, 151, 197
poor nations *see* Third World
population growth 4, 24, 25, 26, 55, 197; and food supply 54, 55, 56–7, 72–3, 74, 76; and land use 61–2; and unemployment 129
postal systems 97
poverty 183, 197; Misery-Go-Round of 5
power, centres of 123, 130
Prebisch, Raúl 128, 136
Prestel 105
primitive cultures 21–3
printing 108–9
producer interests 128
production and waste 151
productivity and wages 134
Project Icarus 43
Pronk, J P 138
protectionism 128, 138, 200
protein scarcity 69–71
Protestantism 51, 52, 164, 165, 173
PTT's 94, 95
public spending 125, 138
Pulse Code Modulation (PCM) 99

quality of life 145, 150, 156–7

Radhakrishnan, President of India 168
radio communications 2, 3, 48–9
Rance, river 83
raw materials 199
rayionalism 159, 164, 175
reading, elimination of 47
Reagan, President Ronald 181, 184
recession, economic 128, 137, 199, 200
re-cycling 151
Red Sea mining 82
regionalism 191
religion: blocs 159–63; cross–fertilization 163; traditional 159, 162, 169; and values 51–2
reproduction *see* fertility
research, stimulation of 138
Ribbentrop, J von 179
right-wing ideologies 182–5
Ritchie-Calder, Lord 205
robots 102–3
Romania 160
romantic monism 164, 165, 166, 167, 168, 169, 171, 173, 174, 175
Roosevelt, President F D 5, 180

Sakharov, Andrei 27, 179
Salgado Peñaherrera, G 137
sanitation 148
Santa Claus Machine possibility 33, 36–8, 39, 41, 48, 50, 51, 52
Satellite Business Systems (SBS) 97
satellites 1–2, 48, 88, 108
satisfaction, attaining 44–5
Scandinavia: diet 57; politics 180, 181
scarcity: equilibrium of 24, 25, 26, 30; new 121, 124, 138
Schmidt, Helmut 180, 181
Schmitt, Walter R 83
Schumacher, E Fritz 50, 131
science and religion 175
seas *see* oceans

seaweed culture 80, 81
secretaries 101
secular beliefs 158, 160, 163–4
selfishness 116
self-reliance, and interdependence
  151–2, 204
Self-Reproducing Robot Rocket
  Ship possibility 33, 45–7
selling, future 105–6
separatism 195–6
Shinto 161
shopping, future 105
social democracy 140, 179–80
Socialist International 140
social policies, economic effect 127
social systems, alternative 37–8,
  155–6
social unrest and ideology 176–7
Socrates 101
soil, and food supply 58–60
Soil Conservation Service 60
solar energy 124, 151
sovereignty 87–8, 124, 204, 208
Soviet Union: agriculture 59;
  development 186–7; fish farming
  81; food consumption 56, 57, 67,
  68, 69, 71; foreign relations 177,
  179; grain stocks 55–6, 186;
  nuclear power 7; power 123;
  religion 160, 167
soybeans 69, 70–1
Space Age 1–2, 194–5
Space City possibility 33, 40–2, 51
space travel 45–7
stagflation 125, 180, 185
Stalin, J 187
standardization, increasing 48
Staring, G J 124
Stettinius, E R 5
Stimson, Henry 5
Stone Age man 21
Sufism 172
summit conferences 206–7
superman, creation 44
surveillance: of oceans 88; total
  48–9

Sweden, prices 133; religion 159,
  160
Synanon 158
synaptic connections 114–15
Syria 171

Taoism 161 167
Taylor, Theodore 36
technological change 91;
  acceleration of 10, 12–13, 16–19;
  and education 112–14, 120; and
  ideology 191; and new growth
  153–4; possibilities 33–52;
  prediction of 31–2; and religion
  165
telecommunications 90–111, 153;
  corporations 94; development
  94–5, 96; in education 113, 119;
  entertainment 106; government
  involvement 93; networks 96–7,
  98–9, 110–11, 114; planning
  95–6; and religion 165;
  ring-main 98, 104
telemail 95, 96
teletext 106–7
television 104, 106, 165
text-information 106–9, 113
Thailand 161, 162, 168
Thammuz, King of Thebes 91
Thatcher, Margaret 208
Theravada Buddhism 168
Third World 3, 176, 177;
  agriculture 59; appropriate
  technology 50–2; borrowing
  200–1; demographic transition
  28; economic growth 28–9, 131
  125–7, 198; exports, 199–200;
  governments 131, 135–7, 183;
  ideology 188–90; importance
  199–200; industry 199; land use
  61, 72–3; migrant workers 126;
  and multi-national enterprises
  130–1, 137; political parties
  188–9; population growth 59,
  197; and technological change
  49–50; trade 128; trades unions
  134–5; unemployment 129, 131

Thompson, Louis 75
Thoth, god 91
Tibet, 166
tidal power 83–4
Tinbergen, Jan 136, 138
toolmaking 21
topsoil 58–60
Total Information System
    possibility 33, 47–8, 50
trade, international 128, 199–200
trade unions 123, 133–5, 138
Transcendent, the 158, 159 160,
    164
transport and land use 61
Trilateral Commission 181
Trivers, Robert 46
Truman, President Harry S 5
Tucker, Robert 183–4
typewriters, future 100–1

unemployment 125, 129, 135
Unification Church 158
United Kingdom: diet 57; land use
    61; living standards 123; political
    parties 180, 181
United Nations 2, 35;
    development 205–6; economic
    policy 126, 136; foundation 5,
    196; and multi-nationals 132;
    organization 3–4; Atomic
    Energy Commission 7;
    Children's Fund (UNICEF) 3;
    Conference on Desertification
    (1977) 59; Conference on the
    Law of the Sea 84–7;
    Conference on Population
    (1974) 129; Conference on Trade
    and Development (UNCTAD)
    126, 128; Educational Scientific
    and Cultural Organization
    (UNESCO) 3, 5; Economic and
    Social Council 3; Industrial
    Development Organization 136;
    International Refugee
    Organization 3; Military Staff
    Committee 7; Relief and
    Rehabilitation Agency
    (UNRRA) 3; Security Council 7

United States: agriculture 58, 59,
    60, 70–1; earnings 182; Federal
    Communications Commission
    92; fish farming 81; food
    consumption 57, 68; as food
    supplier 71–4; foreign relations
    177; grain stocks 55, 56, 63, 71;
    ideology in 182–5; labour force
    27; land use 61; living standards
    149; National Aeronautic and
    Space Administration 83;
    neoconservatism 182–4; New
    Right 184–5; nuclear power 6–7;
    and the ocean 86, 88; politics
    139–40, 180, 181; power 123;
    religion 159, 160, 172–3;
    telecommunications 90, 97, 99
uranium 83
urbanization, changing 102,
    109–10; of land 61–2, 73
Uyl, J M den 138

values: change in 155–6; and
    education 116, 117; and religion
    51
Venezuela, population 72
videodisc 108
video networks 99
video-tex 106–7, 108
Vietnam 168; War 92, 159, 177,
    183
Vishnu 79
Vivekananda, Swami 168
Vonnegut, Kurt 37, 38

wages policy 125, 133-4, 135, 138
Wahhabis 171
war, nuclear 35, 154, 196
Ward, Barbara 195, 202
Warsaw Treaty 192
waste, elimination 151, 155
water: conservancy of 89, 148;
    cycle, manipulation of 39;
    pollution 148
water hyacinth 83
wave energy 84

weather, control of 39–49, 145
Weizsäcker, C F von 128
welfare state 180, 181
Wells, H G 9, 13–14, 44
Weltinnenpolitik 128
Werner Report (1970) 138
West Germany: food consumption
    57; land use 61; politics 140, 181
Western economic policies 137–9
Western ideologies 179–85,
    189–90,191
wheat see grain
White Frontier 163
Whyte, R O 58
Williams, Francis 6
Wilson, C L 124
Woods Hole Oceanographic
    Institution 81
word-processors 100–1; see also
    micro-processors
work, social problems of 37–8, 147

workers: education 115;
    investment in 131–2; and
    micro-processors 103, 104;
    migrant 126
work ethic 51, 52, 164
Workshop on Alternative Energy
    Strategies 149
World Bank 4, 129, 131, 132
World Economic Conference
    (1933) 200
World Food Board 5
World Food Conference (1974)
    129
World Health Organization
    (WHO) 3, 8
World Meteorological
    Organization 4
worldviews and religion 158–9,
    160–1

youth, and future 129, 208